2016

Dear Oliver~
Congrats on making
Eagle! You should be
very proud!
Fondly~
The Rochmans

RUNNING TOWARD DANGER

Real Life Scouting Action Stories
of Heroism, Valor & Guts

Michael Surbaugh
Chief Scout Executive
Boy Scouts of America

Welcome

The Scouting movement has always been marked by young people doing incredible things. Our current and former Scouts are a testament to the magnitude of Scouting's influence. Examples of Scouts impacting our nation surround us. More than half of all astronauts were Scouts. The halls of the United States Military Academies are crowded with former Scouts. Even the decision-making bodies of Congress and state governments are full of former Scouts.

The basis for these incredible achievements is mentorship that prepares young people for everything from the mundane to the unimaginable. Scouting's programs task youth to act valiantly every day, sparking heroism in a variety of shapes and sizes. Most Scouts' courageous acts are more personal and go unnoticed, but some of their acts of heroism are on such immediate display that society must take notice. These are the young men who face peril and run toward the challenges.

Not all Scouts who put on the uniform will face dire situations or save lives, even if they are prepared for such a feat. However, a few young men are faced with such challenges and stand apart as are chronicled in Running Toward Danger. These are a few of the stories of the Scouts who go beyond the call of doing a good turn to do something spectacular.

As the Chief Scout Executive for the Boy Scouts of America, I am proud of these Scouts and all others who act heroically and live out our motto: **"Be Prepared."**

Michel B Surbagh

Real Life Scouting Action Stories
of Heroism, Valor & Guts

RUNNING

MICHAEL S. MALON
Bestselling Author of *FOUR PERC*

FOREWORD by **Hershel 'Woody' Willia**
Congressional Medal of Honor Recip
USMC, Iwo Jima, World W

Presented
David C. S
John K. Sh
& Aaron A. L

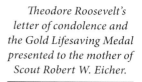

Madam:
I beg to extend to y...
...incere sympathy and my great admiration
...our gallant young son.   It is a
...ible loss and no words of mine can
...en it to you.   All I can do is to ex—
...ss my deep sympathy and my pride as an
...erican in the gallant mannan boy.
Faithfully yours,
Theodore Roosevelt

TOWARD
DANGER

Published by WindRush Publishers
WindRush Publishers and colophon are trademarks
   of WindRush Ventures, LLC

First Edition 2015

ISBN: 978-098590977-2

WindRush publications are available at special discounted
   rates for volume and bulk purchases, corporate and
   institutional premiums, promotions, fundraising, and
   educational use. For further information, contact:

WindRush Publishers
P.O. Box 670324
Dallas, Texas 75367
www.WindRushPub.com

Printed and bound in the United States of America.

Cover design, book design, and layout by John K. Shipes,
   Aaron A. Lake & David C. Scott

Back cover artifacts are used by permission of
   Robert Hannah & Russell Smart

Running Toward Danger is not an offical publication
   of the Boy Scouts of America. BSA images are used
   with permission.

Check out more about this book at:
   www.RunningTowardDanger.com

Get informed and inspired at www.WindRushPub.com

This book is dedicated to every Scout who ever has run toward a call for help.

D. Kent Clayburn
Chairman
National Court of Honor
2015

Statement from the National Court of Honor
Boy Scouts of America ■■■■■■■■■■

Tales of Scouting's remarkable influence on the lives of young people have echoed throughout the course of history. Whether the program is woven into the lives of its youth members for the long term or a short while, its impact is equally as lasting.

In my many years in Scouting, I have met thousands of talented Scouts on the path to success, but on rare occasion I encounter a Scout of exceptional merit. A young leader of this caliber exhibits outstanding bravery and heroism by saving another's life, earning the Honor Medal.

I have the distinct privilege of serving on the National Court of Honor, helping identify Scouts who achieve the extraordinary. Witnessing their extreme valor and courage is the most fulfilling aspect of my role, and I hope you'll be inspired by these heroic Scouts just as I have been.

In this book, you'll read about Scouts who are testaments to the immediate and lifelong impact of Scouting. They embody the effects of a program that offers life-changing experiences you can't find anywhere else.

D. Kent Clayburn

Daniel Carter Beard

National Scout Commissioner
Boy Scouts of America
1932

"It is impossible to read the following accounts without responding to the thrill of the human drama contained in each one of them. These are the deeds for the most part of boys in the 'teens, who forgetful of self, acted with courage and cool-headed resourcefulness when the emergency came.

They are at the same time splendid testimony to the increasing effectiveness of the safety and lifesaving program of the Boy Scouts of America, which aims to reinforce the boy's natural courage with skill and knowledge in handling himself in emergencies of this kind, requiring quick, sure decision."

ACKNOWl

Any book that tackles the final details and obscure events of more than a century is going to require a lot of help; doubly so if this information also is embedded deeply in the dusty files of a giant national organization. For both of those reasons we are extremely grateful for the assistance of a number of individuals (most of them associated with the Boy Scouts of America) and to the BSA itself that allowed us to write this book as a work of unflinching journalism, free of editorial influence.

EDGMENTS

The list of individual Scouters, both professional and volunteer who came to our aid, is a distinguished one. It includes:

Bill Larson, who, with his assistant *Rena McNeal*, edited the second draft of this book. *De Tan Nguyen*, director of Scouting U. *Glenn Adams*, president of the National Eagle Scout Association and sponsor of the Adams Service Project Award for the nation's best Eagle Scout service projects.

With the National Court of Honor: chairman *Kent Clayburn*, staff advisor *Chuck Ezell*, and administrator *Velma Cookes*.

At BSA National Headquarters: Chief Scout Executive *Michael Surbaugh* and public relations executives *Michael Ramsey* and *Deron Smith*. Added thanks to *Steven Price*, archivist at the BSA National Museum and *John Andrews*, Scout executive at the Northern Star Council in Minnesota.

Scout Executive *David Williams* of the Great Smokey Mountain Council in Tennessee and *Tim Anderson*, national Exploring executive. Additional thanks to *Wes Stowers*, president of the Great Smokey Mountain Council.

Two of the nation's greatest collectors of Scouting memorabilia – *Bob Hannah* and *Russell Smart* – were kind enough to let us photograph their Honor Medal collection.

Not least, we want to give special thanks to our two distinguished contributors of the opening statements to this book: *Bill Hemenway*, the great-grandnephew of Dan Beard; and one of America's greatest living heroes, *Hershel "Woody" Williams*. We are hugely honored to have these two gentlemen be part of this book.

Finally, a personal recognition. As a Boy Scout and Eagle, like most Scouts today and a half-century ago, I knew little about the Honor Medal or the Medal of Merit. Of course, I saw the images in the *Scout Handbook*, but they seemed to recognize impossible acts by extraordinary people I never would meet.

In the summer of 2002, I took my family on safari in Africa. One day in the Kalahari, my oldest son, **Tad Malone**, 11, was walking down a path with his younger brother, Tim, when he thought he heard a lizard in a nearby bush. He bent down . . . and went face to face with a black mamba, one of the most dangerous poisonous snakes in the world. With extraordinary presence, Tad froze, then slowly reached behind his back and caught his approaching brother and told him to run and find us and get help. Having saved his brother from certain death, Tad maintained his stand-off with the six-foot snake for a couple of minutes until the mamba, sensing the approaching footsteps of rescuers, turned and slithered off.

That autumn, when I finally signed up Tad with a troop, and mentioned his African adventure, I was told that it was a pity that he hadn't joined on his birthday six months before – as he might have been eligible for a BSA Honor award for lifesaving. I had to dig into the latest edition of the *Handbook* to remind myself of what they were talking about. It was then that the seed for this book was planted. And when, upon finishing my history of Eagle Scouting, *Four Percent*, WindRush publisher David C. Scott and art director John K. Shipes suggested a follow-up book on the Honor Medal – I jumped at the chance. You can see the result of that enthusiasm in the pages that follow.

Life has no shortage of ironies or unexpected shocks. And as I began this book, one evening Tad, now 24, came to the house in a state of shock.

He had been watching the World Series at a friend's house. He stepped outside and when he returned, found his friend unconscious and slipping into a coma – the result of a bad drug interaction between pain pills for a newly-shattered arm and a long term drug prescription. Tad managed to restore the young man's breathing, revived him, called 911, and was ready with samples of the two medicines when the ambulance arrived.

And so, more than a dozen years after my son faced down the black mamba, he again saved a life. He had, once more, run toward danger. And the week I finished this manuscript, Tad learned that he would be a recipient of the BSA's Medal of Merit. I want to thank him for being the living example in my own house of the boys, girls, and men that I write about in this book.

Michael S. Malone
Sunnyvale, California
2015

TABLE
OF CONT

The patch presented to Honor
Medal recipents circa 1940.

ENTS

William P. Hemenway
Great-Grandnephew of
Daniel Carter Beard
2015

Having Daniel Carter Beard as my great-granduncle always has been a bit daunting. Although we never met, I know him well from the many stories I was told over the years from family members regarding his experiences and accomplishments.

Beard lived from 1850 to 1941 during a period in American history that was filled with immense change. He witnessed the Civil War, the culmination of *Manifest Destiny* through continental settlement first expressed in the Monroe Doctrine, the death of President Lincoln, and the close of western expansion. He saw the rise of the "bully pulpit" through the executive actions of his close friend President Theodore Roosevelt, the tragic sinking of the *RMS Lusitania*, and the American entrance into World War I. He survived the Great Depression of the 1930s and experienced the beginnings of Adolf Hitler's world vision. Certainly, Dan Beard lived during fascinating times. But merely living did not satisfy him; he was driven to make a tangible difference in the lives of others.

Beard's father was a world famous portrait artist, an occupation that allowed Dan access to the nation's powerful and elite starting from a very young age. As a man, Beard's own varied travels as a surveyor (and later as an author, artist, and adventurer) provided him introduction to well-known showmen like "Buffalo Bill" Cody, titans of industry like John D. Rockefeller Jr., and politicians like Roosevelt.

Over a 31-year span, he was known as "Uncle Dan" to millions of adoring Boy Scouts due to his affable nature and intense love and respect for young people, wishing them to become modern day American patriots. He revered his heritage and was extremely proud of his ancestors for all the best reasons. In fact, he was a walking, talking anachronism – equally as comfortable wearing his trademark white fringed buckskins on a Pennsylvania mountain range as he was when donning a slick 3-piece suit and strutting down Manhattan's 5th Avenue to BSA headquarters. That was Dan Beard – a man who lived his life straddling the American transition line between two worlds: one belonging to the pioneer, explorer, and adventurer, and the other of the modern city dweller.

PROLOGUE

Like his friend Samuel Clements, better known by his *nom de plume*, Mark Twain, Beard was drawn to the hard life of the boatman – spending some of his early working years traveling on a paddleboat up and down the Mississippi River. He believed that the power of that river was like an "earthly judge," as it measured the strength of a man's resolve to control it. But it also divided the land between civilization and the untamed wilderness.

Symbolically, the mighty Mississippi divided the life of Dan Beard as well. Some of his time was spent on or around it (such as during his early years living in the society-driven city of Cincinnati), while other parts were far away in wilderness camps – paying homage to his pioneer ancestors. Yet the exposure to each permeated his life and built his character through an appreciation of both, giving him a unique and solid foundation for his life's work within the Boy Scouts of America.

He was a member of the BSA's original Committee on Organization in 1910 and put the American eagle on Scouting's fleur-de-lis. He helped develop the National Court of Honor and led it for three decades as its chairman. He was the BSA's National Scout Commissioner for over 30 years, founded Flushing (NY) Troop #1, and served as BSA's unpaid goodwill ambassador throughout the world.

As one story goes: Dan Beard was a VIP guest on the reviewing stand at the 1929 World Jamboree held in Arrow Park, England. To his right, he held in his hand a musket used by one of his patriot ancestors during the Revolutionary War. To his left stood Britain's highly irritated Duke of Bedford. The prickly Duke asked him to kindly remove that firearm from his presence to which the amused Beard replied: "Aw, don't worry a thing about it Duke. This gun hasn't been fired since 1776."

Dan Beard's American spirit was undying and he wrote constantly about its paramount importance to national life within the pages of the magazines of the time. He became focused on forging a new generation of patriots through those columns and was blessed with editors who shared his vision. With their assistance, Beard founded several youth organizations centered on the outdoors, developing frontier skills, and constructing crafts. But these "scoutlike" groups also had higher callings as they taught the preservation of natural resources, promoted the spirit of industriousness, and fostered a higher national citizenship through the serving of others. More importantly, however, these became the tenets embedded within today's Boy Scouts of America.

In its earliest years, the BSA struggled as an organization but its membership never lacked in heroism. As Scouting grew, so did the amazing stories of heroics and self-sacrifice made by many of those Scouts and leaders. And although Beard wanted to recognize these true American heroes, more importantly, he wanted them properly equipped to save other people's lives without compromising their own. As you will read, some of the early reports were sad tales, as young boys perished after inserting themselves into potential lifesaving situations without proper training. But Beard also understood that *his* Scouts simply could not refrain from doing so as every one of them had the heart of a hero.

Now a century later, we know that thousands of boys and girls of all ages, ranks, and backgrounds have heard the call for help and have run toward danger.

This wonderful book describes some of those gripping tales of Scouting heroism, valor, and guts, all the while reinforcing the constant theme that BSA-trained youth are willing and able to serve others just as Uncle Dan envisioned and encouraged throughout his life of dedicated service to Scouting.

But in the end, this aspect of his devotion to youth merely is a fraction of the great legacy that he and his fellow BSA co-founders like Ernest Thompson Seton gave to all of us to protect and to continue. And it is *our* duty to do so – a duty of character that also is inherent within the psyche of American young people. You will find his devotion to his many "nieces" and "nephews," now numbering in the millions, penned within the lines of his famous Recipe for Scouting:

Take a bowl of unbound love for boys; add one pint of absolute faith in American institutions; mix with a cup of milk of human kindness, and two cups of American pioneer blood; one heaping tablespoon of thrills; two tablespoons of romance; half a teacup of Indian traditions; a teacup of fairness and rectitude, a quart of idealism of the Thoreau, Burroughs, and Van Dyke; one heaping of sentiment; the whole seasoned well with patriotism, character, and sportsmanship, stir with the Golden Rule; sprinkle well with the Stars and Stripes and serve Red Hot!

I am humbled to have the opportunity to share this short (and incomplete) introduction of Daniel Carter Beard as the key founder of the BSA's Honor Medal program. He was a great man of broad talents who had a special place in his heart for the youth of America.

But remember, although the stories you are about to read are ripping good yarns of Scouting heroism, you do not have to save a life to be a hero to a young boy or girl.

William P Hemenway

Hershel 'Woody' Williams
Congressional Medal of Honor Recipient
USMC, Iwo Jima, World War II

What makes a hero?

That is a question that often only can be answered after an act of heroism has been performed.

FOREWORD

I know from my own experiences in World War II – in boot camp, on Guam, and most of all, in combat on Iwo Jima – that I never could guess in advance which of my fellow Marines would prove to be that rare individual who would run *toward* the enemy with the heart of a hero. Many of them did but never were recognized for their sacrifice.

Realistically, there really are no obvious traits that distinguish a hero from anyone else before their defining moment. Simply put, heroes are just regular people who are put into extraordinary circumstances, and who respond with valor and commitment.

When I attempted to join the Marines, I was not eligible because I did not meet the height requirements and was given that as the reason. However, that requirement later was removed and I was accepted.

As a recruit in training, I did not distinguish myself from my fellow Marines, and yet, when the moment came in those first days of the Battle of Iwo Jima in February 1945, armed with only a flamethrower on my back, four Marines affording me protection (two of them sacrificed their lives), and seeing many enemy pillboxes stopping my Company's advance, I found the courage within me to move forward. I knew that the lives of others depended on my actions and it was my duty to respond.

The remarkable stories contained on the pages of this book reveal that young boys and girls have within them the same resolve and spirit as older adults. Similarly, I suspect that few of these young people would have been identified as heroes beforehand. Rather, they were just everyday kids, going to school, playing with their friends, hiking and camping with their fellow Scouts, when suddenly the world turned upside down, and each had to make the toughest decision of their young life.

Yet each chose to overcome their fear and run to the aid of others at mortal risk, sometimes at the risk of their own life. This is a testament to both their own character and to their Scout training. Without both, a *rescue* quickly could have turned into a *double tragedy*.

If there is one message that emerges from the scores of stories of heroism told herein, it is that no one knows when they will be called upon to save the life of another. By the same token, no one (especially a young person) knows in advance how they will react at that moment.

However, these Scouts found their hero inside. In the process, they not only saved the life of another (or several) but they also changed their own life forever. Assuredly, the path from that moment to the present is not always a straight one; and the role of an official, honored hero is not a light burden to bear, but who would go back in time and trade that moment for another, darker conclusion?

The fact remains that *millions* of Americans are alive today because, incredibly, generations of young Scouts had the courage to do the right thing at the right moment. And they deserve the public recognition and our gratitude.

Remember, anyone and everyone can be a hero, you must be prepared when you are called.

In the meantime, enjoy this wonderful book of stories about great American heroes and of the national treasure that is the Boy Scouts of America.

Be Inspired and Be Faithful!

Hershel Williams
Medal of Honor

Workers loading
newly-cut timber
onto a horse-drawn
wagon circa 1919.

In the summer of 1918, the
latest of an eventual four ghastly
reports that had been arriving
sporadically over the previous
year arrived in the mail at
the Boy Scouts of America's

INTRO

headquarters in New York City. However, this one was different – it was the final straw. It was the letter that would change American Scouting forever.

The envelope was postmarked "Custer County, Nebraska" and the enclosed letter was written by the Scoutmaster of a troop in the small prairie town of Broken Bow. In the message, the Scoutmaster sadly reported that his troop was likely to fade away now that it had lost its "best Scout" – First Class Scout Russell Grimes, 14-years-old, who had been killed in an accident in which he had shown extraordinary bravery.

The Boy Scouts of America had been anticipating, and dreading, another event like this for some time. So it quickly followed up with the Scoutmaster for details on the accident, and requested statements signed by witnesses. Through these documents, BSA headquarters — and particularly National Scouting Commissioner Dan Beard, one of the co-founders of American Scouting — was able to establish an accurate narrative of events a half-continent away.

It seems that young Grimes had been spending part of his school vacation at his brother-in-law's ranch. One of the projects he was helping with was the construction of an extension to the existing ranch house. On the day of the accident, Grimes had been asked by one of the construction workers if he would be willing to help bring some timber back to the site from a wood lot a few miles away. This would require hitching a four horse team to a long wagon capable of carrying the heavy load. It would be a two man job, the driver at the front handling the horses, and a second rider in the far back managing the wagon's single lever brake.

As the man explained it to Russell, there was some risk to the job, especially should the horses bolt on the way back when the wagon would be fully burdened with the timber. And that, the driver admitted, was a possibility (albeit a small one) since the horses he planned to use on that day were young, excitable, and not fully broken in. Still, he added, the only real risk would be for him in front, on the buckboard, because the fully-loaded timber would all-but encase him and leave him almost no path of escape in an emergency. By comparison, he told Russell Grimes, should the worst happen, you merely need to slide off the back of the rig onto the road. You might get a few bruises, but you'll be fine.

ꓣODUCTION

But why choose young Russell for such an adult duty? The man explained that over the previous weeks he'd been watching the boy work on the ranch and had been impressed by his trustworthiness and reliability – to the point that he now trusted Russell more with the impending task than any of the adult hands. If the wagon gets out of control, he told the boy, the only thing that may save my life will be that brake and you pulling on it with all of your might – and not abandoning me. "Will you stick?" he asked the boy.

Russell promised he would.

By all accounts the trip to the wood-lot was uneventful – other than Russell getting bounced around in the empty wagon as it rolled over bumps and potholes on the dusty road.

But the trip back was a different matter. No one ever will know what it was, but something spooked the already nervous horses – and the scenario the driver most feared suddenly was upon them. The terrified horses bolted, racing down the road in a "frantic, headlong dash" as the driver leaned back and desperately pulled on the reins trying to stop them.

With nearly a century having passed since that awful day, and with the only written record being that of Beard's more than a decade later, it is difficult to capture precisely what happened next. But we have a good idea: the horses screaming and driving each other to greater levels of terror, the pounding of the hoofs on the dirt road, the growing tail of dust behind the accelerating wagon, the driver standing on his heels in the buckboard pulling with all his might on the reins and shouting "Whoa! Whoa!" at the top of his lungs as the logs shudder and clatter around him.

Most of all, young Russell Grimes being bounced around in the back of the wagon, clinging to the brake handle, hearing the squeal of the smoking block of wood on the other end of the brake as it fails to restrain the rear wheel … even as he is being hit by splinters and bits of bark, and perhaps even by entire logs as they slide and bounce off the tail of the wagon.

Beard: "Russell did not need the driver's shout, as the man strained and tugged at the reins, to bring him into action; he was pulling with all his weight on the handle of the brake … He might have jumped from the back of the wagon and got off with no more than a slight bruise or two; but he had promised to stick, and he was game."[1]

Game or not, there came that moment, faced by many Scouts, when Russell Grimes had to make a split-second decision between self-preservation and the duty he felt to others. Only those who have made a similar decision know how they will react. The rest of humanity can only wonder – and dread the moment when they will face the same choice. Russell chose to stay at the brake and accept the consequences.

The fate of both men now rested with the driver and his ability to keep the horses running in a straight line until, after a few hundred yards, they finally tired out and slowed. But it wasn't to be: before they could exhaust themselves, the horse team suddenly swerved. As the horses shrieked, the wagon skidded off the road and overturned, flinging both man and boy away from the wreckage.

The driver was severely injured and hospitalized. But he would live. First Class Scout Russell Grimes suffered a different fate for being steadfast: catapulted through the air he came down hard on exposed rock, fracturing his skull. He never regained consciousness. The rescuers agreed that by staying at the brake to the bitter end, and slowing the wagon just enough, the boy likely had saved the driver's life – at the cost of his own.

The Question:

What possesses a person – especially a young boy or girl, with limited experience and an entire life ahead of them – to commit themselves to saving the life of another? Even more, voluntarily enter a situation that might put their own life at risk – even leading to their death?

It was a question that haunted Dan Beard in the early years of the 20th century – and has haunted Scouting ever since.

Scouting famously had been founded in January 1908 in the United Kingdom (UK) by Lord Robert Baden-Powell, hero of the Second Anglo-Boer War in South Africa at the end of the 19th century. He was worried about the "softness" of Edwardian period British boys (especially those living in big cities) and found a solution in camping and living in the outdoors. He developed his revolutionary model from his observations of boy messengers and military scouts during the protracted, 217 day siege of the small British garrison of Mafeking he commanded on the African veldt, upon which he had made his reputation.

Less known is that in creating the Boy Scouts (his wife would help found the Girl Guides/Scouts soon thereafter), Baden-Powell had drawn heavily upon two American outdoor programs for young men; in particular, the Woodcraft Indians,

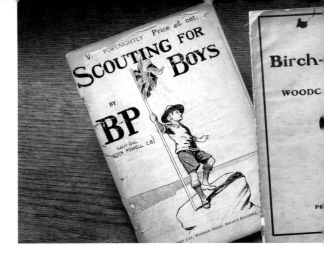

created in 1902 in Connecticut by famed artist-naturalist-author-lecturer Ernest Thompson Seton – and to a lesser degree, Beard's Sons of Daniel Boone, formed in Ohio in 1905. Seton's founding publication, the *Birch Bark Roll of the Woodcraft Indians*, with parts copied by Baden-Powell to an almost scandalous degree, emphasized not only just the outdoors but also character development and bravery in the face of adversity and danger. The story of Baden-Powell's own "scouts" at Mafeking reinforced this message of courage and the duty to assist others in need.

It is important to note that in all three programs (and in all three handbooks for those programs) important recognition was given to members that exhibited bravery in the service of others.

For Seton, it was one of two "Red Honors" – a "coup" or "grand coup" – whose presentation was decided upon by the Woodcraft Council. In his *Scouting for Boys*, Baden-Powell drew upon his interest in medieval chivalry; he often wrote and talked about the Knights of the Order of St. John in Jerusalem and how they wore a black identifying armband and dedicated themselves to performing first aid on people they rescued from danger. Baden-Powell's first honors for lifesaving were the recipients of the "Albert" and "Edward" medals.

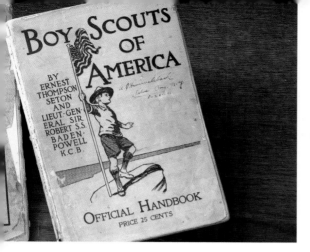

Baden-Powell's initial 1908 Scouting for Boys *and Seton's 1906* Birch Bark Roll *that formed BSA's first* Official Handbook.

Beard brought his own, distinctly contemporary, recognition to his organization's young heroes. His Sons of Daniel Boone handbook offered two awards: the Theodore Roosevelt "Top Notch" award for being heroic to women and children; and the Admiral Dewey Top Notch, symbolized by an anchor, for heroic water rescue.

Thus, even before its founding, the three organizations that would define the future Boy Scouts of America not only were already recognizing young heroes in their ranks, but through Seton – and especially Beard – were forging a uniquely American style to this recognition.

Meanwhile, in the United Kingdom, the commendations and medals for bravery, from Chief Scout Baden-Powell himself, gained considerable publicity and would grow in intensity – and

gravity – with the outbreak of World War I. Setting the standard, Baden-Powell personally volunteered for duty only to be turned down by Army chief Lord Kitchener, who said that he "could lay his hand on several competent divisional generals but could find no one who could carry on the invaluable work of the Boy Scouts." It wasn't long before British Boy Scouts were volunteering in droves for any kind of military service. With millions of British men heading for France, and defense work undermanned at home, British government officials agreed.

In keeping with the precedent set two decades earlier in South Africa, British Scouts

served as military messengers and coastal guards. And it was in this role that 15-year-old George Taylor was killed during the siege of Scarborough – the only active Scout to die during the war – and was buried with full military honors at a service attended by his fellow Scouts.

An American Design

The Boy Scouts of America was founded in 1910 and operated largely under the rules established by British Scouting. If Ernest Seton's greatest contribution was in influencing Baden-Powell in Scouting's creation, Dan Beard's was in defining the distinctly American attributes that distinguished the BSA. Thus, he called upon the memories of the nation's historic heroes such as Washington, Boone, Crockett, and Kit Carson, along with more recent figures that included the active outdoorsman President Theodore Roosevelt and national hero Dewey, to serve as iconic role models for young Scouts.

As national Scout commissioner (the #2 volunteer in the organization behind the BSA president), Dan Beard had another duty: that of presiding over the National Court of Honor. The Court, which exists to this day, was first assembled in the earliest days of the BSA program. As noted, its first duty, then and now, was to pass judgment upon the worthiness of applications for national Scouting honors. As such it was the pre-eminent counterpart to the hundreds (and later thousands) of individual troop, district, and council boards of review held on regular schedules around the country to determine the fitness of individual Scouts for merit badges and ranks, as well as adult volunteers for such local awards as the Silver Beaver.[2]

In the BSA's early years, this National Court of Honor had a secondary task: certifying Scouts for the Eagle Scout rank. And a third: approving merit badge applications. But its true recognition remained as the BSA's sole protector of the integrity of the Honor Medals for Lifesaving.

Beard himself seems to have played an important role in the creation of the BSA Honor Medal program, and to have largely defined the criteria for recipients of its awards. The medal itself took three forms: Gold, Silver, and Bronze, *(see below)* the levels corresponding to the degree of hazard faced by the recipients in earning the award.

The design of all three, as defined by Seton, essentially was the same: a Maltese Cross made from the respective metal and bearing at its center the fleur-de-lis/Eagle/twin stars of the basic BSA emblem (i.e., the Tenderfoot award), in turn hanging from two links attached to the BSA scroll (i.e., the Second Class award) bearing the Scout motto of "Be Prepared." At the top of the cross was imprinted the word "Honor" – and on some medals "Boy Scouts of America" imprinted on the bottom.

Besides the choice of metal, the most obvious distinguishing difference between the three medals was the ribbon. Other Scout medals at the time – notably the Eagle Award – adopted the standard "dangle" form of ribbon connecting the medal's hallmark to the medallion below. But for the Honor Medal the BSA chose an equally common form and design that is all-but forgotten today. This was the "drape" – in which the medal lay atop the face of a swallow-tail ribbon that rested flat against the pocket.

For the Honor Medals, each featured a pair of these draped ribbons falling from the metal scroll. The Bronze Lifesaving Medal had a red ribbon; the Silver Lifesaving Medal a blue ribbon; and the Gold Lifesaving Medal lay atop a white ribbon double drape. The awards themselves appear to have been fabricated by the Dieges & Clust Co. of New York; though some of the earliest (pre-1915) were made by the TH Foley Co., a firm forever connected to the first Eagle medals. Even more than early Eagles awards, these first Honor Medals are exceedingly rare, as few ever were awarded, and today can be spectacularly expensive for collectors.[3]

Along with their Honor Medals, Scout recipients also were presented with an over-sized, parchment-like, certificate announcing their achievement, and signed by Beard himself. Even fewer of these early certificates survive today.

Mentor of Honor

If Daniel Carter Beard seems to appear everywhere in the early stories of the Honor Medal, it is in part because he appears almost everywhere in Scouting itself during those founding years. Modern Scouts, looking at the old photos of an aging Beard dressed in fringed buckskins and campaign hat wielding a tomahawk, are likely to find him more exotic and amusing than impressive. But, in fact, Beard was a formidable figure who can be credited more than anyone for creating the BSA and building it into an enduring national institution. Indeed, few figures in American history can be credited with having left such a deep impression on the nation's culture and daily life.

Beard succeeded for a number of reasons. For one thing, as one of the two most influential co-founders of the BSA (the often difficult and mercurial Seton being the other) Beard's word held unequalled sway in the organization. This proved crucial to keeping Scouting from drifting from its core philosophy toward the many competing interests – such as militarism, segregation, and political activism – of the era. Beard was a master politician and marketer; he knew how to get things done in the rapidly growing organization, and those theatrical buckskins proved a brilliant exercise in branding for the young BSA.

Beard also was an excellent and prolific writer – his prose is simple, clean, and eminently readable even today. It never speaks down to his largely boy readership. Not surprisingly, many of his works became the founding corpus of Scouting's woodcraft literature. Indeed, much of the early history of the Honor Medal that underlies this book's opening chapter comes from Beard's *Boy Heroes of Today*, published in 1932. [Beard later revealed, with much regret and no less resentment, that the main text of the book had been entirely ghost-written and that he had not been consulted by Chief Scout Executive James E. West prior to the decision to publish. However, the opening chapters are most certainly his – not least because of the quality and passion of his words.][4]

Less known is that Beard also had been a superb illustrator before founding the Sons of Daniel Boone. He even had illustrated several of Mark Twain's books, most notably *A Connecticut Yankee in King Arthur's Court*. And if not quite as talented as his cartoonist older brother, Frank Beard, Beard still was talented enough to precede J.C. Lyendecker and Norman Rockwell in giving Scouting some of its early iconography. [Beard came from a remarkable family: his sister, Lina Beard, helped found the Camp Fire Girls.]

As national Scout commissioner, Beard assumed leadership of all of Scouting's field activities in January 1911, and thus freed the bookish Chief Scout Executive West to focus on the crucial tasks of turning the BSA into a real, and financially stable, institution. West's task was to rationalize the organization and gain accreditation from the U.S. Congress; Beard's was to build the organization internally and establish its standards and culture. And though the two men rarely got along, they proved to be a formidable team.

Perhaps Dan Beard's greatest contribution to Scouting was that he was both consistent and enduring. Already in late middle-age when the BSA was founded in 1910, he still managed to stay vital and engaged with the organization until his death at age 90 in 1941. By then he was the walking, talking, buckskinned embodiment of Scouting – and the living repository of its history. Just as important, he was able to watch over and protect for decades those initiatives he found important and valuable.

One of those initiatives was the creation of the three Honor Medals for Lifesaving. By all lights, a small and highly exclusive program with only a handful of recipients per year, it never should have survived inside a young, fast-growing, resource poor, existentially challenged organization like the early Boy Scouts. This is especially so in the face of scores of other worthy programs with much greater constituencies demanding their share of attention, youth, and resources.

And yet, the Honor Medal program of the BSA survived. It did so in part because it was the ultimate realization of some of the basic principles – duty, helpfulness, bravery – enshrined in Scouting's basic tenets. But even more, it survived because it stirred something deep in Daniel Beard's soul. Its awardees, especially those who had died rescuing others, haunted him – to the point that (more than twenty years after the creation of the award) when Beard finally sat down to write the foreword to *Boy Heroes of Today*, the veteran writer would find in its recipients the embodiment of the core beliefs that had driven his lifelong commitment. The Honor Medal Scouts validated his signature effort to acknowledge their actions:

Dan Beard walking in a Manhattan parade circa 1918.

Your national Scout commissioner has sometimes feared that his exalted idea of the possibilities of boyhood and his firm belief in the existence of a spark of divinity, or 'inner light,' in the breast of everybody, is not shared with him by all of his compatriots. Nevertheless, he is convinced that no one can read this book of self-sacrifice and sublime courage without being impressed with the firm conviction that the chivalry, devotion to duty and sacrifice of life, freely made by these Scouts, must be prompted by a spiritual urge beyond the comprehension of a materialistic mind.[5]

Contemplating the many young men who had risked – even lost – their lives in selflessly trying to save others (often people they didn't know) the veteran writer found himself reaching for words equal to his emotions:

"The Christlike heroism of our magnificent Boy Scouts is beyond human analysis. We simply are overcome with a sense of awe and compelled to stand hat in hand!"[6]

With his commitment to lifesaving as central to, yet distinct from, the rest of Scouting (combined with a stewardship that covered the BSA's first thirty years) Daniel Carter Beard guaranteed that by the time of his death the Honor Medal program would become such an inextricable part of Scouting, so synonymous with Scouting at its best, that it never could be excised from the program. And so it remains to this day.

But, before it could become an institution of its own, the BSA Honor Medal program would face the biggest challenge in its history. One that would question the very nature of heroism itself. And, ironically, it began with that tragic death of First Class Scout Russell Grimes.

Answering the Call

This book is the history of that award – and of the remarkable young (and not so young) men (and women) who have earned it over the last century and more. The BSA Honor Medal is, in many ways, even more than the Eagle, the most respected and admired of Scouting's awards. Yet it is the least well-known (and the least understood) of them all – not just to the general public but to Scouting's own members.

We have written this book in order to clear away that ignorance and confusion – but most of all, to celebrate those remarkable individuals who, when called to save a life – even at the risk of their own – have not turned away, or become a spectator, but have run toward that person in need.

This is their incredible story.

"Courage is not the absence of fear, but rather the assessment that something else is more important than fear." - Franklin D. Roosevelt

CHAPTER

What Makes a Hero?

"I saw that his hands were burning [as] I ran toward him."

Scout Dorris Giles after rescuing a boy being electrocuted in 1913.

1

By 1919, the BSA's National Court of Honor had bestowed upon Scouts and leaders a total of 38 Silver Lifesaving Medals, 205 Bronze Lifesaving Medals, and 133 Letters of Commendation.

Needless to say that in that first decade of American Scouting there were many more Scouts who had saved the lives of others "from the jaws of the grim destroyer,"

(as proclaimed by one contemporary newspaper) than there were recipients of any BSA heroism award. One reason was due to the number of Scout lifesaving incidents that occurred before the Honor Medal or the National Court of Honor were created. For example, **Frank Holstein**, 17, of Harrisburg, Pennsylvania, saved his friend and fellow Scout Harold Earp, also 17, from the swirling waters of the Susquehanna River in July 1911. He never received an Honor Medal for his heroics.

Nor did 13-year-old **Henry Draper** of Westwood, Massachusetts, who, in early 1911, saved Joseph Abel from a freezing death after the 9-year-old broke through the ice while skating. Nor did **W.S. Ritchie**, 18, at Camp Kenilworth in Marlton, New Jersey. He was part of a Philadelphia troop staying in bungalows and two-story houses on site. Spotting Samuel Harper, 13, on top of one of the houses and sweeping the roof with a broom, Richie sensed this was a dangerous situation and raced into the building. In fact, Ritchie had just finished climbing the second floor stairs when there was a sudden crash. He sprinted forward and caught Harper just as he broke through the roof headfirst – saving the younger Scout from snapping his neck.

A February 19, 1911, wire service story in the *Salt Lake Tribune* recounted these last two rescues and announced that both Scouts would be nominated for awards from the BSA's "Hero Medal Award commission" but there was no such commission yet formed, and so these three acts were lost to history.

That May in 1911, Scout **Tony Brown** was on a canoe expedition in upstate Wisconsin when another canoe, carrying Scout Clarence Loescher, capsized. Brown dove into the raging river. Despite being pulled under twice, Brown managed to save Loescher. The timing is surprising, since the state's first troops had been formed only weeks prior to the rescue. Local Scout leaders nominated Brown for a national heroism medal – but apparently not from the Boy Scouts of America.

Bronze Lifesaving Medal winner Harold Wood circa 1912. Wood was honored for a drowning rescue.

Scout Wins Three Badges In Service Four Years

HAROLD WOOD, 14 years old, and a scout for four years. He has been awarded merit badges for life-saving, for first aid and has been given one honor medal. He is a son of Charles S. Wood of Crafton.

In Prentice, Ohio, Scout Orin Dahl saved a boy from drowning in a creek. He swam with him to shore and "worked with him until he was restored." The Scoutmaster, "H. Lothian," wrote to the local paper asking its advice on how to apply for an award from the BSA as "[Orin], therefore, is entitled to a life savers [sic] medal." Scoutmaster Lothian apparently never got an answer, but his plea was reprinted in newspapers throughout the country courtesy of the national newswire services.

It only had been four months since January 1911 that the Boy Scouts of America, seeing the need to address honors and awards of this magnitude as well as to create the BSA's rank system, formed the Committee on Badges, Awards, and Equipment to fully "Americanize" the still largely UK-derived program.

ORTH GRIMM, who will be recommended for honor medal of Boy Scout movement—the highest gift.

BOY WAS A HERO

But what would these honors and awards be?

One was the Eagle medal, Scouting's highest achievement – and thus one that was required to be signed off at the National office in order to maintain the BSA's high standards. It originally

During World War I, Orth Grimm was presumed killed-in-action. However, a letter written to his mother arrived a year later. He had been captured as a prisoner of war.

was, as suggested by Seton, to be called the Silver Wolf award. But in deference to Western ranchers (to whom the wolf was a nemesis) and as part of the "Americanization" process (since the Silver Wolf medal was a UK Scouting award reserved for its highest achievers and heroic youth members), BSA's ultimate rank was redesigned to match our national symbol – the Bald Eagle. The other honor was an award program for saving lives – a subject of such public interest that it had to be adjudicated by a yet-to-be-created panel of exemplary men known as the National Court of Honor.

In the earliest newspaper stories of 1910 that described the founding of the BSA, there was mention of the creation of awards for "acts of heroism within the ranks of the organization" and that these awards (twenty different types in one report) would be "given for such deeds as stopping a runaway horse or saving a life." Later that year, the *San Francisco Call* newspaper would report that, according to BSA Chief Scout Ernest Thompson Seton, the award would take the Bronze, Silver, and Gold Lifesaving Medal forms that eventually would be ratified by the BSA – as well as a gilded Medal of Merit for performing

20 good deeds, including such acts as (once again) stopping runaway horses, helping a bogged-down automobile, and assisting an old lady take in her wash (perhaps presaging the famous Scouting cliché of helping an old lady cross the street). The Merit of Medal idea soon would disappear – only to reappear more than a decade later with a different set of requirements.

It wasn't until August 1911 that the BSA's Committee on Badges, Awards, and Equipment – soon to become the seed of the National Court of Honor – held one of its last meetings. Members included Chairman Dr. George J. Fisher, Gen. George W. Wingate (an attorney and inventor of organized rifle practice), Dr. C. Ward Crampton, Beard, Seton, and A.A. Jameson (one of the editors of the inaugural *Boy Scout Handbook* and the *Scoutmaster Handbook*). One of the first items it addressed that meeting was the new Honor Medal program.

But why the rush to national standards for the newly conceived heroism award? The precipitating event, it seems, was the report of a drowning rescue in Brooklyn, New York. Shockingly, when the BSA investigated the story, the rescue turned out to be staged. Scouting could not let that happen again, and the only way to guarantee that "heroism fraud" did not succeed was to codify that any final approval of an Honor award be at the national level.

Soon after (as if to make up for lost time) the National Court of Honor began to award Honor Medals in a hurry.

First to Answer

Official Scout history records the first BSA Honor Medal as having been awarded to 13-year-old **Charles Scruggs** of Cuero, Texas, who was a member of the Elks Patrol, Cuero Troop Number 1. Scruggs saved the life a fellow troop member, Burns Hardy.

As Hardy, himself, later described the event:

"It was nearly 5 p.m. We had been in the water for some time, when I swam out from the shallow water to where it was pretty deep, about 30 feet from the shallow water. I thought the water was shallow. Charles Scruggs called to me that I had better look out, that the water was deep there. When he called, I started to swim back and let down my feet. I then went under. I then tried to get up. I got my head over the water. I came up again, and then Charles came swimming up. He caught me under that arm and swam out to shallow water with me."

"After I went down the second time I was frightened. When I went down it felt as if my head was getting full of water. I believe that I should have drowned if Charles had not come up and helped me out."

"... No one but Charles Scruggs and I saw what happened, for the other boys were not nearby, where they could see us ... I told Charlie not to say anything about it."

Luckily, the next morning at school, Hardy told his friend Albert McHenry what happened – and Albert passed it on . . . until the story finally reached the BSA's headquarters. And so the story of Charles Scruggs as the first (Bronze) Honor Medal recipient remained for more than a century.

However, during the detailed and exhaustive research performed for this book, we discovered that due to confusion over a *Boys' Life* article, Charlie Scruggs was, in fact, the *fifth* Honor Medal recipient. According to a number of newspapers nationally, he and sixteen other Scouts were awarded their Honor Medals at the October or November 1911 meeting of the National Court of Honor. Even the date of Scruggs actual rescue of Burns Hardy, May 25, 1911, was not the first to be recorded.

In fact, one month earlier, at its September 1, 1911 meeting, the National Court of Honor had awarded its first four Honor Medals (again Bronze) to four Minnesota Scouts for their heroics the previous summer. They were presented to the young men on September 8 by the governor of Minnesota at a large and public ceremony covered in the press. As for the actual dates of their rescues, one of the Minnesota Scouts, George Moyer, saved a person from drowning on May 9, sixteen days before Scruggs' rescue.

Who then is the first Honor Medal recipient? This title now goes to First Class Scout **Walther Llewellyn Jerrard** of St. Cloud, Minnesota, age 16, who also saved a person from drowning. His story was the first to receive a positive vote from the National Court of Honor on September 1, 1911.

This confusion about the precedence of early awardees is understandable. The Boy Scouts of America was just a year old (and its first national headquarters office only had opened on June 1, 1910), its current membership was about 61,495 boys, its symbols and ranks still were in development, and many of its rules still were unwritten. And yet, young Boy Scouts already were bravely risking their lives to save the lives of others.

By the end of 1911, as many as thirty other Scouts would be honored for similar acts of bravery – a phenomenal figure, given Scouting's then small size. Equally impressive, given that there were as yet just a few thousand Scout troops in existence, was the geographic range of the troops to which these young heroes belonged: Nashville, Tennessee; St. Paul, Minnesota; Watkins, New York; Lone, Washington; and, as noted, Cuero, Texas.

Nearly all of these brave Scouts were honored for the same action: saving another person from drowning (an early bias we'll discuss later). But there were several exceptions. Easily the most memorable story of the "First Five" awardees is **Edward Grout**, a 14-year-old Scout from Dayton's Bluff, Minnesota. Grout had led his troop on a hike to Battle Creek (just east of St. Paul). Once there, the group was inspired with the notion of damming

He braced himself just in time for the shock of Rogers sliding over the edge.

As in a scene out of an action movie, Edward Grout gripped the tree while Floyd Rogers dangled over the precipice, clinging to him, while below their fellow Scouts looked up in horror. Then, inevitably, the tree slowly began to give way and pull out by its roots. As he felt the sapling go, Grout found a projecting rock upon which he could rest his feet and, straining with all of his strength, pulled Rogers up onto the rock with him. As he did, the tree tore loose and tumbled to the creek below.

the creek – and they set about gathering and piling stones to do so. As they did, Grout and another Scout, Floyd Rogers, decided to follow a path that led them to an overlook of the dam as it was being built. Grout's notion was to dig out the soft sandstone and undermine the path to let rocks tumble to the water below.

Unknown to Grout as he worked, Rogers walked along the route above him. Now undermined, the path instantly gave way. Grout jerked back just in time from being hit by the falling rock – and watched as Rogers pitched headfirst through the air toward the lip of the cliff just below them. Shouting Floyd's name, Grout reached out his left hand and caught the other boy by the wrist. At the same moment, he reached back and grabbed the only thing he could to save him – a small oak sapling growing out of the rocks.

The Medal Flap

Since BSA was so young, some early details were lost until now. Long-forgotten correspondence uncovered late during the production of this book offers a fascinating glimpse into the chaos that characterized the earliest days of the Boy Scouts of America – and the birth of the Honor Medal.

On September 6, 1911, J.A. Wauchope, Scout commissioner of the Ramsey Council #1 in St. Paul, Minnesota, no doubt was thrilled to receive a letter from BSA Executive Secretary (soon to be re-named Chief Scout Executive) James E. West notifying him that BSA headquarters in New York City had just shipped by special delivery four of the brand new Bronze Lifesaving Medals to Minnesota Scouts, who had earned the award in the preceding months.

The names of the recipients were Walther Jerrard, Glenn Dudley, Edward Grout, and George Moyer. Three of the four had saved others from drowning, and the other from a fall off a cliff. The rushed shipping was in response to Wauchope's appeal that he needed the medals in time for a ceremony in which Governor Eberhart of Minnesota would pin them on the young heroes in several days at the Minnesota State Fair *(see below)*.

At the left is Executive Secretary Moffatt; at the right Go hart. The scouts from left to right are Edward Grout, Wa George Moyer

So far, so good. The Boy Scouts of America, still less than two years old and dealing with both rapid growth and tough competition, had fulfilled every claim it had made about this prestigious new award – and had gone the extra distance to deliver the medals under a tight deadline. And, underscoring the organization's attention to detail, West's secretary, Samuel A. Moffat had even told Wauchope, "a medal of some different make or design would be exchanged" for whatever substitute or mock-up was used for the ceremony.

But 1912 would prove a very different experience for Commissioner Wauchope and Minnesota's Honor Scouts – one that, until a single letter exposed the truth, the behavior of national BSA managers seemed increasingly inexplicable.

It began on January 15, when Wauchope writes a note to national headquarters asking, after nearly four months, if there has been movement on the development of the new medal designs. He appears never to have received a reply.

Then, on January 27, 1912, Commissioner Wauchope sends a formal letter directly to Executive Secretary West about the state's newest Honor Medal candidate: "Herewith find enclosed application for Life Saving Medal for Joseph Fendall. Will you please have this matter acted upon at once by the National Court of Honor so that we can have the medal here to be presented during the visit of General Baden-Powell and yourself. The presentation will be made one of the features of the afternoon program."

Commissioner Wauchope understandably assumed that, given the events of the previous year, as well as the fact that the BSA had published a precise description of the three Honor Medals (Bronze, Silver, and Gold) and their requirements, those awards actually existed – and that the requirements were precise and explicit.

Wauchope includes with his letter a statement by Fendall's Scoutmaster, "Rev. Fosbroke," attesting to Fendall's heroism noting that, based on the BSA description of the Honor Medals, that "I am absolutely convinced that this is a most deserving case and that the boy should receive the highest honor medal" – that is, the Gold Medal.

BSA headquarters, no doubt in part because of the planned presence of both the Chief Scout of world Scouting and the Chief Scout Executive of American Scouting, responds quickly. On February 2, 1912, James West himself writes to Wauchope to say:

"It gives me great pleasure to inform you that the National Court of Honor has authorized the award of an Honor Medal to Master Joseph Fendall who is a patrol leader of White Kangaroo patrol, Troop No. 31, St. Paul."

Good news . . . until the last line of the note: "Under separate cover I am sending you a Bronze Medal for use in this case."

That wasn't what Wauchope wanted to read. Not only did he and Rev. Fosbroke believe that Fendall was worthy of a Gold Medal – or at least a Silver – but he also wanted to put on the best possible show for his distinguished guests . . . not to hand out a third-class award.

So Wauchope decided to press his luck – and in the process learned more about the state of the BSA than he probably wanted to know.

On February 20, he writes a "Night Letter" (a form of special delivery of that era) to Secretary Moffat, saying: "Scout Master Fosbroke thinks medal for Scout Fendall should be Gold according to manual. Wants to gold plate it here. Any objections[?]" One wonders if Rev. Fosbroke really felt this way, or just Wauchope. Either way, the response is swift and decisive.

Within 24 hours, a telegram blasts back to Wauchope from Moffat: *"Do not change medal awarded by national organization letter follows."*

It is followed the same day with an official letter from Moffat. In explaining his order to cease and desist, Moffat lets the cat out of the bag with the real explanation for Joe Fendall's receipt of a Bronze Medal [emphasis added]:

"Honor Medals, as you must know, are only awarded by the National Organization and the right to determine the kind of medal awarded in each case must be left to the National Court of Honor. You will note that there are three classes of Honor Medals; the Bronze, the Silver, and the Gold. At this writing *we have not yet secured medals in Gold and Silver but for the time being are issuing Bronze medals in every case. When the Gold and Silver designs have been decided upon some of these cases will be reconsidered and a Gold or Silver medal substituted for the medal already sent. . . In the meantime we do not think it a fair proposition for anyone locally to re-gild one of our badges and take from the National Court of Honor its right to determine this matter."*

As with the case of the first Eagle Scout, Arthur Eldred, whose own application had just encountered a similarly unprepared headquarters staff, BSA National had announced an important new award, complete with specific requirements . . . then assumed it wouldn't have to actually make the award for years. And then, when America's Scouts had proven even more remarkable than anyone imagined, the BSA could try only to freeze the process, prevaricate, and stall until it could respond. Commissioner Wauchope's pressure (and ambition) had forced the BSA's hand – and national headquarters had been forced to admit that it hadn't lived up to its own ambitions.

In late July 1912, Commissioner Wauchope nominated another Minnesota Scout for an Honor Medal: Norman Moffat, 14, the son of a blacksmith, for saving a Curtis Fadden from drowning. Again Wauchope includes an affidavit from the boy's Scoutmaster. But now he is reduced to pleading that the National Court of Honor consider giving Moffat the "appropriate medal to which his heroic action entitles him."

That November, Wauchope tries one last time. In a letter to West, Wauchope notes that, at this point, several Minnesota Scouts had performed acts that made them eligible for Honor Medals and all, apparently, had received Bronze Medals – despite several having met the requirements for the higher level medals. "You understand," Wauchope concludes, "that I am writing this for information and not in the spirit of criticism."

West's reply merely asks whether all of the Scouts had received their medals.

There is no record of any of those early Minnesota Scouts having ever retroactively received Silver or Gold Medals, whether Edward Grout ever received a new medal or whether, despite West's promises, the BSA National Court of Honor ever took up the matter.

1, Raymond I. Tifft; 2, C. B. Haley; 3, Charles P. Harris; 4, James Avent; 5, William M. Hoyt; 6, C. Benson Dushane; 7, Bosley Ensor; 8, Gordon Cummer; 9, Carl Cooper; 10, Frank H. Sykes (Silver Medal); 11, Virgil Chambers; 12, Charles W. Starr; 13, Leman Conrad; 14, Harold S. Wood; 15, Fred Roming; 16, Earl Cummins; 17, Benjamin Barnes; 18, William Waller; 19, W. J. Burns; 20, Jack Scheetz.

More Early Medal Recipients

Also listed among the first fifty awardees for Bronze Lifesaving Medals was **Henry Eichner**, about which little more is known other than that he belonged to a troop in Brooklyn, New York, and that he saved a little girl by pushing her out of the way of an oncoming car.

Though we know the names of these early heroes, in most cases, we have little other information beyond the date and general nature of their rescue, and sometimes their age or rank. What we do know often leads to more questions. Consider Bronze medalist #17, **J. Fred Roming** of Troop 7 of Baltimore, Maryland. Not only did he earn a Bronze Lifesaving Medal for saving a drowning person on April 10, 1911, but he earned a second one, details unknown, a year later.

We also know that in August 1911, **Walter William Waller** of Brooklyn, age 13, saved a person from drowning – an event that certainly received considerable publicity in that media center because the following January he was asked to meet the arriving Lord Baden-Powell on the gangplank in New York City harbor and present him with a letter of welcome from President William Howard Taft. Baden-Powell noted young Waller's Bronze Lifesaving Medal with approval. Taft himself later would present three Honor Medals to a Scoutmaster and two Scouts in Nashville, Tennessee, for saving multiple people from drowning. Weeks later, in St. Paul, hero Edward Grout would serve as Baden-Powell's personal aide for his visit there.

Scout William Waller greets Baden-Powell at New York harbor in January 1912

Baden-Powell met another Scout that January day on the New York gangplank – and was so impressed he stopped to talk at length with the young man. He also is a member of this list for the Bronze Lifesaving Medal (#32) that he would earn six months after this encounter. Of all of the names of the first 50, his alone stands out: **Arthur Rose Eldred**, soon to become America's first-ever Eagle Scout.

Eldred had one of the most remarkable careers in Scouting history. Born in Brooklyn in 1895, he still was a young child when his family moved to Long Island after the death of Arthur's father. From that point on, the boy was raised by his mother and his brother Hubert, who was a decade older.

Both mother and brother perpetually worried that young Arthur didn't have enough structure or discipline in his life and was at risk of getting into trouble.

So, in 1910, when Hubert learned of a new organization called the Boy Scouts of America, he decided to investigate.

The BSA wasn't, in fact, the first such organization that Hubert looked into (in those years, Baden-Powell's model had inspired numerous individuals across the United States to create similar Scout-like organizations). Instead, he started with the American Boy Scouts but was put off by its militaristic culture of endless drilling and marching that characterized the local ABS troop.

CHIEF SCOUT SETON PRESENTING THE HONOR MEDALS AT THE BIG SCOUT RALLY.

Chief Scout Ernest Thompson Seton and National Scout Commissioner Dan Beard present the Honor Medal to Arthur Eldred and Merritt Cutler at their Court of Honor held on Labor Day 1912.

The First Eagle Scout in This Country.

So, Hubert Eldred decided to charter a troop of his own and went to Manhattan to file the requisite paperwork at the BSA's headquarters, then located at the YMCA building at 124 E. 28th Street. He liked what he saw – and soon was commissioned as the Scoutmaster of Troop 1 in Oceanside, Long Island, with Arthur, now 15, as the troop's first Scout.

Should you wish to read more about the story of Arthur Eldred's meteoric assault on the first Eagle award, it is told in the book *Four Percent*. Simply put, his achievement remains unequalled. Somehow, this shy kid with a shock of black hair, in a troop with few resources and little adult leadership, in an org-anization still trying to find its footing against considerable competition, and working from a temporary *Official Handbook* (as the first edition of the BSA's *Handbook for Boys* was still being authored), still managed to earn more merit badges than

entire states full of Scouts. Eldred completed the requirements for Eagle years before the BSA had predicted such a candidate – indeed, even before the award was designed.

The sudden arrival of the over-achieving Arthur Eldred threw the Boy Scouts of America on its heels. No matter the bureaucratic obstacles put forward to slow his advance – including the most intimidating board of review in Scouting history, featuring Seton, Beard, and Chief Scout Executive James E. West – the young Eldred pushed through. Finally, in the summer of 1912, West admitted defeat. Arthur Eldred officially was designated as the BSA's first Eagle Scout. With that first admission came another: West told Eldred he would have to wait until fall for the receipt of his Eagle medal because it had yet to be designed.

Thus, Eagle Scout Arthur Eldred had to spend the summer of 1912 cooling his heels awaiting his official ceremony and the receipt of his medal. So, like other summers in his Scouting career, 17-year-old Arthur decided to go to camp across the Hudson River in Orange Lake, New York. And it was there that fellow Scout Melvin Daly decided to wade into the shallow water near the bank.

Daly was a popular member of the troop. Before this moment, his most memorable Scouting experience had been walking through the snow to a troop meeting in nearly sole-less shoes because he had spent his shoe money on his first Scout uniform. Now, as he waded out into Orange Lake, Melvin Daly suddenly stepped off an underwater ledge and disappeared beneath the water's surface.

He managed to claw his way back to the surface and scream for help before he disappeared again. Among all witnessing the unfolding tragedy, only two figures broke into a run for the lake's edge – stripping off shoes and clothes as they went: fellow Scout **Merritt Cutler** and Eagle Scout Arthur Eldred.

Eldred got to Daly first. Swimming to where Melvin last had appeared, Eldred dove down. He found Daly in the mud at the lake's bottom. Grabbing the boy and pushing off, Eldred pulled his way back to the surface, then pushed Daly's limp form high enough to get the boy's face above the water. There, Eldred was met by Cutler, who also gripped Daly and helped swim him to shore. It was at that moment that Melvin Daly revived. Confused and terrified, he flung his arms around Cutler – and in a death embrace, the two boys again sank beneath the surface.

As a future World War I combat veteran, a survivor of the Spanish flu, a distinguished government official, a lifelong supporter of Scouting, (to date) the patriarch of three generations of Eagle Scouts –

and, of course, the first Eagle himself – Arthur Eldred would accomplish many important things in his life, and survive many dangers. But no act he ever took, nor danger he ever faced, was greater than the one he met in the next few moments.

Already exhausted, he again dove to the bottom of the lake and there found the two boys still locked together and struggling. Eldred pulled them apart; then, assuming that Cutler was in the better shape, again grabbed Daly and pulled him to the surface. Unlike Cutler, Eldred had trained in lifesaving for his Eagle, and he knew enough to spin around the flailing Daly to stay out of his reach, grab him in a cross-chest carry, and swim him to shore. Bystanders now had come down to the water to carry in the coughing, choking boy.

Eldred had saved the boy's life. But he wasn't done. Looking back out, Arthur saw that Cutler, battered by the struggle with Daly, now was losing his

Eagle Scout Theodore Gaty, circa 1914.

own fight and was within moments of drowning. Without hesitation, an exhausted Eldred dove back in. He reached Cutler in time and rescued him.

Thus, in a matter of minutes, Arthur Eldred, biding his time over the summer awaiting the presentation of his Eagle award, had saved the lives of two of his fellow Scouts. Eyewitness accounts and subsequent affidavits and reports confirmed everything Eldred had done. So, even as his Eagle paperwork slowly made its way through BSA headquarters, Arthur's Honor Medal form followed closely behind.

If today Arthur Eldred's name remains obscure, even among Scouts, the blame rests with the BSA itself. Like most new institutions, particularly non-profits, it was more concerned with survival – especially recruiting and fund-raising – than with keeping careful records at the time. The main internal BSA public notice of his Eagle award was in the merit badge honor roll in the August 1912 issue of *Boys' Life* magazine. Instead, most of the articles lauding Eldred's achievement appeared in several newspapers, including the *Brooklyn (NY) Daily Eagle* and the *Kingston (NY) Daily Freeman*. Other local newspapers across the country printed the story after it hit the wire services. *The Freeman* described the tall, self-effacing young man as "a sturdy, well-built, keen eyed little fellow." Only the *Daily Eagle* carried a photograph of the first Eagle.

It wasn't for nearly a half-century (by which time the Boy Scouts of America was a national institution with millions of members) that historians began to look back and reconstruct the organization's early years. And, since in the interim the Eagle Scout had become an iconic figure in American culture, there was a new interest in learning about the very first one. They found his name in the BSA's papers: Arthur Rose Eldred. But then, adding to the slights of the previous fifty years, those historians – and eventually Scouting itself – appended the wrong photo to the story. The image was that of the 38th Eagle Scout,

Theodore Gaty Jr., whose square-jawed handsomeness apparently fit what everyone thought the first Eagle Scout should look like.

It wasn't until 2005 (93 years after Arthur Eldred earned his Eagle and 54 years after his death) that Gary Twite, a commissioner with the Chief Seattle Council, found a pair of photographs of the real first Eagle. In it Eldred poses, with no little embarrassment, in front of his house wearing his uniform in September 1912. Most viewers focus on the Eagle Medal he wears on his left breast pocket. Tattered, but still intact, it currently resides in a place of honor at the National Scouting Museum in Irving, Texas.

Far less noticed is the Bronze Lifesaving Medal that hangs next to it on Arthur Eldred's uniform. It is a reminder of a feat just as remarkable as his Eagle. And while Eldred's tattered Eagle medal is now is seen by thousands of visitors each year, his Honor Medal is not with it.

Silver among the Bronze

In addition to those scores of Scouts who earned the Bronze Lifesaving Medal in Scouting's first three years, nine earned Silver Lifesaving Medals for saving a life at extreme risk to themselves. The first of these was Scoutmaster **Frank H. Sykes** of Philadelphia, Pennsylvania, who saved a lady from a suicide attempt by drowning on September 16, 1911, in Atlantic City, New Jersey. Again, drowning rescues dominated, as they accounted for seven of the first nine Silver Lifesaving Medals.

Scoutmaster Frank H. Sykes, circa 1911.

That Arthur Eldred could save two lives and only be awarded a Bronze Lifesaving Medal; and that at the time of Russell Grimes' heroic death seven years later no Gold Lifesaving Medals yet had been awarded in an organization of more than 1.3 million members, suggests that considerable confusion remained (even after almost a decade) about the purpose of the Honor Medal, its award requirements, and even about the nature of bravery itself.

The Honor Medal program wasn't alone in the BSA's program as being relatively undefined in those early years. The two ranks below Eagle; Star and Life, would begin as separate rank paths

to Eagle, then, once aligned, would exchange positions – all in Scouting's first decade. Even the Eagle medal itself wasn't immune. As late as 1915, the BSA still was polling its members whether there should be an even higher rank, such as a "Double Eagle" or a "Golden Eagle." From 1913-1915, *Boys' Life* magazine actually referred to it as the "Silver Eagle."

As for the Honor Medal itself, so demanding were its requirements that *no* Gold medals were awarded during Scouting's first six years. Much of this confusion was due to Dan Beard himself. He had helped bring the Honor Medal to Scouting from his former organization; he had

embedded it into the new institution; he had protected it and ensured its survival. He presided over the National Court of Honor that adjudicated the awarding of Honor Medals; and he signed the Letters of Commendation to its recipients.

But at the same time, like all busy executives (and Beard essentially was the BSA's chief operating officer for its first two decades), he only had a limited amount of bandwidth to deal with Scouting's varied operations and almost none for those operations that seemed to be doing well. Like many senior executives before and since, he conducted managerial triage: abandoning those programs that were destined to fail, ignoring those that worked, and focusing on those that were faltering but still could be saved.

Although the Honor Medal program was small, it fell into the middle group. The record suggests he left it alone. He stated his position on the requirements for the awards and left the other members of the National Court of Honor to deal with the rest. The National Court of Honor, like all bureaucracies, tried to operate without imposing on the boss – and when in doubt, tried to guess his position on the matter. And that, of course – ironically, for an award for bravery – almost always meant taking the most conservative and safe path in their decisions.

This strategy would have been more successful had Dan Beard's own opinions about bravery not reflected his (and society's) own ignorance and bias.

Three of these opinions that seem odd to us today ruled out the awarding of BSA Gold Honor Medals for much of the first decade. One of these, perhaps arising from the strong religiosity of Beard and most of Scouting's founders, was the belief that true sacrifice all-but required the death – the martyrdom – of the Scout performing the rescue. A second seems to have derived from the Ten Commandments ("Honor thy father and mother") as Beard strongly believed that no Scout ever should earn an Honor Medal or Letter of Commendation for saving a family member (especially a parent) because that was a child's duty, and shouldn't require any moral decision on the Scout's part.

Elaborating on this last viewpoint, Beard told the National Court of Honor in 1916:

I should like to explain to the Scouts that no medals will be awarded them for acts which are undeniably and strictly in the line of their duty. For instance, a Scout saves his mother's life and sends in an application for an honor medal. In a case like this the Chairman of the National Court of Honor has always written to the effect that in place of claiming an Honor Medal, the Scout should get down on his knees and thank Almighty God for the opportunity offered him to prove his devotion and affection for his parent, and at the same time make known to her that her son is not only affectionate and dutiful but brave.[7]

Dan Beard's third belief in those early years (and widely held at the turn of the century that seems more like a cartoon image today) was the pseudo-scientific notion of the era that a person wasn't really drowning until he or she sank beneath the surface for a third consecutive time, preferably after screaming for help. As foolish as this sounds today, we shouldn't dismiss this notion too arrogantly: even now, few people realize that a drowning person is as likely as not to be quiet and moving very little, rather than assume the standard image of a terrified figure crying out and thrashing around.

Indeed, by 1916, Beard himself knew better (one application even describes a victim as going down for a *fourth* time) and was complaining about the endless appearance of the phrase in Honor Medal applications:

> *Another thing I should like to have pointed out to the Scouts is the fact that the superstition about its being necessary to go down three times before one is drowned is only a bit of superstition or folklore. A person may go down a half-dozen times and not drown or go down once and not come up again. This superstition is so firmly fixed in the minds of the boys that their otherwise good reports of rescues are often marred by the introduction of what they believe to be the truth, that the party rescued was 'going down for the third time.'*

Reading the minutes of the National Court of Honor during those earliest years of Scouting, it is easy to see the impact of Beard's opinions on Honor Medal deliberations – and on the Scout parents and leaders who apply for the award. The Scout who saves a parent, even at extreme risk to themselves, never appears in these applications; apparently they already have been winnowed out. Meanwhile, more than one affidavit from a witness attests that the rescued party "was going down for the third time," as if checking off that box.

But the most telling effect of Beard's biases can be found in the awards tally. Again, despite the nearly 200 Silver and Bronze Lifesaving Medals bestowed by the BSA through 1917 (most of them in the later years), *none* are Gold.

Not only does this seem statistically unlikely on its face, the fact is that we have just read of an act of bravery that surely involved enormous risk: Arthur Eldred's rescue of his two fellow Scouts. If Eldred didn't face a high likelihood of dying saving Daly, he surely did when, exhausted, he dove back in to save Cutler. And yet that act was deemed by the BSA only to deserve a Bronze Lifesaving Medal.

And there were other acts of bravery of the highest order during those years that still are preserved in the documents that the National Court of Honor scrutinized. For example, in the months following its February 1913 meeting, where it banned alcoholic beverages from troop meetings, set the time requirement on the Second Class rank, determined the role of patrol leaders, established troop committees, and supported district and council camporees – the Court took on the task of judging nine Honor Medal applications:

• Scout **Harold Fitch Miller** rescued Scout Henry Bradley, who had fallen through the ice at frozen Baddacock Pond in Groton, Massachusetts. Miller himself had been on the ice, knocking around a ball using a bent piece of wood as a hockey stick. When he heard Bradley crash into the water, Miller quickly ran around the pond to him, crawling on his belly on the thin ice, all while still clutching the stick. He had only a few seconds to reach Bradley, as the struggling Scout didn't know how to swim. Finally, after touching Bradley with the stick, Miller convinced him to hold on. Then, still flat on his stomach, Miller crawled backward, dragging Bradley with him.

• Scouts **Burton Allen** and **Rolle Vaaler** rescued cousins Harold and Analem Nelson, both 13, at the old logging dam on the Rum River near Milaca, Minnesota. The cousins had been playing on a sandbar in the spillway of the dam when they slipped into the fast-moving water. Harold Nelson, a "fairly good swimmer," attempted to save Analem, a poor swimmer, but found himself in trouble and abandoned the attempt in order to save himself. At this point Allen and Vaaler, who had warned the cousins of the risk, dove in to help. Rolle reached Analem first but the drowning boy pulled them both under. When they again surfaced, a choking Rolle pushed away just as Burton Allen arrived. Allen dragged an unconscious Analem to the bank 75 feet downstream. There, joined again by Rolle Vaaler, the two Scouts stretched Analem across the sluice beam "and worked his arms and got the water out of him."

• In Geneva, Indiana, Scout **Mack Burdge**, 12, saw a youngster, Kenneth Whiteman, floundering in a stream into which he had fallen. Whiteman was a poor swimmer and, according to the local committee investigating the near-tragedy, "was going down for the third time." Burdge grabbed a fallen, 12-foot tree branch nearby, held it out over Whiteman, and yelled for him to grab it. The boy did as he was told and Burdge, nearly slipping into the water himself, hauled him ashore.

• At Camp Mohawk in Harpers Ferry, West Virginia, Scout Charles Gross decided to swim across a nearby canal. He not only was a poor swimmer but he also told no one of his intentions – until he was discovered going down ["for the second time" in one eyewitness report, "for the third time" in another] in the 12-foot-deep water. Assistant Scoutmaster **William Charles Reed**, returning from a nearby swimming hole with a group of other Scouts, heard Gross yelling for help, dove in, and saved him.

Most subsequent applications exhibit similar themes.

- In Paducah, Kentucky, a Scout troop was camping at a lake shared by a nearby resort. According to the application, one of the resort guests started to drown and yelled for help. The troop's Scoutmaster, sitting nearby with a group of his Scouts, turned to them and said, "Go get him." Three boys jumped up and "with lightning speed" dove in. The drowning guest managed to death grip one of them but was too tired to hang on. Scouts **Henry Robertson**, **Jimmy Wilhelm**, and **Emmet Quick** hauled him to shore and each earned the Bronze Lifesaving Medal.

- Included in another application is another, darker, narrative. On an iced over mill pond in Davis, West Virginia, a group of Scouts, along with two teenaged girls were skating together. One of the Scouts, with one of the girls, went off to explore the far end of the pond and broke through the ice. The first rescuer (as he grabs the girl's wrist) broke through the ice as well. Then, two Scouts ran to a nearby log and managed to drag it into the open water and yelled for the victims to grab it – which the girl managed to do. One of those two Scouts then ran to find the assistant Scoutmaster nearby, who, on hearing the news, rushed to the pond, made his way onto the sinking log, and managed to save the girl. The third Scout escaped as well. But the first boy, despite efforts to resuscitate him, died. Scouts **Owen S. Curran** and **Wade I. Wilson** each earned the Bronze Lifesaving Medal. Assistant Scoutmaster **Ray Slider** earned the Silver Lifesaving Medal.

Boys clear ice on a frozen Michigan pond in 1910.

Here are the three other (successful) applications at that February 1913 meeting – all awarded the Bronze Lifesaving Medal – and all water rescues:

• Scout **Roy B. Craig** at Stinson Lake in New Hampshire watched a young woman dive from a small boat to swim the forty feet to shore – only to see her take two strokes and sink. He dove in to save her only to have her pull him down. He finally managed to break her grip, surface, and pull her unconscious body to shore.

Scout Walter McCarthy saved two men who fell through thin ice in December 1912.

• Scouts **Loring Williams** and **Charles Goldfus** from Minneapolis saved a man from downing in Lake Wapogasset.

• A 17-year-old Scout, **Walter James McCarthy** of Springfield, Vermont, who lived on the Black River, saw two workmen taking a short-cut home across the ice and fall through. He ran out on the thin ice with a rope and pulled one man to shore with the help of some bystanders. McCarthy then ran out a second time and did the same for the second man. Unknown to him at the time, the first man rescued was a gear shop foreman with a wife and two children.

As one studies these applications, the commonalities are evident – and they lead to one obvious question: did almost every Scout rescue in the early 1900s involve someone drowning?

The answer probably is "yes" and "no."

"The past is a foreign country," writes the novelist L.P. Hartley. "They do things differently there."

The United States of a century ago, though we can recognize and identify with many of its features, nevertheless was a place where children were free to spend their days wandering the woods and fields, diving into ponds and lakes, and even skating on ice with little or no adult supervision. There were few fences around factories, mills, and dockyards. Perhaps most importantly, there was little formal training in swimming, much less lifesaving, with most boys and girls never progressing further than learning how to paddle around a swimming hole.

This wasn't new: historians have found that in 16th century Tudor England half of all accidental deaths were drownings – thanks to a lethal combination of large populations of non-swimmers working and playing in proximity to unguarded bodies of water ... a situation that changed little over the next three hundred years.[8]

Put these factors together and it becomes obvious why there is a preponderance of applications that feature people of all ages putting themselves in precarious aquatic situations, and then discovering they can't swim. Then they are saved by a young Scout who has learned how to swim at camp – but not before he also is almost drowned because he has no training in aquatic rescue – lifeguard training mostly was reserved for older Scouts working on their Eagle rank. Meanwhile, there often are adults looking on, but refusing to go in the water themselves – likely because they too can't swim. And, perhaps, in a world of epidemics of childhood diseases and industrial accidents, no antibiotics, still primitive medicine, and almost no emergency assistance, some in the crowd are a little less sanguine about taking the risk of being a rescuer. In the end, both rescuer and survivor, bearing names like Vilma and Mack, are rescued by men in wagons or carried off to nearby houses to be stripped of their wet clothes and, more often than not, given an alcoholic beverage to cut through the chill. Most then are taken home and put to bed. Few ever visit a doctor or hospital. In cities and towns just a couple decades past being on the frontier, you still are expected to shift for yourself.

Two Boy Scouts of Hood River, Or., Get Bronze Medals for Brave Deed

Roger Simpson at the left and Edwin Sonnichsen.

Bronze Lifesaving Medal recipients Roger Simpson (left) and Edwin Sonnichsen both of Hood River, Oregon, in 1912.

But there is another answer as well: people in every organization quickly learn what the people at the top want – and do their best to give it to them. All of those "went under for the third time" comments in the affidavits are a clue. When Dan Beard thought of Scouts saving lives, he thought of lifesaving in the sense that we do: in the water. And so, it is very possible that Scouts saved lives in other situations and scenarios during those years – and never applied for an Honor Medal because they assumed they were ineligible.

As early as 1915, during those polls about Scouting's rank program, one respondent, a "Charles D. Hart" of Pennsylvania, proved prescient. He called for "a medal like the Victoria Cross, *very*

difficult to get that any Scout may receive for special heroism not only in lifesaving." It would be several years before anyone was willing to listen.

The actual Honor Medal nomination form underscored this bias. Though it emphasized that "It is of the utmost importance that in any case of rescue whether from drowning, from death by fire, electricity, or from being run over, explicit details should be given that will enable the committee to decide as to the degree of the award" everything in the application was oriented toward water rescues. In other words: if you expect to get a medal for anything but saving someone from drowning, you'd better die in the process. And if that wasn't enough, the point was driven home by a list of questions that included: *Did you have*

a boat? What was the dept of the water? And What wa the condition of the bottom i.e. was it covered with weed or snags?

Needless to say, most po tential applicants got th message.

Nevertheless, one non drowning rescue applicatio did manage to reach the Na tional Court of Honor tha year. The story it told wa terrifying – and, to our moc ern eyes, a glimpse into wha might have been scores c equally astonishing rescue on dry ground for which ap plications never were writter much less read.

On a sweltering first da of July in Houston, Texas, a about 4:30 in the afternoor young Ralph Landgrebe, a was playing in his yard wit a friend when they found length of wire used by Ralph father as an entry gate t keep horses in a vacant lo Ralph convinced his frien

An electric trolley car in 1913.

o throw the wire over the overhead cable that passed down the center of the street or the trolley line in hopes of starting a fire, or at least some sparks.

When the wire failed to produce the desired result, Ralph decided to run out and pull down the illegal wire before the next trolley passed by. He jumped up and caught the end of the wire. And when he came down, his feet landed on the rail embedded in the street. The result was a massive short-circuit of electricity that left the boy in a crumpled form on the rails, is smoking hands still holding the live wire. His frightened friend ran home.

Riding by at that moment was Scout **Dorris Giles**, a 14-year-old paperboy delivering the *Houston Chronicle* in his route across the north side of the city. He saw Ralph Landgrebe run out of his parent's house and into the street, heading for the wire. He yelled for the boy not to touch the wire, but as Ralph later would recount (no doubt translated by an adult), he heard Giles' warning "but the wire just seemed to jump out at me."

"I put up my hand to keep it out of my face; my hand grasped the wire and I was helpless. My other hand raised of its own accord and grasped the wire too."

The boy instantly was wracked with agonizing pain and fell to the ground. There, through a charged haze ("While I could not move a muscle I knew everything') he saw Dorris Giles approach. Giles: "I saw that his hands were burning [as] I ran toward him." Dorris grabbed the boy's leg and tried to pull him away. Landgrebe momentarily felt his agony abate, only to return suddenly. Dor-

ris Giles, holding the boy's leg, had created his own short circuit – and the blast of electricity had thrown him on his back in the street.

"I got up feeling very dazed and weak," Giles later recalled, "and I was afraid to touch him again because I knew I would get hurt if I did – but I [also] knew that he would be killed unless I got him away." But now he had a plan. Running to his bag, Dorris grabbed a newspaper and returned to Ralph. This time, holding the unfolded newspaper in his hand as an insulator, he again grabbed the boy's leg. It worked.

At that moment, Ralph's older sister Jessie looked out the window, saw what was happening, and ran out of the house. She appeared at Dorris' side – and even as he warned her off, she reached down to grab her brother. The resulting shock knocked her off her feet. "When I got up Dorris was pulling [my brother] off the car track towards the ditch."

Dorris told Jessie to run back to the house and telephone a doctor but by the time she got there a neighbor already was making the call. So she went back out to the accident scene. There, an injured and mourning Dorris Giles gave her the news she most dreaded: "He is dead."

But at that very moment, Ralph, who had been unconscious since being pulled from the tracks, woke up, heard his own death pronouncement, and sat up. Within moments he was on his feet leaning against his sister, while Dorris held the boy's burned hands. They led him home and placed him in the parlor on the family davenport, then wrapped wet towels around the boy's hands. Ralph eventually was taken to St. Joseph's Infirmary to have his burns treated, then sent home.

Ralph's father, J.W. Landgrebe, later reported that the boy's right palm was burned nearly to the bone, its third finger nearly burned off; while his left forefinger also was burned to the bone. Furthermore, he had a few bruises on his head and back.

"Twenty-four hours afterwards he [still] was so full of electricity that your fingers would tingle if you touched him, recalled Ralph's father." When visitors sympathetically smoothed his hair, Ralph would complain that he "hurt all over" – even at the top of his head.

As for Dorris Giles, who had braved and survived the voltage of an electric chair, he apparently finished his paper route that afternoon and went home for dinner. All that he ever said about the aftermath was that "my right arm ached all evening from the shock."

In the subsequent coverage of the event in Dorris' own *Houston Chronicle* – "Chronicle Newsboy is Hero; Rescues Victim of Live Wire," – the manager of the Houston Electric Company, who most certainly appreciated the risk Giles had taken, said:

"From the facts which have been presented to us in this case it seems to me that the action of young Giles is a fine piece of heroism ... It also brings out the tremendous value of the Boy Scout Movement in this country in educating boys just what to do in cases of emergency."

Back in New York, the application, affidavits, and newspaper clippings were met with skepticism. No one doubted what Dorris Giles had accomplished – there was too much evidence for that – but the actual event had been so extreme, the danger so great, that the National Court of Honor wondered if the boy actually understood the suicidal risk he was taking. It took a committee formed in Houston to investigate the case, and a subsequent letter sent from the superintendent of Schools to certify:

... Dorris Giles really understood the danger to which he was subjecting himself, that he met this danger knowingly, that his act was undoubtedly the means of saving the life of Ralph Landgrebe, that the action was one which required coolness, and skill as well as courage, as is evidenced by the fact that after the first unsuccessful attempt to remove the live wire, he recalled having learned in his Boy Scout work the fact that paper is a non-conductor of electricity and to use his newspapers in removing the live wire.

The National Court of Honor apparently was satisfied with this reply and Dorris Giles was added to the list of Scouts approved for consideration for Honor Medals and Letters of Commendation.

Improvisation

The difference between how the public imagined that these final judgments were made (and how they actually occurred in a meeting room at Boy Scout headquarters in the Manhattan YMCA building) was a wide one. As late as 1918, Beard would admit in a letter to BSA president Colin Livingstone and his executive board cohorts that "at present the National Court of Honor exists only on paper and the chairman thereof handles nothing but the life-saving department" with the assistant of two BSA headquarters staffers serving as secretary and administrative assistant – "but it is hoped that sometime in the near future the National Court of Honor will be regularly organized and able to function and be of great service to the Scout Movement."

Potential awardees and their families filled out multi-page applications (and often notarized statements from themselves and other eyewitnesses). However, for American Scouting's first decade, the actual Honor Medal decision-making process essentially came down to Dan Beard and Ernest Seton sorting through the stack separately (as the two men did not get along) and making their medal selections. The results were recorded by the "secretary," who was, early on, Chief Scout Executive West. More than 200 Honor Medals were awarded in this manner.

Two Candia

The casualness, even improvisation, of this process is on full display in a November 10, 1913, memo laying out the decision-making process for that year's Honor Medal nominees. For one Scout, the record shows that the nomination was delivered to Seton and Beard in late September, and back to Beard a second time a month later.

On October 18, Seton recommended a boy for a Bronze Lifesaving Medal; and because there is "No reply from Mr. Beard yet," the new secretary, Mr. Milton B. Sackett, a former Scoutmaster who holds the distinction of being the first adult volunteer ever to earn a BSA merit badge, stepped in to vote for the Bronze as well.

Indeed, for such a notoriously unpredictable figure, Seton appears to have been quite dutiful in making his Honor Medal votes while Beard – probabl

onor **Badges**

Bronze Lifesaving Medal recipients Scouts John A. Norman (left) and Henry Eichner.

)ecause he was busy try-ng to keep the BSA pro-ram alive – is consis-ently absent. There also s a clue that diplomacy)etween Scouting's two)rickly founders was as mportant in these votes s the actual quality of he applicant. Thus, re-,arding the application f assistant Scoutmaster Villiam Charles Reed f Geneva, Maryland mentioned earlier as the escuer of Scout Charles)ross), Seton states: "It s a poor case as the res-uer was not in danger,)ut I say Bronze if Mr. 3eard does or else only

a Letter of Commen-dation." In two other cases, where Seton and Beard disagree – one where Beard wants to give a Bronze Lifesaving Medal and Seton just a Letter of Commenda-tion; the other where Beard wants to give the Letter of Commen-dation and Seton no national recognition at all – the cases are held over "for a meeting of the entire Court," which likely is code for putting Seton, Beard, Sackett and the Court's fourth member, A.R. Forbush, in the same room to hash things out.

And what of Dorris Giles of Houston, Texas, the young Scout who risked lethal levels of electricity to save another's life? As of November 6, 1913, only Seton had replied – and had nominated the boy for the Silver Lifesaving Medal, which Giles ultimately would receive. That even Giles is considered ineligible for the highest Lifesaving Medal explains why there would be no Gold Lifesaving Medal awarded for another four years.

The First Loss

In early 1914, *Boys' Life* carried a tragic story – one made even more touching by the accompanying photograph of a very young boy with a wistful expression, blond hair, a bill-less cap, and wearing what appeared to be an oversized swimming robe.

His name was Homer Hathaway – and he was, as the headline announced, the first American Scout to die trying to save a life:

> *"The Christmas season was saddened for the Boy Scouts of Oconomowoc, [Wisconsin], as the result of the drowning of one of their number on Lake La Bella in their town. A crowd of Scouts and other young people had started out to skate and play hockey on the lake. One man, George Grokosky, who was skating by himself, crossed the ice and went through.* **Homer Hathaway** *and Russell Eddy, both of Troop 1, rushed to his rescue..."*

They didn't make it. Before the two boys could reach Grokosky, they too broke through the ice. Now all three were at mortal risk.

LEFT:
Homer Hathaway in 1913.
ACROSS:
The Bronze Lifesaving Medal presented to Dudley Cook for rescuing George Grokosky on December 22, 1913.

Another, quick-thinking, Scout named **John Dudley Ray Cook** – "a new member of the troop," grabbed a rope and threw it first to Russell and then Grokosky somehow pulling them out of the freezing water and onto ice thick enough to hold them.

"He then tried to reach Homer in the same way but could not do it. In order to get him, Dudley had to go in himself and swim to Homer, who sank just before his rescuer reached him, and did not come up again."

By now, the boys' Scoutmaster and other adults had reached the scene. They dove for Homer Hathaway and, after an hour, managed to bring his body to the surface. Attempts at resuscitation proved fruitless.

"The funeral was held the day before Christmas, and the greatest honor was shown by the Scouts of Homer's troop. The whole troop acted as honorary guards, while the six members of his patrol were pall-bearers. At the grave, the boys planted an evergreen as a token of their perpetual remembrance of their heroic brother Scout. The Scout call was given by the bugler over the grave as a last farewell to the Scout who lost his life in trying to save another."

Dudley Cook received the Bronze Lifesaving Medal for his heroic actions. And Homer Hathaway? Dan Beard and the Boy Scouts of America seemed to have no idea what do about a boy who, largely because of his youth and lack of training, had died during the rescue. The Gold Lifesaving Medal that had been reserved for just such a supreme sacrifice was withheld. It appeared that Homer's death just *wasn't* good enough for the honor. No record of Hathaway appears in the official records of the National Court of Honor. Instead, he was forgotten for more than a century – until now.

A Time for Heroes

Like several other initiatives in the BSA's first decade (most famously Eagle Scouting, but also supporting War Bond solicitations, tree censuses, scrap metal and rubber drives, and putting up posters - *see below*) the Honor Medal program took on a life of its own, capturing the imagination of the general public.

Heroism was in the air in those years. One obvious reason was the gathering clouds of war in Europe – and the clash of millions of men under arms that began in August 1914. Every day, the news was filled with stories of brave and heroic acts by French, British, Russian, and (while America remained neutral) German soldiers. After May 1915 and the sinking of the *RMS Lusitania* those drumbeats began to be heard in the USA.

At the same time, the newspapers regularly carried accounts of the recipients of the Carnegie Medal for heroism. In 1904, as part of his historic burst of philanthropy, steel baron Andrew Carnegie placed $5 million into a fund dedicated to honor civilians who had committed acts of great bravery in the service of others in their private lives (and when needed) to support their families or help those heroes with medical costs.

The precipitating event for this gift was the worst mining disaster in American history – at the Herwick coal mine in Western Pennsylvania, near Pittsburgh – where an explosion of trapped methane in the mine killed 179 miners, leaving just one badly burned survivor. Two men working nearby, Daniel A. Lyle and the mine engineer Selwyn M. Taylor, upon hearing the explosion, immediately raced into the mine to help. They died as well.

On hearing of Lyle and Taylor's sacrifice, Carnegie was so moved that he immediately had medals minted privately to be awarded to the men's families. And soon after, he created the Hero Fund that still operates today and has awarded nearly 10,000 medals and $75 million in grants in the century of its existence.

In an age of limited insurance and workman's compensation, the Carnegie Honor Fund was a revelation, a last resort, and an *angel of mercy* to those people who were suffering for having done the right thing. Not surprisingly, in its early years, the Fund and its medal recipients received considerable media attention. And, in fact, it wasn't uncommon for some of the more illustrious of BSA's Honor Medal recipients to be considered for Carnegie awards.

There is no evidence that the creation by Beard, Seton, and Carnegie of their respective awards was anything but the coincidence. And it isn't surprising that a decade later in the 1910s that the general public typically equated these two Honor Medals. Thus, the same *Houston Chronicle* article that lauded Dorris Giles' Boy Scout training also quotes the manager of the local electric company as saying "It is an action worthy of consideration by the Carnegie Hero Fund Commission."

Because of their similar charters the Carnegie medals typically went to adults (mostly men) and the BSA Honor Medal to boys. It seems inevitable that the latter would be seen as the "Carnegie for Boys." This too added to the status of the Honor Medal – and the expectations for it. And so, while Scouting's the Honor Medal program remained little more than a boutique operation inside the organization – a tiny, but distinguished sideshow – in the outside world it loomed far larger in the public's mind. This was not a situation that could last much longer.

BOY SCOUT HERO

ROBERT CRUIT,
The young Takoma Park Boy Scout, who, at the risk of his life, rushed into a fire, carried out a little girl whose clothes were aflame. He burned himself, in extinguishing the fiery garments. His companions are to ask that a hero medal be awarded him. Boy Scout headquarters are considering the request.

And at the end of 1918, the BSA's Honor Medal program found itself in crisis and in desperate need of reformation.

Why? Because, now heroic young Boy Scouts were dying – one after another – and their extreme valor no longer could be ignored.

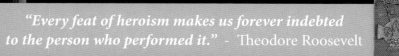
"Every feat of heroism makes us forever indebted to the person who performed it." - Theodore Roosevelt

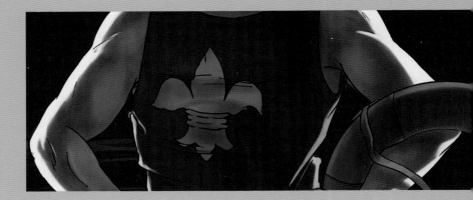

*"All I can do is to express
my deep sympathy and my pride
as an American in the gallant boy."*
Theodore Roosevelt, in a letter of condolence to the
mother of Scout Robert W. Eicher Jr. in 1917.

The Ultimate Sacrifice

CHAPTER

Thirteen years after the events of 1918, when he sat down to write the opening to *Boy Heroes of Today* (the first official history of the Honor Medal), Dan Beard still seemed bewildered by the stunning events of that year and still was trying to make sense of what had happened.

For nearly a decade, the heroism recognition program had progressed nicely on its own accord. So well, in fact, that as noted, Beard sometimes didn't even bother to approve the award decisions made by Chief Scout Ernest Seton and the National Court of Honor's junior members. Furthermore, over the years, the entire process had become much more systematized, most notably in the creation of a nomination form that severely circumscribed the eligibility of candidates for medals and commendations. Most of all, the number of awards given each year continued to grow at a steady rate – suggesting that the program was well-known to Scouts around the country, or that the percentage of Scout heroes was growing commensurately with the membership of Scouting, or (from the most romantic perspective) that Scouting was making America's boys braver and more competent.

Thus, in April 1918, Beard proudly could report to BSA President Livingstone (in the same letter in which he notes the National Board's skeleton staff) that:

In 1917, we bestowed honor medals for heroism in life saving, 35 this year against 24 of last. The Chairman is glad to report that there appears to be in the field, a better understanding of what we mean by heroism, as indicated by fewer applications made by those not deserving medals than there has been in previous years. In many of the cases the boys have shown great heroism and a remarkable advance in their ability to think and act quickly and intelligently when confronted with critical conditions involving possible tragedy. This shows that the Scout training is accomplishing great results in character making, and doing much to minimize danger by teaching how to act in the presence of it.

He also threw in a final pitch for the National Court of Honor:

. . . here is the great opportunity of the Boy Scout Movement and the real and vital necessity of a live and active National Court of Honor, for that is the Court that should set the standard for achievement in all that is great and noble.

He soon would come to regret that boast. But for the moment, Dan Beard had a nice little program receiving considerable publicity, while earning both the BSA and himself no little credit. Best of all, it seemed to run all by itself. Indeed, he was feeling so good about the situation that he couldn't resist a little flourish (and name dropping) at the end of his report:

"Mark Twain often said 'Education and environment can bring a body up to believe in anything.' This report and the disastrous effects of German [war] propaganda verify Mark Twain's saying, and also forces on us the realization of the immensity of the responsibility which rests upon our shoulders. We must be a force, a vital force, for the propaganda of right living, of honor, chivalry and patriotism . . ."

What Beard had *failed* to report was that during the year discussed three other Scouts already had *died* in the act of trying to save another and had not been recognized by the National Court of Honor. Three months later, when Beard received the news from Nebraska regarding Russell Grimes' death in the wagon accident, he no longer could ignore this shocking jump in number of Boy Scout deaths. The National Court of Honor had to act.

Many anticipated this moment would come, it now being four years since the sad drowning of would-be rescuer Homer Hathaway. After all, hadn't the National Court of Honor reserved the Gold Lifesaving Medal for just such a scenario?

But it was Grimes' death that seemed to hit Beard the hardest, not just for its shocking nature and the boy's lonely death, but because Beard, as Scouting's chief advocate, understood the tragic story's potential to destroy everything he had worked for over the preceding two decades.

Even a dozen years later, the boy's story still was rolling around in Beard's mind. Why had Grimes found himself in that lethal situation? Had Scouting somehow failed him? Had the 14-year-old, First Class Scout not been trained sufficiently to know what to do?

"It was not a foolhardy or impossible task that Grimes had undertaken," he writes. "He was familiar with horses and wagons. He could drive an automobile, knew the value of brakes and their importance in an emergency. Riding behind in the jolting wagon when it was empty, and taking the bumps when it was loaded down with logs, Russell conducted himself as well as any adult helper might have done."

What's more, Beard told his readers, "The situation had the possibility of real danger, but no one regarded it too seriously."

But, of course, the situation had proven serious indeed; the possibility of real danger suddenly became the reality of it. Now a young man had been lost forever. And how close the line had been between success and tragedy:

"Had the horses stayed on the roadway a minute or two longer the driver might have brought them under control again. In that case the driver probably would have remarked at the end of the trip, 'That's a game kid!' One or two people might have heard of it and patted the boy on the back. But Russell Grimes had lost his life."

Perhaps the reason Dan Beard still was meditating in 1932 on Grimes' untimely death was that in 1918 he had little time to do so. In short order the previous year, three other Scouts had died attempting to rescue others, and each had presented a different challenge to the quiet status quo of the BSA's Honor Medal program:

• **Robert W. Eicher Jr.** died in the summer of 1917 in a much reported tragedy. His was the first application to reach the BSA's headquarters asking it to award the boy with a Gold Lifesaving Medal. Just 14-years-old and a Second Class Scout, Eicher was, in Beard's words "a poor swimmer, had no life-saving experience whatever." Eicher was picnicking with his family and some friends. After lunch, one of the girls in the group, who had just learned how to swim, decided to join some of the other girls down at the nearby Loyalhanna Creek. As none of the other girls knew how to swim, the girl – Eicher's friend, 15-year-old Ada Mazie Hugg – decided to demonstrate her new skill for them.

Moments later, young Robert heard screams, including his own name. He ran to the sound to find Ada flailing desperately in the fast current and whirlpools. No one else came to her aid. Of the seven people at the picnic, only Robert knew how to swim. Though he'd only had limited training in lifesaving, the boy didn't hesitate and dove right in. In doing so he made a fatal mistake: he didn't take a few seconds to remove his heavy sweater or shoes. He instantly was weighed down and fighting the current.

Still, incredibly, Eicher did manage to reach Ada, who already was sinking under the water, and briefly hold her head above the surface. But the current and the weight of his clothes quickly overcame him. The pair, with Robert desperately trying to get Ada to shore as they disappeared again and again under the water, quickly was swept downstream. When their bodies were found, Eicher still was gripping Ada's arm.

August 29th, 1917.

My dear Madam:

I beg to extend to you my most sincere sympathy and my great admiration for your gallant young son. It is a terrible loss and no words of mine can soften it to you. All I can do is to express my deep sympathy and my pride as an American in the gallant ~~mmmmm~~ boy.

Faithfully yours,

Theodore Roosevelt

Mrs. R. W. Eicher,
Jeanette, Pa.

This is the first Gold Lifesaving Medal (with reverse inscription) ever awarded. It was presented to the mother of Scout Robert Eicher after she received a letter of condolence from Theodore Roosevelt.

The story of the doomed boy and girl quickly became a major news item across the East Coast. Three weeks after the tragedy, the story got a second boost, when the boy's grieving mother received a letter from former President Theodore Roosevelt, who had read the press coverage and felt compelled to write. The note said:

"I beg to extend to you my most sincere sympathy and my great admiration for your gallant young son. It is a terrible loss and no words of mine can soften it for you. All I can do is to express my deep sympathy and my pride as an American in the gallant (crossed out the words 'young man') *boy."*

That edit at the end of TR's note contained volumes. No matter how much he was lauded as a heroic young man, Robert Eicher still was very much a boy – a boy who had, for all of his bravery, done a foolhardy thing by jumping into the stream without first looking for another way (branch, pole, rope, etc.) to effect Ada's rescue, without

running downstream to make the swim shorter, and most of all without stripping off his shoes and extra clothing. Roosevelt knew all of this, and so did most of the adults who read the news coverage of the tragedy. He was nothing more than a boy, they told themselves. He didn't know what he was doing. Robert

Eicher's doomed rescue attempt certainly hadn't been meaningless – no such sacrifice ever could be – but it came very close to being pointless. What began as a single tragedy had become a double one.

Robert Eicher Jr. was buried in the Jeanette (PA) Memorial Park, where his carefully tended tombstone still can be seen. It reads:

Robert W. Eicher
1902-1917
A Boy Hero
Who Gave
His Life for
Another

"I Tried to Do My Duty as a Boy Scout, Mother"

SOUTH ORANGE, N. J.—The Boy Scouts of America are pledged to "do a good turn daily." This "good turn" is done both to man and beast. It ranges from filling mother's wood box to feeding a hungry dog. There is no limit to its scope. Gordon Seyfried, a boy scout twelve years old, ran up against something new in the way of doing his daily good turn. He found his mother's maid in the act of shooting herself.

Gordon saw his chance to do a good turn. It was not only his chance but his duty, as he saw it. So he tried to tear the revolver from the maid's hand.

The revolver was discharged. The bullet passed through the maid's body,

A news item in the Maurice (IA) Times *describing the heroic death of Scout George Seyfried. He was awarded the 4th Gold Lifesaving Medal.*

As his name-dropping of his friend Mark Twain suggests, Dan Beard was no country rube but rather a man accustomed to operating in the halls of power and dealing with the powerful men who inhabited them. When he wasn't in buckskins, Beard favored tailored suits and elegant dinner meetings. And, as attested by the fact that he had taken a tiny group surrounded by a host of competitors and helped turn it into the largest youth organization in American history, Beard also was a master politician.

Like all great politicians (not to mention great outdoorsmen), Beard always had his ear to the ground, listening for the changing vibrations of the popular will, sensing the next shift in the culture, detecting incoming threats before they appeared. And now, with the death of Robert Eicher, Beard could see in the letters to editors and hear in the comments of his powerful peers, a disquiet about the young man's death. Why had the boy been so heedless of the risk? Why hadn't he been (and this must have been especially painful for Beard given the Scout Motto) better "prepared?"

Then came news of a second death:

• **Edward Samuel Goodnow**, a 16-year-old Scout from Springfield, Massachusetts, managed to save another Scout from drowning, before himself drowning. It was the second loss of a Scout in a water rescue – the heart of the Honor Medal program.

It got worse.

The third death was one of the strangest, and saddest, events in the history of the Honor Medal:

• **George Gordon Seyfried** of South Orange, New Jersey, was a tiny boy. Just 12-years-old, he had joined the Scouts just a few months before and still was a Tenderfoot. On that fateful day he happened upon the family maid ("servant" in some accounts), a strapping young woman much larger than Seyfried. She had just fallen out of an intense love affair and was "despondent and desperate" – in fact, had resolved to end her life. When young George encountered her, she already had obtained a revolver and was holding it to her chest, preparing to pull the trigger.

Beard later writes:

"Scout Seyfried knew nothing about handling a situation such as this. He grabbed the girl's wrist, and tried to wrench the gun from her hand." In fact, all that he managed to do was flatten the gun against the maid's chest. *"In the struggle the gun went off, and the bullet passing through the girl's left breast struck him in the neck,"* the bullet lodging there.

With the bullet having glanced off her ribcage, the maid survived. But it was a different story for little George. His mother, weeping over him, asked why he would attempt such a thing. Peering up at her, Gordon Seyfried whispered, "I saw her with a pistol and tried to do my duty as a Boy Scout, Mother." Moments later, he was dead.

It was a story almost too sad to read. It not only shook the leadership of the BSA, but, together with his growing sense of a changing public image of Scouting, appears to have begun to change something inside Dan Beard as well. The echo of that change still can be heard in his description of George Seyfried's death years later:

"Without that spirit – the spirit that willingly takes the great risk in an emergency – what use would be the knowledge of the best means to make water and fire rescues, to resuscitate, and the many other things the advanced Boy Scout learns?"[7]

Unprepared

Boy Scouts across the nation were exhibiting extraordinary bravery, performing astonishing acts of heroism, and rescuing victims in sometimes terrifying predicaments. But too often these boys were rushing into those potential lethal situations without either the right judgment or the proper training and preparation to effect a successful rescue of the victim while surviving the event themselves.

Had Scouting done these boys a disservice? Certainly many of those boys who had jumped into an emergency were "born heroes" in the sense that they exhibited certain traits and attributes – physical assuredness, empathy, a different assessment of risk, a deep sense of duty and responsibility – that all but compelled to them to commit to the rescue. In addition, many of these and other Scouts carried a skill set with them at a young age (swimming and lifesaving in particular, but also first aid and leadership) that gave them the confidence to keep calm and know what do in an emergency situation.

But it is a big leap – sometimes literally – between having the ability to be a successful rescuer and actually becoming one. And now the question was being asked: Was Boy Scouting, with its seemingly endless stories of heroes and its requirements and merit badges in aquatics and first aid, actually convincing young men to race heedlessly into dangerous situations for which they hadn't the maturity, the temperament or the sufficient skills to succeed, or even survive?

To this question, the Boy Scouts of America (and in particular Daniel Carter Beard) had no ready answer. Perhaps there was no answer, only a recognition that Scouting could not retreat from its core philosophy. After all, what would it be without its message of bravery and skill – trustworthy, loyal, and brave were points of the Scout Law; to help other people at all times was at the heart of the Scout Oath; most of all "Be Prepared" was Scouting's motto – but an empty shell, and little more than a social club? No, Scouting's only choice, the right choice, was to move forward, become better at what it already did well, to prepare Scouts of all ages to better deal with emergencies, and ultimately, to rethink the very meaning of heroism itself.

For now, however, in mid-1919, the program's only choice was to investigate, and then render decisions upon these first four "true" candidates for the Gold Lifesaving Medal (with Homer Hathaway now long forgotten), announce the awards, and then wait for their stories – and the concerns they created – to fade.

Today, more than a century into its existence, and after having survived wars, demographic shifts and numerous controversies, the Boy Scouts seems among the most durable of American institutions.

But that wasn't the case in 1918. The BSA at that point just was eight-years-old with about than 1.1 million members. Other Scouting competitors had largely faded away but they still could be revived if the BSA foundered. While it had managed the exclusive and critical step of obtaining a Congressional charter, that charter easily could be revoked if a major scandal made the BSA a political liability. While Scouting enjoyed enormous reservoirs of goodwill for its recent work on war bonds and war materials drives, there were a number of important national figures – not the least of which was Theodore Roosevelt himself – who had not yet forgiven the organization for not becoming an explicit training program for budding soldiers.

So, rather than being an overwrought response to a tense situation, Beard's reaction seems measured and prudent.

Had they known his plans, not everyone would have agreed with Beard's decision. American Scouting still lived in the shadow of Baden-Powell, the founder of the international Scouting Movement and eventual Chief Scout of the World. Several years earlier at the BSA's founding event on September 23, 1910, at New York's Waldorf-Astoria Hotel, an event attended by both Beard and Seton, the old general had said, "The heroism that is being displayed by Boy Scouts is wonderful. Every day I get reports of life saving. They do not hesitate to jump into the water. They know that it is their business to go in and do the job."

*An image from 1912 depicting Boy Scouts
utilizing the Two-Person Carry rescue technique.*

Over the years Baden-Powell also had written:

"A Scout will sacrifice his life to save his 'pal' or even a stranger, for the matter of that – especially if the stranger is a woman or a child" **and** *"Remember...(and Be Prepared if ever should it be necessary)...to endure hardships, help one another, and meet death bravely – not caring for your own safety so long as you are carrying out your duty"* and most of all *"If a fellow is not capable of sacrifice he should not call himself a man."*

Reading those passages at the end of the decade, Dan Beard must have shaken his head. It was hard to argue that a message hadn't been given to America's Scouts – a call to action across the nation that now almost would be impossible to excise from the program. There was no choice, Beard realized. He would go forward with Scouting – but now his inspirational quote from Baden-Powell would be a different one: "Every boy has just as much a chance of being a life-saving hero if he chooses to prepare himself for it." (*Scouting for Boys*, 1910).

Beard would spend the rest of his career focused on that "preparation." And Scouting would take up the torch and carry it to the present day.

Revise and Restructure

There now was a clear path forward. The first step would be to deliberate on the applications and move on. The BSA's National Court of Honor ultimately agreed that all four young men had met the requirements for the Gold Lifesaving Medal. Each of the medals was engraved on the reverse side, in italic script, with the name of the Scout and his dates of birth and death. The medals then were mailed to each Scout's home council and from there delivered to the Scout's family.

Within weeks, the BSA also proudly announced a new partnership with the Red Cross to teach all Scouts to swim. The timing was not a coincidence.

In the end, the crisis Beard feared never materialized. Americans chose instead to honor the sacrifice of the four remarkable boys and move on. Dan Beard was relieved. But he also knew that if the current pattern continued, the controversy would erupt anew – perhaps in a much worse way. He resolved to not let that happen – even if it meant reforming Scouting itself.

[As an aside, it is interesting to note that, in fact, there were nominations for *five* Scouts who died serving others that arrived at BSA

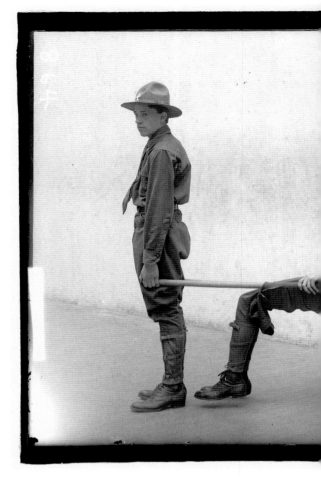

headquarters in the fateful years of 1917 and 1918. This last nomination was for **John Langbourne Williams II**, the scion of one of the leading banking families in Richmond, Virginia. When the Spanish Influenza epidemic hit Richmond, Williams, a 15-year-old First Class Scout, volunteered to help the sick at the local emergency hospital. There, while in the discharge of his duties, the boy contracted the disease himself and died soon thereafter.

Moved by his "unselfish desire of high order to serve humanity in the community in which he lived" and by the fact that "as a true Scout he lived fully up to the Scout Oath," was efficient, fully "prepared" and "faithful unto death," the Richmond BSA Council prepared a resolution of acclamation and sent it to Williams' parents

(John's father would outlive him by 33 years), local media, and BSA's National Headquarters.

There is no record of the National Court of Honor addressing this resolution. Why? Probably two reasons. First, the nature of John Williams' sacrifice, though noble, was far from the Court's then-current notion of what constituted "rescue" – and not something it wanted to address in that troublesome year, much less add another name to the Gold Lifesaving Medal list. Second, as long noted by historians, the Spanish Influenza pandemic, coming as it did so soon after the disasters of World War I seemed to induce a kind of global amnesia about its existence – despite the fact that it killed an estimated 50 million people worldwide. Humanity seemed to want to forget about it – and did so for more than a generation.

And so, the memory of John Langbourne Williams II, a true hero, found itself caught between a bureaucracy in crisis and a world in denial, so his sacrifice was forgotten. Until now.]

Blue Ribbon Board

One of the advantages of having a small board filled with people empowered to make big decisions is that, in times of crisis, you can move very quickly. The BSA's National Court of Honor did just that.

In spite of his admission about the actual number of active members on the Court, Beard had long packed its membership roll with a number of distinguished figures – who, until this point, likely had considered it little more than a ceremonial position; the usual "we'll put your name on the masthead, but you won't be required to do anything" offer made by most non-profits. But now, obviously, things had changed and Beard appears to have reeled in the Court to do some serious work.

The members of the Court now included (besides Seton and Beard) BSA President Colin H. Livingstone, Deputy Scout Executive Dr. George J. Fisher (the man who made volleyball an American sport), science writer Frederick K. Vreeland, and the famed writer and explorer of upper Labrador, Dillon Wallace. Most interesting were the two other non-Scouting Court members: explorers Belmore Brown and Colonel David T. Abercrombie (whose name survives today in the outdoor clothing company he founded in 1892, Abercrombie & Fitch).

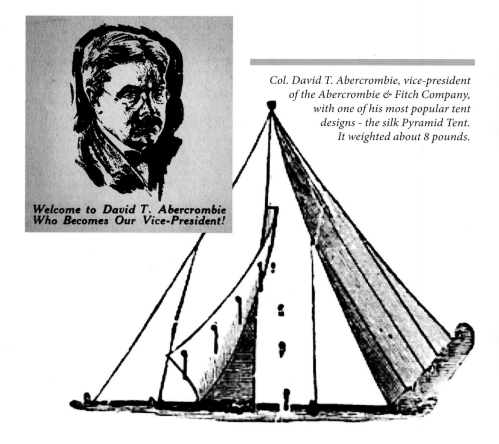

Welcome to David T. Abercrombie Who Becomes Our Vice-President!

Col. David T. Abercrombie, vice-president of the Abercrombie & Fitch Company, with one of his most popular tent designs - the silk Pyramid Tent. It weighted about 8 pounds.

Col. Abercrombie was born into a Scottish immigrant family in Baltimore in 1867 and who dreamed of adventure from his youth. As soon as he graduated from engineering school he took a job as a surveyor and civil engineer for a number of railroad companies, mapping previously undocumented sections of the Appalachian Mountains from North Carolina to Kentucky. It was in the field during these expeditions that Abercrombie began to create rugged outdoor clothes for himself and for his fellow crew members.

Soon, his increasingly popular clothing was joined by other camping gear. His brother recalled:

[David's] inventive genius enabled him to make a practical solution to most every problem of the prospector, huntsman, camper, and woodsman. He was one of the best woodsmen, in its broadest sense, of his time. When sheet aluminum was first made, he was the first to utilize it in the manufacturing of camp utensils, nesting kits and other useful articles for the camper. This application was soon followed in general use in home kitchen ware.[8]

This idyllic existence ended in 1892, when Abercrombie developed severe farsightedness (he would wear thick glasses the rest of his life) and, at just 25, he was forced to retire from surveying. It was Abercrombie's fellow surveyors who suggested that he pursue a new career designing and making his outdoor clothes and continue to invent new camping gear. The young man took their advice. And after six years of working for manufacturing companies, Abercrombie decided to open a retail store of his own. The David T. Abercrombie Company opened its first store in 1898 on South Street in Manhattan selling everything from safari clothes and tents to fishing poles and rifles.

The store was an instant hit, becoming a popular outfitter for wealthy and worldly New Yorkers. Shrewdly, Abercrombie decided to go to them by moving the store uptown to its now legendary home on Park Avenue. Soon, Abercrombie could name among his customers the likes of polar explorer Robert Peary, future President Theodore Roosevelt, and the BSA's co-incorporator, William Dickson Boyce. Soon, no expedition to any of the wildest and explored regions of the Earth travelled without Abercrombie clothes and gear. At the outbreak of the Spanish-American War in 1898, Roosevelt not only outfitted himself, but also the entire Rough Riders in Abercrombie-produced uniforms.

One of Abercrombie's most loyal customers was an attorney named Ezra Fitch. In 1900, Fitch abandoned his practice to join Abercrombie as partner in the soon to be re-named Abercrombie & Fitch Co. Unfortunately, it took only a few years for the partnership to crumble (Abercrombie wanted to stick wth the outdoor business, Fitch wanted to expand the business into new markets). So, in 1907, Abercrombie left the company he'd created (the one that survives to this day) to found a new company, specializing in textiles, aptly named the David T. Abercrombie Co.

Though all-but forgotten today, this new enterprise proved to be his second great entrepreneurial success. After the outbreak of World War I, he was named director of the New York Packing Depot and awarded the rank of Major. Abercrombie's success at the Depot (including some far-reaching innovations in folding, packing, and a new kind of waterproof paper) was estimated to have saved the U.S. government $85 million in a single year. He finished the war as a Lt. Colonel.

The presence of Col. Abercrombie, a legendary outdoorsman, a current national hero, and a friend to the most famous outdoorsmen of the era, gave the newly configured National Court of Honor a heightened professionalism, responsibility, and rigor in the public's eye…exactly the image Dan Beard now wanted to present.

Mountaineer and world explorer Belmore Browne in 1920.

Living Heroes

The first (and most obvious) task was to rethink the rules regarding the Gold Lifesaving Medal which now in retrospect seemed both misguided and more than a little ghoulish. It was obvious – especially in light of the recent bad publicity – that there was no true correlation between the risk involved in a rescue and the survival of the rescuer.

That vote likely occurred in late 1919, because by April 8, 1920, in the BSA's *Annual Report*, Beard advises: "In regard to the Gold [Lifesaving] Medal, we believe that we should not wait until the boy is dead before presenting him with a Gold [Lifesaving] Medal, as has been the custom." From now on, Scouting's highest award for saving a life would not always be associated with the death of a brave young man.

The next step was predictable – the inevitable response of a large institution to bad publicity attached to one of its high-profile products: *reposition and rebrand*. Scouting's existing lifesaving medals now carried too much public baggage, the extraordinary good works they celebrated now were too tarnished to fully restore to their former glory. And, as any executive knows, there's no better time for a complete reconstruction than at just such a moment. And no better way to do this than all at once in a clean sweep.

And so, no doubt at Beard's suggestion, the National Court of Honor officially ended its Bronze, Silver, and Gold Lifesaving Honor Medal program. Replacing it would be two awards: one for saving a life at considerable risk to one's self; the second for saving a life at extreme risk to oneself.[11] Further, they would both share the same design – a medallion hanging from a more modern ribbon (like the Eagle Medal) topped by a single metal bar inscribed "Boy Scouts of America" – the only difference being that the higher medal would be distinguished by a pair of crossed palms attached to the ribbon. They both would be referred to as the "Gold Honor Medal," with the higher one bearing the extra words "with crossed palms."

To design this medal, Beard turned to the other famous non-Scouting member of the National Court of Honor.

Belmore Browne is a name little known today except among collectors of North American landscape paintings. And though, in 1920, he was at his height of fame, Browne was in fact better known as an explorer and adventurer. It was this singular combination of outdoorsman and artist that made Browne the perfect person to design the new Honor Medal.

Born in the Catskill Mountains in upstate New York, Browne, in a trip unusual for the time (1888) and at just age eight, travelled with his family on a sightseeing trip to Alaska. The memory of that trip stayed with him the rest of his life. In his twenties he returned to Alaska in a series of epic adventures that established Browne as a world-class outdoorsman.

Such was his reputation by the turn of the century that Browne was invited to serve as a hunter, writer, illustrator, and specimen preparer for a series of expeditions by the American Museum of Natural History. The result was a collection of drawings and paintings that made his name as an important naturalist and artist. As part of those expeditions, Browne explored the Stikine River region and parts of the Alaska and Kenai Peninsulas. He returned to the Stikine in 1904 and 1905 on two more personal expeditions.

Having helped to put new regions of Alaska on the map, Browne now turned to a new interest: mountain climbing. His initial success in this new endeavor was being part of the first group, in 1907, to successfully climb Mount Olympus in Washington State. But his real obsession was to be the first person to climb Mount McKinley (Mount Denali). As the world watched, in three epic assaults – in 1906, 1910, and 1912 – Browne and his team got within reach of the summit (in the last attempt they were within 125 feet) before being driven back by blizzards. The book he wrote about those three expeditions, *The Conquest of Mount McKinley*, was a best-seller and remains a classic work on mountain climbing.

After serving in World War I, Browne retired from the strenuous life to focus on his painting. In time he would become one of the country's pre-eminent wildlife and natural landscape painters. His work still is prized by collectors, who pay large sums for his works, and many of his paintings are in permanent museum collections; including at the Smithsonian Institution.

It is hard to imagine anyone more perfectly suited to design a medal

to be awarded for heroism and bravery. Belmore Browne proved up to the task. His new BSA Honor Medal was a masterpiece – one of the finest and enduring designs in the history of American medals. Whereas other famous medals of the era are notable for the achievement they recognize (including the Eagle Scout Medal and the Nobel Prize medallion) or how they brilliantly capture the aesthetics of the era (the Distinguished Flying Cross and the Air Medal), the BSA's Honor Medal stands apart. It is quite timeless – as contemporary today in the early 21st century as it was in the early 20th.

Browne no doubt would be proud that his design has proven so enduring (he died in 1954), but even he probably couldn't explain why.

One thing is for certain, the Honor Medal is memorable on the first glance, and the thousandth. As required by Dan Beard, it

is a "modern" medal. Tha is, there is no back drapin ribbon; rather, the medal lion hangs directly fron the ribbon that is rect angular at the top wher it meets the rectangu lar gold bar reading "Bo Scouts of America" an pinched together at th bottom by the ring tha holds the medallion.

The medallion's out side ring, in gold (thes days gold over silver), wa comparatively conven tional: the Boy Scou fleur-de-lis insignia at th top, beneath it a laure wreath around the centr emblem, two small star at two- and ten-o'cloc (representing, as with th Scout emblem, "truth" an "knowledge"), and at th bottom the words "FO SAVING LIFE." Dign fied, even elegant, but ir distinguishable from mos awards of the era.

But then, geniu Browne decided to pu at the center of th medallion not som heroic figure or Gree god or other icon – convention for centurie or such awards – but something wholly unexpected: a bright, three-colored, image n shiny enamel. Not just any image, but vhat appears to be a three-lobed variation n the Chinese Taoist symbol of the Yin-'ang, minus the interpenetrating dots – he traditional image of the connectedness of nature. Further, instead of the usual black and white, Browne chose to make the three swirling forms three different colors. Why? Because, as Browne explained, they represent the three likely locations where Scout rescues occurred: red for fire, blue for water, and white for land.

elmore Browne's expedition to the summit of Mount McKinley in the Alaskan Territory in 1912. Jote his use of Abercrombie's Pyramid tent design.

Then a misstep: Browne initially chose for the medal a ribbon of red, white, and blue. It took 9 years (and Honor Medals from that era are exceedingly rare and valuable) but this ribbon's choice eventually showed its flaws. For one thing, the ribbon was identical to that found on the Eagle medal – which visually diminished the importance of both of Scouting's two supreme awards. Just as important, aesthetically, the tri-color stripes clashed with three-lobed design in the medallion, creating a visual chaos.

But Browne got it right the second time: his brilliant replacement was a ribbon of rich, blood red – and drawing from the title of Stephen Crane's great Civil War novel, *The Red Badge of Courage*. This symbolized the sacrifice, sometimes in blood, made by the recipients of the medal.

But one does not need to understand the symbol-ism of the Honor Medal's medallion to be struck by its aesthetic power. In the 1920s, its simplicity and primary colors must have been a visual knock-out,

Belmore Browne's first design of the BSA's Lifesaving Medal utilizing the red, white, and blue ribbon used from 1921 - 1930.

unlike anything many viewers ever had seen. In the 1960s, it seemed amazingly timely – in tune with the Eastern mysticism of the Counterculture. Even today its self-contained boldness hints at deep cultural archetypes that still make it a stunning sight. Nearly a century after its creation, Browne's BSA Honor Medal seems more timeless than ever.

Was Belmore Browne trying for this kind of immortality? Sure, that's what an artist does. Did he expect it? Most likely not. But in the end, he pulled it off. And when the Honor Medal hangs from a Scout or Scouter's uniform pocket, compared to other medals it looks utterly modern as if it was designed last week.

A third medal, the BSA Heroism Award, was designed to fill the gap left by the disappearance of the Bronze Lifesaving Medal for Scouts who saved the lives of others with minimal risk to themselves. It featured a simple design – a red and white ribbon with no top bar, bearing a medallion that featured the Scout medal in intaglio (an image created by carving, cutting or engraving) paired with an olive branch that curved around its right side. The outer ring, in red enamel read in white letters across the top "For Meritorious Action" (later "For Heroism"), and on the bottom "Boy Scouts of America." It remained in service for 89 years, until it was retired in 2013.

Twenty-five years later, in 1945, the Heroism Award would be joined by a matching medal that substituted gold/blue/gold ribbon, with

Fresh Start

The BSA wasted no time in announcing this program change. The official news was delivered in an article entitled "Gold Medals Only" on the first page of the July 1921 edition of *Boys' Life*, located immediately above the latest Honor Roll of Bronze, Silver, and Gold Lifesaving Medal recipients. After describing the retirement of the old medals, as well as the "strikingly handsome" new one, the article drove home the arrival of the new program by announcing its first recipient: Dale V. Collier of Rock Island, Illinois, for "saving two persons from drowning, January 28, 1921, in a thrilling ice rescue:

The BSA's current Honor Medal design utilizing the all-red ribbon first introduced circa late 1930.

he top lettering on the red enamel ring reading "For Meritorious Service." This medal (that replaced the Letter of Commendation) came to be called the Medal of Merit and still is in use today. It is awarded to a Scout or Scouter for "some outstanding act of service of a rare or exceptional character that reflects an uncommon degree of concern for the well-being of others."

The Heroism Medal and Medal of Merit both were dignified and elegant in their design. The Boy Scouts of America now had a awards equal to the bravery and sacrifice made by its recipients.

The Scout, while going on an errand for his mother, saw three men walking on the ice on the river and break through when about 70 feet from shore. Dale seeing a boat nearby jumped into it and with a board broke the thin ice and reached the first man, pulling him into the boat that rapidly was filling with water. He broke his way through the ice 300 feet down the stream from where the first man had been rescued and reached the other two just as the ice broke which they were holding onto with their hands. The two men reached the edge of the boat, one on either side, and with the help of the boy held on until people who had come to the rescue could get another boat out to them. Both men went into unconsciousness soon after they were taken out of the water and more than two hours was required before the first man became conscious. The second was sick for 5 days. Dale did not cease his efforts at resuscitation until the doctor arrived and ordered him home.[9]

With the new medals, Daniel Carter Beard now had the vehicles with which to restart Scouting's heroism award program. In doing this, he was depending upon one of the most defining, but least discussed, characteristics of Scouting: its rapid membership turnover. In those days, before Cub Scouting (founded in 1930), the typical Boy Scout joined at age 12 and remained Scouting until about age 18 (though they could continue to work on their Eagle almost indefinitely if a Life Scout at 18). At that point, because there also was as-yet no Exploring or "Senior Boy" program, they "aged out" of the organization. Those that came back as adult Scouters typically didn't do so until they were married with teenaged children – usually twenty years into the future.

Thus, Beard knew that in radically revamping the Honor Medal there would be almost no one left in the BSA after five years who remembered the old Bronze, Silver, and Gold Life saving Medal program – much less the controversy of 1918. That meant that, if he moved quickly and sweepingly, the door not only was open to replace the medals, but also to revamp Scouting's entire commitment to improving the first aid and safety skills of Scouts to survive any rescue into which they threw themselves.

So, even as the National Court was creating the new Honor and Medal of Merit family, the BSA was rethinking both its rank requirements and its physical facilities to reflect a greater emphasis on safety, and to teach it at an earlier age. The original 1911 rank requirements for the BSA included only an elementary "first aid and bandaging" requirement at Second Class and the ability to "swim 50 yards" at First Class – as well as, importantly, "Describe or show how to save life for 2 of these accidents: fire, drowning, runaway carriage, sewer gas, ice-breaking, or bandage an injured patient, or revive an apparently drowned person."

1912 Scouts demonstrating first aid with a bandage.

In 1917, the First Class rank now required Advanced First Aid ("panic prevention, various accidents, runaway horse, mad dog, snake bite, dislocations, unconsciousness, poisoning, fainting, apoplexy, sun stroke, heat exhaustion, freezing, sun-burn, ivy poisoning, bites/stings, nosebleed, earache, toothache, object in eye, stomach ache or cramp, chills") and now both Swimming and Lifesaving merit badges were required for Eagle as well as its preliminary rank of Star (soon to be switched with Life).

By 1927, Beard's new emphasis on safety (and after the usual delays of passing major changes through an established bureaucracy) was making its mark. Now there was a new Second Class requirement: "Demonstrate the practice of 5 rules of safety." Nine years later, the BSA added Safety as an Eagle-required merit badge. In time, nearly every one of the approximately 150 merit badges would feature a requirement about safe practices.

But this new obsession with Scout safety went far beyond rank requirements. Beard set out to make safety the secondary focus of almost every Scouting activity – a philosophy that still colors the program today. He instituted carefully managed safety and rescue programs at every Scout camp in the nation. He had the BSA publish a pamphlet, *Every Scout a Swimmer* that not only taught young Scouts how to swim but also explained elementary lifesaving skills. The BSA also didn't hesitate to apply negative reinforcement: it didn't refrain to label a young non-swimmer (in a play on then-notorious Prohibition saloons) as a "sinkeasy."

At the Dan Beard Outdoor School, a facility he founded in Hawley, Wayne County, Pennsylvania, Beard created a joint venture between the BSA and the Camp Fire Club of America, with former President William H. Taft as its honorary chairman (future inventor and business tycoon Howard Hughes would become one of its early participants). The staff developed an intense training program designed to turn a non-swimmer into a proficient one in the course of a single summer. It served as a test bed for similar Scouting programs.

Meanwhile, the Eagle-required Swimming merit badge not only required extensive distance swimming, but also skill at the side stroke and backstroke – the former used in water rescues, the latter to enable an exhausted swimmer to rest. And, in an echo of the Scout Law, the BSA published "Twelve Points for Swimmers." It began with advice about confidence, "breathing rhythmically," balance, the importance of learning different strokes, and the enduring myth about not going into the water after a meal. But then it dug deep into a series of rules that young Scouts today still are required to know: the buddy system, safety devices, spotting underwater obstacles, knowing the depth of the water, and resuscitation techniques. The final law was:

Keep learning. Devote a little time, whenever you go into the water, to practice some of the techniques of lifesaving.

The Eagle-required Lifesaving merit badge now required a Scout to show proficiency at diving to the bottom in seven feet of water, towing a victim in four different rescue carries, undressing in water (no doubt in response to those Scout rescuers who had drowned because their clothes were water-logged), swimming 100 yards, and demonstrating different techniques for escaping a frantic victim (the other major cause of Scout deaths).

Just a few years before, Scouting had accepted that a certain number of deaths among brave rescuer Scouts was inevitable. Now, under Dan Beard's guidance, that attitude had reversed to one of zero tolerance for incompetence. Scouts still occasionally were going to die (inevitably in extremely high risk situations) but not for lack of skill or training ... not if Scouting could help it. Even if it meant devoting precious institutional resources to swimming programs and safe facilities. And even if it meant providing (in the form of Eagle Scouts) the equivalent of several thousand newly trained lifeguards every year.

SCOUT MAHER

Second Class Scout Ralph J. Maher received the Silver Lifesaving Medal for a water rescue made on August 12, 1915, in Pittsburgh, Pennsylvania.

By the August 1925 issue of *Boys' Life*, the BSA proudly could announce that the previous summer 14,000 boys had been taught to swim in America's Scout camps, "and that this year an even more determined effort will be made to eliminate the 'sinkeasy' from the list of Scout campers."[10]

Apparently to drive the point home, the article – "Swimming to Seamanship" (it also included a pitch for Sea Scouting) – went on to tell the story of a recent Gold Honor Medal recipient who, unlike his predecessor, both succeeded in his rescue … and survived:

If the Scout executive of Lawrence County (PA) had wanted to demonstrate the value of discipline in Scout training, and the heroic metal of the Scouts of his Council, he could not have found a better opportunity, or made a more telling or dramatic display than what happened in the course of the day's work last year at Camp Kennedy's Mills.

A large number of visitors were present this day – the opening day – and lined the banks as the boys swam in the muddy and swollen Slippery Rock Creek than ran through the camp. Suddenly in the middle of the stream Wallace and McDonald – the latter a poor swimmer – were seen to struggle and go down. The Scout executive's shrill whistle cut above the noise made by the shouting, gamboling, high-spirited boys having their daily swim. It was the whistle for 'Attention!' – and each boy stood where he was – silent, ready for orders, all except a new Scout, who rushed in to the rescue, lost his head and grabbed at the strugglers. Wallace, to break this boy's hold, kicked him in the stomach, sending him over with a back somersault, under the water, unconscious.

Sam Fisher, sitting on the raft (not yet in the water) was told by the Scout executive to bring McDonald in, and **Ed Raney** swimming upstream was ordered to go to Wallace's help (as both these boys were certified lifesavers in the American Red Cross). The people on the banks were thrilled with the swift strokes Fisher used to come up from behind McDonald and tow him ashore using the brace carry.

Almost simultaneously, Raney took Wallace, who with marvelous gallantry had been standing on the bottom of the creek holding McDonald up, determined to save him at any cost, and who consequently was in a bad way and unconscious, brought him in with a cross chest carry. It was necessary to work fifteen minutes on Wallace before he could be revived.

During this time another drama, equally gallant, was being played unnoticed. **William Fike**, the untrained Scout who had jumped into the water, had now slipped beneath the surface. James McMurdo, another trained Scout, dove in after him. The creek was so muddy that McMurdo only could locate the unconscious Fike by feeling around with his foot. Bringing him up, McMurdo swam with the boy to the other side of the creek. The onlookers scarcely realized what McMurdo had done.[11]

That was just the start. A few pages later, the letter from Chief Scout Executive James E. West (published in *Boys' Life* in "The Scout World" column) told this same rescue story a second time – either the result of bad editing or intentional message reinforcement. And, in what had to be a coordinated message, early in the same issue, Remington Arms, promoting its Model 24 take-down rifle and its official Scout folding pocket knife, took out a full page ad that featured an elaborate illustration of two figures in a mountain lake, their faces upturned and barely out of the water, one of the figures obviously rescuing the other. An inset photograph showed

BSA's first Chief Scout Executive James E. West in 1910.

a stern "Scout **Lawrence Nelson**" of 1743 Sheridan Street, St. Paul, Minnesota, (privacy and security issues not being the concerns they are today) in his broad-brimmed campaign hat and large neckerchief. The headline reads "Gold Medal for Heroism" and read:

As he enjoyed the simple pleasures of wading near a river bank, Scout Lawrence Nelson heard a piteous cry for help. Turning he saw a little girl being swept away in the swirling waters of the river current. Without a thought for his own life and safety, Nelson swam to rescue the frightened child. In a hysterical panic she seized him around the neck, with the result that they both went under. Scout Nelson, struggling heroically, succeeded after a time in quieting the little girl, and in getting both their heads above the water. He then swam with his burden. It was not an easy rescue, and they both were thoroughly exhausted when they reached the shore.[12]

Scout Lawrence Nelson
1743 Sheridan Street,
St. Paul, Minn.

Below the photo of Scout Nelson was the illustration of a Remington pocket knife – "Official Knife, Boy Scouts of America" – with its blade, bottle opener, spike and can opener displayed, and an arrowed pull-out showing a small shield emblazoned with "The Remington Award for Heroism." Its caption reads *"The Remington Arms Company presents the Remington Award for Heroism – a Scout Knife with a shield engraved as above and his name engraved on the reverse side – to each winner of the Heroism Medal."*

Remington, which produced Scout knives for the BSA from 1923 until its sale in 1939 (and then returned in 2009), only produced these special Remington Heroism Award knives for two years, 1923-25. We only can assume that when Beard

saw this bit of coattail riding by the famous gun maker on Scouting's own award – especially the "Remington Award for Heroism" part – the company was told to cease and desist. Needless to say, the few such knives ever awarded are hugely valuable today. One 2006 commenter on a knife collector's fan site described it as "the Holy Grail" of pocket knives.

Sydney J. Wilson
2900 Pingree Ave
Detroit, Mich.

*First Class Scout **Sydney J. Wilson** after he saved a family of 4 from drowning in Detroit, Michigan, in 1924.*

Institutional Amnesia

Within little more than a decade, Dan Beard accomplished a complete reconstruction of the BSA's already famous Honor Medal program for Scouts who successfully had saved the lives of others. To do so, and almost without anyone noticing, he had changed all of the rules. The three medals had been replaced by two, one of stunning design. And like the Eagle, the top award would remain supreme – any achievements beyond would be recognized by the addition of palms. Moreover, the medals would give equal value to the saving of lives in all situations, not just in the water or through ice.

Most of all, the highest Honor Medal award would not be awarded only to those Scouts and Scouters who died in the course of the rescue. Rather, the review process would take a reverse approach: assessing the level or risk, and then equally rewarding those brave souls who survived the dangerous rescue of others by keeping their heads and putting to use their Scout training.

Finally, to back up this change in perspective, Scouting itself changed its rank requirements, inserting added requirements in first aid, swimming and lifesaving, and general safety at almost every level. This was matched by expanded aquatics and safety programs at every Boy Scout camp around the country.

The result was that the BSA became the most safety-oriented youth program in history. It also became the nation's largest reserve of emergency and disaster volunteers. Now, in those desperate rescue situations, it wouldn't be just brave young Scouts running to the calls for help, but *trained* Scouts to undertake a well-planned rescue.

Best of all, and to Dan Beard's great satisfaction, fewer of those brave Scouts were dying in the process.

The new Scouting Honor Medal award program was made official at the January 9, 1924, executive committee meeting of the National Court of Honor. It was Frederick Vreeland, who chaired the newly formed Honor Medal committee, who presented the new vision:

Scout Earl Lifshey of Brooklyn, New York, after receiving the Bronze Lifesaving Medal (right, with inscription) *in early 1916.*

Scout Lifshey

It appears unjust to put a premium on unpreparedness by recognizing the heroism of a boy who incurred serious risk of his own life because of a lack of training, while another Scout skilled in life saving methods might effect a similar rescue without corresponding risk.

Your Committee feels furthermore that the Scout who shows resourcefulness and preparedness in life saving methods as the result of his Scout training should receive special recognition.

… Should a high degree of Scout training lessen the personal risk the nominee is not disqualified, but on the contrary the Court will give special recognition to demonstrated skill in life saving methods and Scout resourcefulness.[13]

With those words, Scouting's Honor Medal program changed its trajectory – and embarked on the path upon which it still travels.

"Courage is resistance to fear, mastery of fear." - Mark Twain

3

Blue, Brown, and Green

*"I never saw such a
brave thing in my life."*
Jack Bassford of Carmel, California,
when describing Air Explorer Brookner W. Brady
who swam to the aid of his friend being
attacked by a shark in 1952.

CHAPTER

As these words are being written, more than 13,000 Scouts and adult Scouters have earned BSA Honor Medals and Letters of Commendation for lifesaving – including the Bronze, Silver, and Gold Lifesaving Medals, the Belmore Brown-designed Honor Medals (red/white/blue ribbon; red ribbon; plus the additional crossed palms variety), the Heroism Medal, and the Medal of Merit. Over a hundred of these medals were earned in 2014, with only 75 Honor Medals, and just a handful with Crossed Palms.

Among Scouting's awards, this is an exceedingly small number. Over the past century, 120 million Scouts have earned 120 million merit badges, and currently earn them at a rate of a little more than 2 million per year. By comparison, Scouting's supreme advancement award, the Eagle Scout rank, has been earned by more than 2.2 million Scouts, or more than 50,000 Scouts per year in the 21st century.

Yet, despite their tiny relative numbers, Scouting's Honor Medal and Medal of Merit recipients have had an outsized impact. Not only do they represent the very embodiment of the Scouting Spirit – and often its ultimate sacrifice – but also they have had a material impact on American life. For this book we conducted a statistical analysis, including standard variables regarding genera-tion length, family size, and other factors, and determined that there currently are over *five million* Americans alive today because they – or one of their parents, grandparents (or even great-grandparents) – were saved by a Boy Scout.

Five million. Together these survivors and their progeny would constitute the 23rd largest state – larger than Alabama, South Carolina, Louisiana, and Kentucky, among others. And they would populate a United States city as large as Chicago and Houston *combined*.

Is there any voluntary activity in American life that has saved more lives over the last century? In the world?

Perhaps the YMCA Lifeguard program has, but it typically pays its lifeguards, many of whom happen to also have earned the BSA Lifesaving merit badge. Indeed, one would be hard-pressed to find any voluntary *adult* program that has saved so many lives.

It is an achievement – never looked for, met without hesitation, and requiring almost limitless reservoirs of bravery – that is literally unmeasurable. How many of the survivors – and children and grandchildren of survivors – have gone on to change our world in some material way? How many of their future descendants will do so as well?

The Challenge of Categorization

The challenge in recounting the history of Scouting's Honor Medal recipients is the same today as it was when Dan Beard (or more precisely, BSA's writing team) sat down to scribe *Boy Heroes of Today*: How do you tell the stories of heroic rescues in a way that both honors the achievements of the young men who took the risks and that yet doesn't become an endless – and ultimately tiresome – list of all-but indistinguishable rescue stories. That was challenge enough in 1932, when there were just a few hundred Honor Medal honorees; it is far more challenging nearly eight decades later when the number of honorees is one hundred times greater.

The truth is that *every* Honor Medal story is worth telling – but there simply are too many to tell. Moreover, many are much alike. That doesn't diminish their singular value but it does make them, when aggregated, wearying to read.

This is a pity, because every one of these stories, by definition, contains at least one moment of extreme peril when one person, the victim, experiences the terror of looking directly into the face of imminent death. Many are in extreme pain, all (if conscious) are desperate and, likely as not, paralyzed with fear.

The other person, the rescuer, usually is stunned at the sudden apparition of a person about to die – likely something they never have before seen. Not only must this person recover from the initial shock. . . but then choose not to back away, or stand and stare, but to run towards the scene and place themselves into deep discomfort (smoke, freezing water, fire, etc.) at their own peril.

At the same time (and this is crucial in the story of the lifesaving rescues) the rescuer, by entering the situation, has assumed tacit *responsibility* for making the rescue successful. Bystanders – even more skilled ones – may back off from their own rescue effort, moving to a support role (or less) when seeing that someone else already is on the scene. That means that the rescuer, even while racing to the scene, must draw upon his or her reservoirs of training – and trust that they remember their past lessons correctly. After all, they now have committed to making the rescue a success.

Once in the thick of the rescue, the rescue and rescuer form an instant relationship that may lead to the survival of both, the death of one of them, or the death of both – all of which will be determined in a matter of seconds. The difference between success and failure, life and death, can hinge on the tiniest choice. A drowning person usually is so desperate that he or she will clutch anyone who approaches in an embrace that will doom them both – so the rescuer must approach from behind or below. If from the front, the rescuer must spin the figure around to get him or her in a cross-chest carry or under the chin or by the hair in a hold from which they can't resist. It is a delicate dance that quickly can turn tragic, especially (as we've already seen) with an inexperienced rescuer.

Scouts demonstrate how to construct a stretcher using a uniform tunic during a first aid drill in 1911.

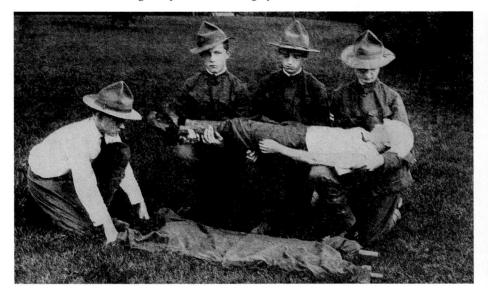

By the same token, a burning car can seem relatively safe – right up to the moment the heat causes the gas in the fuel tank to vaporize suddenly and turn into a bomb. Fallen beams can seem stable – until they suddenly shift and collapse. A room can look secure until one realizes too late that it is filled with carbon monoxide or another invisible gas.

Even for a trained rescuer, the actual moment of rescue can contain its own perils. The goal almost always is to remove the victim from the dangerous situation and into the hands of emergency personnel who can stabilize and treat the victim – all the while escaping injury or death to the rescuer. Unconscious victims pose a special problem because they are dead weight and there is no time to revive them until they are in a safe location. Thus, they can impede the escape from danger and increase the likelihood of the rescuer becoming yet another victim.

Some rescues, even when immediately successful, ultimately can become failures. Victims sometimes die during rescues, or survive for a few days, then expire from injuries. And while this has no bearing on the value of the rescue, or the Honor Medal, it certainly can have an effect upon a youthful rescuer. Most never have seen a dead person – and now that person is someone whom they attempted to save. It is easy to see how self-recriminations can follow: What if I had done something a little different? What if I had been better trained in lifesaving or first aid – or remembered better the training I did have? That the victim would have died anyway without the rescue attempt offers little consolation. Some degree of trauma is inevitable and perhaps hits the adult Scouter even stronger, who feels a greater sense of responsibility to have done the right thing.

But even if the rescue is successful, dealing with the experience sometimes can be difficult. The surreal aspect of the rescue itself: one moment life is moving along normally and the next instant the life of another human being (and perhaps your own) depends on extreme physical action and split-second decisions. The appreciation of the rescued and the acclaim of the world, both in their own way can be an emotional burden, especially in the inevitable after-effect of feeling unworthy of the attention, and of wanting to forget what happened.

Every one of the thousands of Honor Medal stories contains some, or many, of these attributes – though few of those aftermaths ever are reported. Instead, we read the headlines and the commendations, the inscriptions and the encomiums; and we almost never learn the real stories of what happened to the hero and the rescued in the days, weeks, and years that followed. Was the event just a brief moment in their lives, soon forgotten except for the occasional reminder by a scar or a pinning on of the medal or a fear of water or fire? Or were the scars deeper and more lasting – for rescued and rescuer – that never really healed? Did the aging Scouter proudly point at the medal or square knot on his uniform chest and describe the events of a singular day forty years before – or did he never speak of it?

Perhaps it is best that we don't tell those complete stories of the Honor Medal recipients. Because, in the end, what really matters is that instant when the Scout sees an imminent tragedy and chooses to intervene. To do so without hesitation, as many Scouts have done, is heroic enough; but to hesitate for that split-second as they recognize the real nature of the peril and their inadequacy for the task and then *still* charge in, is courage of an even higher order. *That* moment is what really matters – not what happens the moment after, or the moment after that. It is that instant that Scouting honors, and for which it prepares every Scout. And it is the reason those millions of Americans are alive.

Scout George Griffith,
3246 George Street,
Chicago, Ill.

*First Class Scout **George Griffith** received the Honor Medal for lifesaving during an ice rescue in Chicago, Illinois, in 1924.* ■

Types and Times

There are two ways to tell the story of Scouting's Honor Medal recipients: thematically and chronologically. When BSA's managers decided to officially produce *Boy Heroes of Today* in 1931 and focus solely on Gold Lifesaving and Honor Medal recipients, they chose the former style – in part because the award was less than 20-years-old, and partly because it enabled them to circumvent the crisis of 1918. The only clue of that difficult period was the choice to devote an early chapter to "Heroism and Training," the latter term being Scouting's newest obsession.

The first chapter, "First Awards," begins with the story of Russell Grimes and the wagon. In Chapter 2, "The Great Sacrifice," the narrative jumps to 1930, giving short shrift to the award recipients during the missing decade. Then "Heroism and Training" – with only a systematic look at the different contemporary Honor Award recipients. It quickly becomes obvious that *Boy Heroes of Today* isn't just a celebration of Scouting's bravest but in fact a reset of the whole narrative.

And that narrative is organized thematically, by types of rescues. Given the aquatic bias of those early years, it isn't surprising that the next five chapters of rescue stories are entitled: Quiet Waters, Raging Torrents, Angry Seas, Sea Scout Tradition, Scout Ways, and Frozen Waters – basically every permutation of water rescue imaginable. Even a chapter on Honor Medals earned by Scouts in American territories is mostly about water rescues. Only at the end of the book does the narrative finally turn to other rescues – from fires, blizzards, and (water again) floods. Still, that is a breakthrough of sorts, as the book chooses to celebrate Honor Medal recipients who still are alive to wear their medal.

Eighty-five years later, with thousands of Honor Medal recipients now on Scouting's rolls, it still is useful to look at categories of rescues, but also at a far broader spectrum of rescue types – not just in water, but in a vast range of scenarios unimaginable in the early 20th century. It now also is possible to look at types of *rescuers*: young and old, trained and untrained; as well as the impact on these rescues and rescuers by the changing face of society and technology. Finally, there is a story to be told about the secondary effects of the Honor Medal, the distinct culture it has developed, notably through the unlikely vehicle of a hugely popular comic strip.

It is those themes, each in turn, that this book now will address and when appropriate, we will present the stories of these brave Scouts and Scouters chronologically to their era.

BOY SCOUTS OF AMERICA

July 25th, 1921.

Scout Cornelius Gilsing,
Troop #10,
710 W. Miami St.,
Logansport, Indiana.　　(Thru S. Ex. Raymond O. Loftus)

My dear Scout:

We take pleasure in notifying you on behalf of the
National Court of Honor that you have been awarded a
Bronze Medal for your bravery in rescuing Edmund Dietl.

The intrinsic value of this medal is small, but that
which it stands for should mean so much to you now and in
the future. It shows that you as a true boy scout were
prepared to do your utmost even though it may have resulted
in the loss of your own life.

You will, we are sure, prize this medal very highly, and
it will always tend to keep before you the great lesson of being
prepared to render service in an emergency.

The medal is being sent through Mr. Loftus under separate
cover.

With congratulations from all the members of the National
Court of Honor, I am

Fraternally yours,

BOY SCOUTS OF AMERICA

Daniel Carter Beard,
Chairman.

DCB/DR

Scouting Expands

For its first 20 years, the Boy Scouts of America consisted solely of Scouts – that is, boys between the ages of 12- and 17-years-old. That's what Chief Scout Executive James E. West wanted, believing that any program for younger boys would detract attention from a program that still was fighting for acceptance.

Not everyone agreed with that strategy. As early as 1911, Chief Scout Ernest Thompson Seton, drawing upon his earlier experience with the Woodcraft Indians, proposed a junior program that he presciently named the "Cub Scouts of America." West ignored that proposal.

Meanwhile, young boys, seeing their older brothers in Boy Scouts, wanted to emulate their experience and pushed for the creation of their own groups around the U.S. The demand soon became so great that West surrendered – at least to the point of licensing, in 1916, Robert Baden-Powell's *Wolf Cub Handbook* for younger Scouts.

The book proved hugely influential. Hundreds of Wolf "packs," largely led by mothers, sprang up in the years that followed. Dan Beard, ever the patriot, complained that it was unseemly for American boys to use a British handbook. He only partly won his case.

Meanwhile, West at last agreed and ordered the creation of the Boy Rangers of America. It selectively used parts of Scouting, such as the Scout Law, but also carried a heavy American Indian theme. Over the next decade, while the program grew ever-more popular, it also lived up to West's fear of a second, distracting organization. So, in 1930, Boy Rangers adopted Seton's original name, aligned its program more closely with the BSA, and became the *Cub Scouts of America*. Today, the Cub program has more than 1 million members and it is the primary feeder organization into the Boy Scout program.

Not surprisingly, from the first moment of the organization's existence Cubs began to exhibit the same heroic behavior found in their older brothers in Boy Scouts. From the very beginning, there was no doubt that Cub Scouts soon would be making rescues of their own, and no question that they, too, would be eligible for Scouting's medals for saving lives.

That still is true today: those young boys who are lauded by local news agencies for dialing 911 or poison control or awakening family members in a burning house, are quite likely Cub Scouts. Indeed, since 1930, an estimated 1500 Cubs have earned Honor Medals, Medals of Merit or Certificates for having helped save another person's life.

This isn't coincidental. By the time of Cub Scouting's creation, 12 years after the crisis of 1918, Scouting had developed and field-tested sophisticated first aid and safety programs. It also had learned, from those early deaths of Scout rescuers, that no age was too young for this training. Thus, when Cub Scouting officially was launched, it came fully freighted with simple first aid training, water safety rules, and accident prevention programs.

Those programs only have grown more sophisticated over the decades – this despite the fact that Cub Scouting largely is an indoor program and held in private homes. For example, even at the youngest level – 6-year-old Tiger Cubs – the Safe and Smart Elective Adventure recognizes that even if a boy is unlikely to find himself in a dire situation, he very well may encounter one and choose to help:

1. Memorize your address, and say it to your den leader or adult partner.
2. Memorize an emergency contact's phone number, and say it to your den leader or adult partner.
3. Take the 911 safety quiz.
4. Show you can "Stop, Drop, and Roll."
5. Show you know how to safely roll someone else in a blanket to put out a fire.
6. Make a fire escape map with your adult partner.
7. Explain your fire escape map, and try a practice fire drill at home.
8. Find the smoke detectors in your home. With the help of your adult partner, check the batteries.
9. Visit an emergency responder station, or have an emergency responder visit you.

BSA's current Medal of Merit.

If that seems a lot for a young boy, consider this story from 1975:

- As the Baptist Temple bus neared the end of its delivery of Sunday school students in Alliance, Ohio, the wife of the driver sat in the front talking with two teenagers and 8-year-old Cub Scout **Richard Hoover Jr.** Suddenly, Hoover burst from the group and raced down the aisle. He alone had noticed that the back door still was open from the previous drop-off – and the driver's 3-year-old daughter had somehow made her way back there and was standing at the threshold of the opening as the highway raced by beneath her feet. One bump, one tap on the accelerator, and the little girl would have been thrown out. Hoover grabbed the girl and yanked her back at the last second, slamming the door shut as he did.

Or this story from 1977:

- Eight-year-old **Jimmy Brown** was walking with his mother, Jo Ann Brown, to a Cub Scout banquet in Williamsport, Pennsylvania, when a mugger appeared seemingly from nowhere, knocked Ms. Brown to the ground, and tried to rip away her purse. As they struggled, 70 pound Jimmy leaped on the mugger's back – hitting the man so hard that he dropped the purse and ran away empty-handed. Mother and son both were cut and bruised, but safe, and they continued onward to the banquet.

In many ways, the story of Cub Scout Honor and Merit Medals are especially compelling precisely because one hardly expects boys so young to assume such enormous responsibility – or even to consider that they might have the requisite skills to accomplish a successful rescue. But as the Tiger Cub safety requirements show (and these requirements become ever-more sophisticated as a boy ages and advances upward to Arrow of Light) Cub Scouts are more prepared from the very start not only to aid in a rescue, but to succeed at the task and not lose their own lives in the process.

By the time a Cub reaches Webelos (the bridge from Cubs to Boy Scouts), he will have constructed an emergency preparedness kit, been trained in basic first aid, practiced making emergency calls, made a safety presentation to his family, participated in nationally certified safety programs, and even been warned about Internet predators. It can be said that, when it comes to safety, Cub Scouts are the best trained pre-adolescents in the United States. And, lest the reader assumes that these "rescues" are limited to calling emergency numbers or enlisting the help of adults – it always is important to remember that Scouts of all ages perpetually surprise adults at what they can accomplish. Consider these stories of Cub Scouts, all ten-years-old and under:

• A farmer took his grandson, Mark Wilson, and Mark's cousin, Cub Scout **Ramie Carroll**, 9, to a farm near Sweatman, Mississippi, to look at a new model of cotton picker in action. After the demonstration, the farmer drove the fully loaded picker to a nearby trailer to dump the load. What the farmer didn't realize was that the two boys were playing in that trailer when he dumped all 3000 pounds of cotton on top of them. By sheer luck, a neighboring farmer had just driven up, witnessed what had happened, and ran towards the men shouting. The three men together hurriedly raced to pull the two boys out of the cotton pile. They found Ramie quickly, but it only was after they overturned the trailer did they finally discover the seemingly lifeless body of Mark. Checking the boy's breathing, pulse, and heartbeat (and finding no signs of life) the three men sadly accepted that the boy was dead. But Ramie wouldn't accept their conclusion, and grabbing his cousin, he began to perform the mouth-to-mouth resuscitation he had learned in Cub Scouting. He refused to give up until, miraculously, his cousin revived.

• Karl Bergsma was working on his car at a service station in Staatsburg, New York. He was leaning over the engine compartment and running jumper cables, when the car's battery exploded – spraying his face with acid. His son, Cub Scout **Scott Bergsma**, 9, who had been helping on the car, grabbed his father's hand and led him to a nearby sink, positioning his father so that a continuous stream of water poured into his eyes. Once his father recovered from the initial shock and could rinse his own eyes, Scott ran to a nearby phone and called the local Rescue Squad, giving them precise descriptions of both the emergency and his location. Then, he called his mother, told her what had happened, and instructed her to notify the nearby hospital that they would be on their way. Then, continuing his almost superhuman coolness under fire, Scott rode with his father in the ambulance, continuing to flush his eyes until the hospital personnel took over. In the end, Scott was credited with having saved his father's vision.

• Cub **Scout Dane Miller**, 8, watched in horror as his 3-year-old brother, Danny, climbed into the family car and, imitating their parents, yanked the car's transmission out of "park." The car began to roll down an incline. Dane, without hesitation (despite knowing that he was a hemophiliac and risked bleeding to death with even a small injury) took off running in pursuit. At the last moment he managed to dive halfway through the driver's window and slam the stick back into "park." But by this time the car was moving too fast; the gears were stripped and, though momentarily slowed, the vehicle kept rolling – right through a barbed wire fence. The impact knocked Dane from the car – leaving him battered, bleeding, and tangled in the wire. He had deep lacerations on his neck, arms, and chest. Meanwhile, the car came to a safe stop on its own with little Danny unhurt and laughing at his wild ride. Now at risk of bleeding to death, Dane was rushed to the hospital, where he underwent extensive blood transfusions. Happily, he survived.

TRUMAN GIVES BRAVERY MEDALS

President Truman stands with a proud 10-year-old Coral Gables, Fla., boy, Parker Edward Stratt, after pinning a Young American Medal for Bravery on his Scout uniform in a White House ceremony at Washington Tuesday. The President also helps Margaret Galassi, 16, right of Springfield, Ill. show off her bravery medal which she was given for saving seven children from a burning home near Buffalo, Ill.

(AP Wirephoto)

And, most incredibly:

• In September 1951, 10-year-old Cub Scout **Parker Edward Stratt** was fishing for minnows with his friend Gerry Susan Gustafson in a rock pit near Coral Gables, Florida. Suddenly, an alligator burst through the surface of the water, clamped its jaws onto Gustafson and began to pull the girl into the pit. Parker tried to grab Gerry by the hair and arm, but only could hold on briefly for fear that the alligator, which now was spinning in the water, would rip off the girl's arm. It pulled Gerry underwater multiple times but Parker managed to pull her back to the surface. Then, as it flipped on its back, the gator momentarily lost its grip on the girl and Parker made his move. Hooking his feet in an exposed root, he stretched out into the water, grabbed the girl under each arm and pulled her out – just as the alligator lunged again. . . and missed. Though Gerry's arm was broken and bleeding profusely from bites, with Parker's help she still managed to scramble up the muddy bank – both of them knowing that if either slipped they would end up again in the creature's jaws. But their trial wasn't yet over. Parker managed to seat Gerry on the handlebars of his bicycle and ride her to the hospital in town. There, the doctors managed to save the girl's arm. On June 24, 1952 in a Rose Garden ceremony, President Harry S. Truman presented his own award for bravery to Parker Stratt.

Today, on average, America's Cub Scouts save a person's life every month. It is a statistic that counters the standard image simply of little boys in blue uniforms being tended to by their mothers, while racing wooden cars down a Pinewood Derby track. Cub Scouts can be action heroes, too.

97

Rethinking Heroism

Not surprisingly, in the two decades that followed the revision of Scouting's Honor Medal program, the nature of the award recipients slowly changed as well.

For one thing, thanks to the BSA's now-extensive first aid, swimming, and safety training programs, the number of young and unprepared potential Scout rescuers unknowingly putting themselves in mortal danger plummeted to the point that the National Court of Honor's *1936 Annual Report* proudly announced:

*Scout **Martin King** and his father, whom he saved from asphyxiation in 1931.*

Increasingly the records show that the benefits of Scout training are being realized. In the great majority of cases, the Scout showed not only courage, but knowledge as well. It would be an unfortunate policy to suggest to boys that they put themselves in danger if they were not in a position to render assistance, and only add another victim to the accident. Scouting makes it possible for boys to secure the necessary training so that when the emergency occurs, they will be prepared.

It was during that year that Scouting experienced one of its most devastating disasters – and with it, one of its most emblematic acts of heroism.

• That March, a troop of 20 Scouts and two leaders were camping in a cabin on Whites Creek (a tributary of the Elk River east of Fayetteville, Tennessee) when the stream, quiescent for more than a century, suddenly went to full flood. At 5 a.m., the rushing waters approached the cabin and startled awake Scoutmaster **James ("Jim") Wright** who immediately recognized the threat and awoke the Scouts.

Recalled one boy, "Jim told us to get up and get dressed as quickly as possible, that the creek was up. We began to dress but before I could get on my overalls, water was almost knee deep in the house. I put on my shoes, tied them without lacing, told my brother to hurry, grabbed my lumberjack (jacket) and cap and rushed to the porch.

"Jim said that we could not leave because the water was too deep and swift. We then got our patrols together and stood on benches until the water reached our feet, then Jim told us to get on the roof.

Carl Mee and Joe Brashear stood on the end of the porch and helped Paul Derrick up on top of the house. Carl and Joe would help the boys up and Ted would pull them onto the roof. They helped the smaller boys up first, while some of the boys climbed up the side …"

The National Court of Honor particularly noted that "[a]t no time was there evidence of panic or terror. Scout discipline was maintained under the most terrifying conditions. The stronger helped the weaker, and initiative, resourcefulness, and courage figured the simple narratives."

The Scout's story continues: "After all got up top, Jim came up last and began talking and laughing to encourage the boys. I remember him saying that he felt just as safe as if he was home in bed, but not quite as comfortable. Jim was all the time laughing and joking to encourage us so that we would not lose our nerve."

But their safety was short-lived. Unable to withstand the pressure of the flood, the nearby bridge over the stream tore loose and headed down-river past the troop. A moment later the cabin ("bungalow") shifted on its foundation beneath them. The Scouts' worst fears were about to be realized.

The bungalow upon which the Scouts of Troop 45 rode down Whites Creek in 1929.

"Jim told us to take off our shoes. I took mine off, and was taking off my lumberjack when the bungalow tore loose. Jim told us to lie down. I lay down and grabbed my brother."

As a second Scout on the roof recalled, "With a ringing sound, the bungalow broke up, some of the boys falling in the water when the roof collapsed, part of the roof being carried out in the stream with most of the boys on it. There was a large part of the roof in front of us and the water carried us so fast we overtook this part of the roof and hit it, causing it to fall back over us, and it caught some of the boys in under it, and we started floating again."

First Scout: "The bungalow was roaring and jumping while going down the stream at the rate of about 20 miles per hour, like a bucking bronco and with every jump it was breaking up."

"I was holding my brother when I heard Jack Hamby scream for help. I turned to see him fall in the water, between two pieces of the bungalow. I saw him going down and I jumped in after him. I saw his head go under and thrust my hand into the water and caught him by his hair, pulled him up and got ahold of his arm, then climbed back up, pulling him with me. I got back on top and had him where his waist was level with the top when the two pieces of the bungalow came almost together.

"I thought he would be cut in two. **Ted Derrick** then grabbed him by the other hand and together we pulled him out. Ted asked him if he was unconscious and he said no. I asked Jack if he was smashed up very bad and he said no, but his finger was cut off."

"I then heard Ted holler for me to come and help him. I turned and saw that he was holding my brother [Tom] who had fallen off and was caught under the water. I went to help him. We both pulled with all of our might. Tom looked up at me and I saw death painted on his face. He said, 'My leg is hung.'"

"Just then, whatever was holding him turned loose and we pulled him up on the piece of roof, with his hip out of place and his leg broken. He was as helpless as if he had been in the middle of a stormy ocean."

They were far from safe: "I lay down holding him in my arms. The piece of roof was still in midstream, but all at once it turned into the bank. When it hit the trees it immediately broke up, giving us very little time to climb the trees. I was the last one getting onto the tree, as I was trying to get up with Tom. I cried for the other boys to help, but they were fighting for their own lives and did not hear. We all got into the tree. There were only three of us, then the tree washed up, again leaving us with Tom in the roaring water. Here we all got separated and only Tom and I got into a big white oak tree. I carried him up about ten feet above the water and set him on a limb and stood on the limb holding him."

But the river still was rising: "We stayed with this tree until it went under water . . .

I turned and with a mighty strength that God must have given me for this occasion, made for Tom, getting him to let go of the limb . . . I then made back for the tree which a few seconds ago had been in reach, with a lifeless form in my left arm. I made the tree, carried him up about ten feet above the water, and set him down in between three limbs of the tree – where we were found when help came to us in a boat about midday."

Meanwhile, for the second Scout, a different tragedy was unfolding. They first had to rescue the boys crushed between the two roof pieces: "Tom Douglas was caught by something about his leg, breaking it and pulling him under. Ted Derrick reached over the side, holding him above the water until he was loosened from the parts below and then pulling him onto the raft . . . I did not see [Scoutmaster] Jim after that because he had jumped in after some of the boys. He kept cool all the way through the tragedy, giving orders for all of the boys to hang on to the [roof] raft.

"We then were thrown into a point by the large sluice which went through the woods. The roof hit the trees and was broken to pieces. We jumped for a common-sized pine, but it was washed down and we got in another. Tom Douglas fell there in the water, and could not do anything because of his leg.

Willie Evans, endangering his own life, jumped in the water and got Tom and pulled him in a tree twice. We were wet and cold but the boys did not even say a word because they were Boy Scouts and a Boy Scout is 'brave.'"

Tom Douglas: "… the bungalow split into three pieces and we were all separated. Then I heard our brave leader say, 'Boys, do the best you can.' I lost consciousness until I found myself floating down the creek on a side of the house with Jim and a few more of my dear Scouts." That's when the roof piece crashed together. "I had lost Jim," Douglas recalled sorrowfully. As noted, Willie Evans risked his life to save

Douglas – and together with nine other Scouts they took to the trees when their roof rafts momentarily hung up while being carried through a nearby woods. Three of the huge pines snapped under the pressure of the flood waters, forcing more rescues.

"We then took to the driftwood and waited for six hours … I was very cold, but what was a chill to death?" asked Douglas. "At last a signal came from another Scout, that aid was coming. Three men rescued us and took us to a house where we had wonderful care."

One of those rescuers was **J.C. Acuff**, the local council Scout executive. When he learned of the flood, he knew the troop would be trapped in it and raced to the scene. Once there, he found a small boat and – in the face of

enormous danger – rowed out into the midst of the flood. The current was so strong that it took him two hours to row just two hundred yards. There he found Scout Willard Staples clinging to a tree and within minutes of being swept away.

In the end, seven Scouts were killed in the flood, along with Scoutmaster Jim Wright, who had been swept under while trying to save one of the boys. The National Court took the very significant step of awarding four Honor Medals: to Life Scout **Willis Evans**, 17; to Life Scout Ted Derrick, 15;

THE 7 SCOUTS WHO DROWNE

posthumously, to James T. Wright, Scoutmaster, and to J.C. Acuff, the second Scout executive ever (and the last to date) to earn a Gold Honor Medal [you will read about the first later in this chapter].

According to the meeting minutes of the National Court of Honor, the action of the Tennessee Flood Scouts is "an illustration of Scout heroism and Scout training that is unsurpassed in the history of Scouting." Obviously deeply moved, the secretary adds:

"Boyhood is a wonderful and beautiful period, when human imagination is the strongest, the ideals the highest and the ambitions the most splendid ... These short, simple accounts that follow chronicle the greatest devotion that one human can have for another. Think of the joy of those whose loved one was restored, the gratitude of the victim, the splendid example of courage, training and idealism! Bear in mind that these deeds of heroism were performed by young boys – mere lads in their teens."

TOP LEFT: The monument's inscription plate.

TOP RIGHT: Scoutmaster James Tarwater Wright circa 1929.

BELOW: The surviving troop members at the monument's dedication ceremony in 1932.

NEAR LEFT: The memorial monument.

ACROSS: The 7 Scouts who died in the flood.

Twenty-six other Scouts would earn the Honor Medal that year. As always, most were water rescues. And though almost forgotten in light of the Tennessee Flood disaster (one of the largest losses of life in Scouting history) nevertheless, several still stand out:

- **Charles Bieler**, a 14-year-old Second Class Scout from Jersey City, New Jersey, watched as a father and his 9-year-old daughter were swimming in a nearby bay. Suddenly, a wave from a passing motorboat caused the girl to swallow water. Frightened, she grabbed her father and they both went under. Bieler swam out and brought her into shallow water. Rescuers saved both with artificial respiration. What makes this story memorable is that when asked for his name, Bieler refused to give it, saying that he merely was doing a Scout's duty. Undaunted, members of the crowd searched until they learned Charles' name – and then put him up for an Honor Medal.

- **Walter Fichter**, a 13-year-old Second Class Scout from West Hazleton, Pennsylvania, was walking along some railroad tracks with three buddies when he heard a train coming. They had stopped to watch the operation of the signals when they noticed some younger boys standing on a railroad bridge just up ahead, closer to the oncoming train. They yelled for the boys to look out. The boys responded and ran. But one of the group, a boy of about five-years-old, stumbled and fell on the bridge.

Realizing there was no time to escape, the little boy crawled over to the side of the bridge and hung onto a wooden sill nailed to the end of the railroad ties. By now the train was entering one end of the bridge, and a running Walter Fichter the other. He managed to cross the tracks just a few feet in front of the oncoming train in order to reach the boy on the other side. By this point, the boy was beginning to slip off, holding on now with two hands and just one leg. As the train passed, Walter crawled on his stomach along the side of the bridge until he reached the boy; grabbing him and hung onto him on as the train wheels sliced the track just inches beside them. It was estimated that ten railcars passed the two figures on the track that afternoon with the "wheels and ladders and stuffing boxes of the freight cars" just missing them. A relieved Walter Fichter later would say, "We were pretty badly scared."

- **Wilson Martin**, a 15-year-old Second Class Scout from Brookfield, Missouri, and his friend Harry Scoch, also 15, had been ice skating when they got the idea to explore a nearby, abandoned, ice making plant. Entering, they found themselves in a vast and empty room. Seeing a small door on the far side, Scoch ran for it – in the process hitting and breaking a small pipe "and releasing ammonia and ammonia gas [part of the ice making process] that was in storage in the refrigeration system. The liquid ammonia not only sprayed down the boy's back and legs but he quickly was surrounded by a steam-like cloud of the gas. He fell to the floor with the gas burning his eyes and filling his lungs so that he couldn't even scream.

Scout Martin, though he had no preparation in this type of emergency, ran to his friend. Ignoring the danger, he dove into the fog and, blinded, groped around the floor until he found Scoch and dragged him into clear air.

But more danger lay ahead. Besides the damage to his eyes and lungs, Scoch's clothes were saturated with ammonia and as it evaporated it began to freeze, even as it was burning his flesh. In agony, he tried to tear off his clothes but Martin stopped him. Instead he got his friend to his feet and half-carried him to a nearby house. There, while the home owner called for a doctor, Martin helped his friend out of his clothes. The ammonia fumes were so great that they had to abandon and seal the room they were in. Meanwhile, Martin had to physically restrain the suffering boy from rubbing his burning eyes, which saved his eyesight. Scoch was severely burned and spent several weeks in the hospital; but he lived. Martin was honored for his resourcefulness and cool head in a situation for which even Scouting had not provided training.

• **Roy Griesen** and a friend were fishing near the Gress family farm outside Dickinson, North Dakota, when they heard a young boy screaming that a bull was "eating" his sister. Griesen, a 14-year-old Tenderfoot ran up the creek bank and saw Eunice Gress, 7, on the ground, trapped beneath a bull's forelegs. The bull, which already had gored the little girl, now was starting to kneel in order to attack her again. Eunice tried to sit up, but the bull knocked her down and gored her a second time with its horns. In the process, it also broke the little girl's left arm, splintered one of her legs and deeply gashed her under one eye. The bull's next attack likely would be fatal. Griesen, knowing that drawing the bull's attention would likely mean an attack on himself, nevertheless, spotted a nearby tin can and threw it at the beast. Then, advancing, he gathered up stones and threw them at the bull. The animal was even more enraged by the onslaught of rocks, but eventually retreated. Roy quickly gathered up the girl and ran with her in his arms towards the Griesen farmhouse, where he was met by Eunice's father who rushed her to the hospital.

During the Interwar years, nearly 3,000 Honor Medals and Certificates were awarded by the BSA.

This number stunned even its creators. At one Court of Honor meeting in the mid-1930s, Dan Beard commented that "[t]his figure represents only a portion of the actual lives saved, since again and again a single award has meant the saving or two, three, and even more lives. It would be interesting if we had some way of estimating the sum total of the lasting happiness, which these brave lads have brought to the families and friends of those whom they have rescued."

A Letter of Commendation from Dan Beard to Scout Truman Fleming of Norfolk, Virginia, in October 1928.

Growing Older

It wasn't just at the bottom of the age scale that the BSA began to feel pressure for expansion in its second decade. Similar lobbying was being exerted at the upper age limit of Scouting. As Scouting's own official website admits:

The need for a senior Boy Scout program probably surfaced the second day after Scouting started in the United States in 1910. Actually, in the very first National Executive Board meeting report, there is a discussion about losing older boys. It was no surprise to our founders that older boys needed an age-specific program with challenges appropriate for them. Older boy programs cropped up across the country during those early years, causing the need for national action.

Young men who had enjoyed their time in Boy Scouts eventually faced the prospect of turning 18-years-old and "aging" out of the Scouting program (21-years-old and beyond if they were working on their Eagle rank – a rule that lasted until the 1960s). So popular was the program that a sizable percentage simply didn't want to leave.

Some found a role as "junior assistant Scoutmaster," a position they could keep until turning 21 when they fully could become "assistant Scoutmasters. But many more didn't want to become adult Scouters; nor did they want to watch over 12-year-old Tenderfeet. Rather, they wanted to continue the Scouting experience with their peers, amping up the adventures to match their maturity. Not surprisingly, a number of new organizations sprang up to meet this demand.

The first Scouting initiative to recognize the value and commitment of older Scouts was the Order of the Arrow (OA). Founded on July 16, 1915, as Scouting's camping society, the OA was inspired by both Ernest Seton's Indian lore lectures and Freemasonry. Born at the Treasure Island Scout camp in Pennsylvania, the OA didn't become a national Scouting organization until 1921.

Strictly speaking, membership in the OA still was confined to boys within the Scouting age range, though members could stay through age 20. From the beginning, it carried a heavy complement of adults. It still does: of today's 180,000 OA members, nearly half are adult volunteers.

Sea Scouting, which also allowed Scouts to remain as members until age 21, was nearly as old as Boy Scouting itself, and its early history even more circuitous. It first appears in the United Kingdom in 1909 as a mention in *Chums* magazine (Chum Scouts was a mirror organization of England's Boy Scouts).

But it wasn't until 1911 when Robert Baden-Powell's brother, Warrington Baden-Powell, wrote a handbook for Sea Scouting that the program became a full member of the larger organization. Just a year later, Sea Scouting officially was inaugurated in the United States with the founding crew being located in Philadelphia. Its official launch was featured in the first issue of *Scouting* magazine in April 1912. But by then, other seamanship programs already were in existence (most notably the Rhode Island Sea Scouts) that enjoyed their own support from Theodore Roosevelt. Still, thanks to using the fast-growing Scouting program as a feeder, BSA's Sea Scouting program quickly overwhelmed, and eventually absorbed, its competitors.

The next cohort of older Scouts to be created was by Eagle Scouts. By the mid-1920s, a number of Eagle Scout clubs, brotherhoods, and regional chapters sprung up around the country. The most important was founded by the local council executive in San Francisco, Raymond O. Hanson. Reflecting the then-popular iconography of swords, shields, robes, and chivalry, the group was called the *Knights of Dunamis*. It soon had chapters and several thousand members throughout the United States – performing community service, earning special ranks (most notably the "Knight Eagle"), and holding dances, and other adult social events.

The most important of the Scouting programs for older boys and young men had its start in the Pacific Northwest as a kind of earthbound counterpart to Sea Scouting. Like the Order of the Arrow, *Exploring*, founded in 1922, emphasized camping and outdoor activities. But unlike the OA, it operated externally to Boy Scouting with its own uniforms and, ultimately, ranks. Moreover, because of its relative independence, many Explorer "posts" slowly migrated toward career training as well. Thus, just as Sea Scouts prepared generations of sea captains, and the Knights of Dunamis served as a networking program for future doctors, lawyers, and corporate executives, Explorer posts increasingly attached themselves to police and fire departments, hospitals, park rangers, and other professional programs.

A Knights of Dunamis patch, circa 1960.

Nothing breeds success like success, and by the beginning of the 1930s, the BSA finally was prepared to establish an official program (with full staffing at National headquarters) for older Scouts.[14] The result, inaugurated in 1935, was *Senior Scouts*, which subsumed Sea Scouts, Explorer Scouts, OA, Knights of Dunamis, Rover Scouting (formed in 1918 as an even older service society and was a prototype for the Alpha Phi Omega college Boy Scout fraternity), troop alumni programs, Senior Scouting (an in-troop program), Press Club (a journalism training program), and the Senior Degree Honor Society. Inspired by fighter pilots of World War II, another new program, Air Scouting, was founded in 1941.

Senior Scouting survived until 1949. By then, many of its programs had been diminished in membership by war (18- to 21-year-olds being the prime age for the Draft), differing philosophies (Sea Scouts), and declining membership. For example, Press Club, an offshoot of the Lone Scouting program begun in 1915, never had more than a few members.

BSA's national managers decided to reorganize and condense the various Senior Scouting programs into just one: Explorers (later Exploring) with a standard uniform of a forest green shirt with tie, and featuring the Silver Medal as its Eagle Scout equivalent. Tracking the evolution of the program after that, in all of its permutations, is beyond the scope of this book. That said, it should be noted that older Scouts today (including girls aged 14- to 21-years-old) can choose between *Venturing*, a more traditional Boy Scout program with emphasis on high adventure; *Learning for Life/Exploring*, which is career-oriented, and the venerable *Sea Scouts*. Eagle Scouts of all ages are invited to join the *National Eagle Scout Association* (NESA).

With the creation of Senior Scouting, there seems to have been little discussion about whether older Scouts would be eligible for Honor Medals. After all, the BSA still was reeling from the disaster in the Tennessee flood just a year before – and though there was some debate about a second local Scout executive earning an Honor Medal, there was none about the extraordinary bravery of Scoutmaster Jim Wright. The precedent now had been set: *any* official member of Scouting was eligible for the Honor Medal, Medal of Merit, or Certificate of Merit.

Not surprisingly, in the decades since, "senior" Scouts not only have earned numerous awards for heroism, but because of their maturity and skills, often have done so in spectacular, even unforgettable, ways.

*Fourteen-year-old Queens (NY) Boy Scout **Henry Plimack** poses for a newspaper photo with his family in 1957 after saving 2 girls from drowning in the East River.*

• **Bernard A. Dawson**, 23 and an assistant Scoutmaster in Zanesville, Ohio, was working as a reporter for the local newspaper when he got the call to cover a burning house. Racing to the scene, he found the house in flames, begun by an explosion in the garage. Even as he watched the flame consume three walls of the garage, he learned from the crowd that there was one person, a child, still unaccounted for.

The child, Thomas Callipy, 9, had been watching two men work on a car. Somehow, a can of naphthalene (a highly flammable solvent once used in cleaning fluid) was tipped over onto a hot plate and exploded – setting fire both to the garage and to the two men. Little Thomas, seeing the fireball, ran to the back door of the garage only to find it locked. He quickly collapsed from the fumes and smoke.

Braving the flames, Dawson ran into the garage in search of the boy. He found Callipy unconscious in a back corner under a pile of inner tubes and tire casings that he apparently had used to protect himself. Everything from tires to the boy's clothes now was on fire.

Joined by a second rescuer, Dawson carried the boy to safety. He performed artificial respiration on Callipy, not stopping until an ambulance arrived fifteen minutes later. The child survived.

• After a busy day, the Tulare, California, Sea Scout crew of Ship #66 was resting on the beach on the peninsula at Morro Bay. Because the sea was rough with crosswise breakers creating an obvious rip tide, the Scouts were told not to go in the water. And for that reason, all of the crew's life belts and lines were left back on the ship, which was tied up on the other side of the sand dunes.

There was a cry for help. The crew members currently on the beach – **Jack Cameron**, 23, **William Earl**, 22, **Pat Nowell**, 17, and **Charles Weaver**, 20 – immediately ran toward the sound, spotted figures in the water, and dove in. Earl, the strongest swimmer, was the first to reach the drowning men. However, as he reached for the first man, he was pushed under. But Earl was well-trained and quickly broke the man's hold. He was joined by Nowell – and the two Scouts grabbed the desperate man (who didn't know how to swim) and started to work him to shore. Meanwhile, Weaver swam to the second man (who could swim but had exhausted himself holding up the first) and helped him ashore, with Cameron swimming alongside to help if needed.

As they approached the shore, the second man announced that he could make it the rest of the way himself. So Weaver and Cameron went back to help the first party only to find themselves caught in a riptide. Cameron managed to escape it and was swimming again towards the first group when he came upon the second man (the one who wanted to go ashore by himself) floating face down from exhaustion. Cameron carried him ashore.

Weaver, meanwhile, was being pulled out to sea by riptide. He used his swimming skills and training to work his way sideways to calmer water. By now, the first party was reaching the shore. The remaining crew on the ship had spotted the rescue and now was running across the dunes with lifebelts and lines. They raced to Weaver's rescue but just then he reached shallow water and waded in by himself.

• Working as the flagman for a crop dusting operation in North Spring Valley, Nevada, Explorer **Randy Newman**, 17, was on duty when he watched the plane piloted by Charles Lee Gordon catch a side gust of turbulent air and crash into the plowed field. Gordon, seriously injured, managed to escape the cockpit. But as he did, the plane's fuel tank exploded behind him and slammed him to the ground beneath the tail. He couldn't move – he had fractured both ribs and a vertebra. Gordon now was at risk of burning to death.

Newman ran across the field to the crash and, ignoring the potential for a second fuel tank explosion, crawled under the plane and dragged, then half-carried, Gordon to safety. As he did so, Newman yelled for the other flagman to run to the nearby ranch house and call for an ambulance. He then tended to Gordon (including treating him for shock) until the ambulance arrived.

- In January 1966, three boys in Rockford, Illinois, decided to dig a tunnel through a giant drift of soft new snow that had piled up against a neighbor's garage. All three were inside the tunnel when it collapsed. Explorer Scout **Bart Swanson**, 16, escaped, as did the third boy. But their friend, Brad Joesten, 13, was trapped beneath the pile of snow.

  The two boys immediately began digging with their hands. Eventually, they found Joesten and uncovered his head and shoulders. Seeing that the boy barely was breathing, Swanson sent the third friend running for help and set to giving Joesten mouth-to-mouth resuscitation. He didn't stop until emergency help arrived and gave the unconscious boy oxygen. Bart rode with Joesten in the ambulance to the hospital and was with him when he regained consciousness.

- Sea Scout **Houston "Sonny" Sansome** of Columbus, Georgia, was working in his backyard with members of his Crew on various repair projects. One of the Scouts had gotten pitch on his clothing and was using a gasoline soaked rag to clean the sticky substance off his clothes – not an unusual procedure in 1954. As other Sea Scouts had a fire going nearby, the Scout was warned not to get close to it – but in a moment of carelessness he did just that. The evaporating liquid on his clothes burst into flames. The Scout panicked and began to run wildly around the yard, even as the fireball began to consume him. Seeing this, Sonny Sansome knocked the boy down with a flying football tackle. Then, seeing nothing nearby to use to put out the flames, and without a second thought, Sonny threw himself atop the boy and used his own body to extinguish the fire – badly burning himself in the process. Both young men survived.

- June 1965: Explorer **John O. Johnson**, 17, of Melrose, Minnesota, was driving alongside the town's main railroad line when he happened to glance over and see two-year-old Nancy Reiland sitting alone in the middle of the tracks. At first he didn't believe what he saw, then he quickly spun his car around and raced to the edge of a spur line. Unable to drive any further, Johnson leaped out of the car and bolted towards the little girl. It was at that moment he heard the horn of an approaching train – an express line racing at full speed towards them. At the last second, Johnson managed to grab the girl and leap with her off the tracks. A second later the locomotive roared past.

And this most incredible act, possibly ranking as one of the greatest acts of bravery and heroism in Scouting history, comes from December 1952:

• Air Explorer **Brookner W. Brady Jr.** of Monterey, California, was skin diving with his friend Barry Wilson off Pacific Grove. The water was choppy but exceedingly clear. So Wilson decided to go further out another 60 feet and dive there in the 40 foot deep water. Moments later, he surfaced, screaming for his life. Brookner swam quickly to his aid – only to find the water red with his friend's blood. It was a shark attack. So, Brookner pulled out his sheath knife and dove for Wilson.

He found him just below the surface, unconscious and bleeding heavily from vicious bite wounds. The shark still had Barry in his jaws and as Brookner grabbed his friend with one hand, he began slashing at the shark with the other. He stabbed the shark three times in the eye with his GI trench knife, but the creature continued his attack. Finally, itself bleeding badly, the man-eater momentarily swam off to regroup.

Four members of a skin diving club swimming nearby heard Barry's screams and rushed to help. They could see glimpses of the bloody battle whenever it broke the water's surface. The group included a Highway Patrol officer and two soldiers from nearby Fort Ord. They arrived in time for Brookner to hand his wounded friend over to be carried ashore, while he swam off to the beach to get help. As this hand-off occurred, the men could feel the shark brushing against their legs as it prepared for the next attack.

Sadly, Barry Wilson died of massive blood loss before he could be brought to the beach. Brookner Brady, just 15-years-old, was awarded the Honor Medal with Crossed Palms.

SHARK VICTIM—Barry Wilson, 17, of Pacific Grove, left, who was killed by a shark while he was skin diving with a companion, Brookner Brady, 15, of Monterey, right. Story on

Scouter Heroes

As you will recall, the first Silver Lifesaving Medal was awarded to an adult in May 1912: Frank H. Sykes, a Scoutmaster in Montgomery County, Pennsylvania, for a water rescue made the previous September. And as a general observation, very few adult volunteers received any recognition for lifesaving over the next decade until the time of the Tennessee flood disaster.

But, had there been any question in regard to awarding the Honor Medal to adult Scouters, it was answered with the heroic death of Scoutmaster Wright and the rescue efforts of Scout Executive Acuff. After all, lifesaving was precisely that – and the whole message of Scouting was that *everyone* in the program, from the littlest Cub Scout through the most venerable Scouter, such as Dan Beard, was expected to live up to the founding tenets of Scouting.

That meant adult volunteers too were expected to "be prepared," to be "helpful," and be "brave." And if living up to the Scout Oath, Law, and motto meant saving the life of another person (and perhaps risking their own life in the process) then why should they too not be eligible for Scouting's Honor awards? To date an estimated 10 percent of the 13,000 Honor Medal recipients have been adults: Scoutmasters and assistant Scoutmasters, troop committee members, district and council volunteers, and Scouting professionals. And, as with senior Scouts, the awards earned by these adults have a character of their own.

• Ten-year-old Donald "Tony" McKinney was walking around a farm near Raccoon, Indiana, when he slipped through a hole in a protective grating and fell into a pit serving a grain auger (a screw conveyor that carries grain up a tube for loading into a truck). The boy slid down into the auger blade while it was still in operation – horrifyingly, it cut off Tony's right leg below the knee.

James Pattison, who had just arrived in a truck to dump another load of corn, heard the boy's screams and jumped from the truck's cab and ran to the sound. The 20-year-old assistant Scoutmaster jumped down into the pit, grabbed the boy and carried him up to safety. Then, using his emergency first aid training, applied direct pressure to the wound by clamping his bare hands around the leg stump.

An early BSA Honor Medal with Crossed Palms similar to the one presented to Air Explorer Brookner W. Brady Jr. in 1953.

Moments later, another truck driver ran up, tearing off his shirt. Pattison took the shirt and momentarily releasing his hold, wrapped the boy's leg, and restored the direct pressure with his hands. He remained in this position for the 15 mile drive to the hospital – where doctors credited him with saving young Tony from bleeding to death.

- Early on an October morning in 1972, **Jack English**, 38, a supervisor at the Swier Electric Co. plant in Phoenix, Arizona, had just completed making assignments to his crew when there was huge flash outside the window. The office lights went black and an instant later an employee burst in shouting that one of his fellow workers had been electrocuted.

English, a Scoutmaster for a troop in nearby Glendale, rushed out. As he did a second electric flash illuminated the company grounds – revealing a crane with its load of steel bars, the latter now down by one end on the ground. Beneath the raised end of the bars, English could see the crushed and pinned body of Robert Rehm, 21. Rehm had been manning a chain attached to the bars to keep the load from swinging as the crane operator was moving the bars from one side of the yard to another. In the process he accidentally had touched the crane to a 7,000 volt overhead power line. The resulting short circuit had dropped the crane load on Rehm, electrocuting him in the process.

Taking an incredible risk, English dove under the still-dangerous load to see if anything could be done for Rehm. The young man was unconscious and badly burned. English couldn't tell if he was alive. Nevertheless, even with the risk of electrocution at any moment looming, English managed to pull out Rehm.

He immediately was joined by two other Swier Electric employees, and between the three men, they maintained artificial respiration, heart massage, and shock treatment until a mobile coronary unit arrived. Robert Rehm survived.

- The staff of Nooteeming Scout Camp near Hudson, New York, decided to hold a picnic at nearby Taconic State Park near the base of a waterfall. They were just climbing to the pool at the base of the falls when they heard screams. Looking up, they saw Kathy Ann Tietjen, 16, who had been walking above, slip, and tumble down the cliff. Halfway down, she had become wedged in a crevice on an exposed ledge.

James Keeley, an Eagle Scout and Camp Nooteeming's waterfront director, volunteered to save her. First, he had to swim across the pool. Then, he climbed the steep ledge to reach the girl. After checking her injuries and determining that Tietjen could be moved, he calmed her and treated the girl for shock.

Looking down he realized there was no way for the two of them to get back down the ledge. So, calling for help, Keeley arranged for a rope to be lowered from above. He then tied the girl in a makeshift sling and slowly lowered her to another Scout waiting in the pool below. That Scout swam with Tietjen to the waiting staff members, including the Camp Nurse, who had improvised a stretcher and a crew to take her down the trail to a waiting rescue squad.

- On a windy, moonless night, at the mouth of the Spokane River near Coeur D'Alene, Idaho, **Jack Steve** and his daughter heard shouts for help outside their riverfront cabin. The cries were coming from a vast log "raft" floating in a nearby lumber mill storage area. Father and daughter ran out of the cabin, pushed their canoe into the water, and paddled to the rescue. It was no easy feat: the night almost was pitch black, the densely packed logs were moving in the wind, and their constant bumping together created a continuous rumble that made it nearly impossible to pinpoint the source of the cries.

But Jack Steve and his daughter were expert canoeists and not only negotiated their way through the log raft, but also located the source of the distress: four men. All were in the cold water, desperately clinging for their lives as the logs they gripped rolled back and forth. Carefully, as they risked being capsized, Steve and his daughter pulled the men aboard and paddled them to safety.

The Turning Point

Heroism is an achievement of the moment. After the rescue has occurred, the rescued are carried off to safety, the newspaper stories are written, the honors and awards are presented, and life typically goes on as before for the onlookers and emergency personnel.

For the rescued survivor, the event may in time be all-but forgotten or, conversely, be the stuff of night-mares. Some injuries heal but others never do. They, at least, have the comfort of knowing they still are alive.

But what of the rescuer, the hero? Often this is a child, plucked by events from everyday life, then tumbled through a few minutes of terror, followed by weeks of universal acclaim and honor, only to be thrust back to everyday life for the years that follow. Their moment of bravery may be the greatest event of their lives – one that took place near the beginning, leaving them with decades of a less-eventful aftermath. Some, for whom the events of that singular day remain a nightmare, a quiet life probably is a relief. But for others it is no doubt an early peak they never will reach again. Some are happy to recount how they earned their medals; others put the award away never to discuss again, even with their children or grandchildren. If they return to Scouting as adults, they are entitled to wear a special square knot above their pocket, similar to the Eagle award, religious medal, and other achievements. But the Honor Medal knot is relatively unknown to other Scouters, and thus often goes unnoticed.

But there is one touching story that offers a glimpse into the real meaning of the Honor Medal to its recipients. It is the coda to one of the most famous stories of Scouting heroism.

The Butte, Montana, hiking party in August 1922. Left to Right: Omer Bradford, William Kent, John McCarthy, Thomas Lanphier, Willard Murray, Carl Shiner, Henry Heideman, Wilbur Marvin, Arthur Kiely, Scout Executive Benjamin Owen, and James Weal.

The story begins in August 1922 near Butte, Montana. A troop of nine Scouts along with the Scout executive from Seattle, Washington, set out on a four and a half day hike through the Highland Range of the Rockies. This was a popular trip. It has been reported that some councils even allowed unsupervised older boys to hike the largely unexplored region. Many even discovered new lakes and mountain peaks that were added to government maps.

However, this troop did have adult supervision – Scout executive **Benjamin Owen**. It also had several younger Scouts, the youngest being 14-year-old, First Class Scout **Wilbur Marvin**. As all of the boys had backpacking experience, there wasn't any concern about any of them, even Marvin, not being up to the task.

The first leg of the hike promised to be particularly strenuous: they would climb three peaks, all over 10,000 feet tall: Red Mountain, Devil's Peak, and Table Mountain, all of them interconnected

by narrow "hog's back" saddles. A local prospector met the group and led them part way through the 5,000 foot climb up Red Mountain. He parted ways after lunch, leaving the group to continue their climb. They reached the summit at 2 p.m. as the afternoon wind began to blow.

Scout Executive Benjamin Owen, 1922.

Next up was Devil's Peak. They half-stepped, half-slid down the far side of Red Mountain and started, single-file, across the hog's back to Devil's Peak. As they did so, the sky suddenly darkened and clouds rolled in overhead. It began to rain. Lightning and thunder filled the sky above them. The wind began to howl, and as it did the temperature dropped below freezing and the rain turned into hail. The Scouts were exposed completely. On the narrow saddle and the mountain beyond there was no visible shelter. And they were too far along to go back. The only way out was to keep going forward over Devil's Peak then down the other side to the tree line. It was a bitter climb but somehow the Scouts made it to the crest of Devil's Peak. As they reached the summit the storm began to clear away, replaced by afternoon sunlight.

The Scouts took a short break to regroup and let their soaked clothes begin to dry. But their vulnerability on the mountain top was obvious and they quickly resolved to press on and find a good place to camp. They headed down Devil's Peak and, within minutes, were crossing the second hog's back to the third peak, Table Mountain, a mile and a half away. Again they hiked single file across the saddle and started up the new mountain. What they hadn't noticed in their excitement was that behind them another, bigger storm quickly was blowing in.

Table Mountain to the left and Devil's Peak on the right with an "X" marking the spot of the lightning strike at an elevation of 10,800 feet.

The storm struck without warning. Later, all that the boys could remember was a blinding blue light, the crack of an explosion and the horrifying aftermath. The Scouts lay scattered in a ragged line on the mountainside, some unconscious, others screaming in agony. Everyone had been knocked out by a fierce lightning bolt. Now, as they picked themselves up and took stock, the Scouts realized the magnitude of the tragedy.

One Scout, Henry Heideman, was dead. The lightning bolt had struck him behind the right ear, travelled down his chest and exploded his heart, killing him instantly. Nearby, Thomas Lamphier had been hit in the leg by the bolt that travelled down his shin and burst out from the ball of his foot, leaving a deep burn. Meanwhile, the bolt had travelled around the outside of both Carl Shiner and William Kent. Shiner was left with severe burns on both his back and abdomen. Kent's injuries were even worse. Not only did he have a nasty burn on his right abdomen but a second large burn across his back had melted away the flesh to expose the muscles beneath.

All three boys were in terrible pain. Kent's was the most severe. Delirious with shock, he was thrashing around on the rocks and coming close to the edge where he would fall several hundred feet to his death. It took four other Scouts to hold him down.

Scout Executive Owen and the other Scouts knew they had to move quickly – both to protect themselves from the ongoing storm and to get the three injured boys to safety. According to their maps, the nearest human habitation, Nelson Ranch, was 11 miles away on the far side of Table Mountain, a hike that would require another thousand feet or more of ascent, followed by a descent of five thousand feet.

At the Julius Nelson Ranch where the Scouts received shelter and treatment. Left to Right: Wilbur Marvin, James Weal, Mrs. Carl Johnson, Omer Bradford, John McCarthy, and Willard Murray.

Sixteen-year-old Star Scout **Omer Bradford**, along with the team's youngest, Wilbur Marvin, volunteered to make the trek. Scout Executive Owen took two maps, marked on both a rendezvous point, and gave one to the boys as he wished them luck.

As the pair raced off, Owen organized the remaining boys into two details, one (Eagle Scout **John McCarthy**, 16; Star Scout **James Weal**, 16; and Owen himself) to care for the injured Scouts and the other, led by First Class Scout **William Murray**, 15, to gather all the gear, including tent halves, food, blankets and clothes. These now were scattered all over the hillside and needed to be gathered and taken down to the base of the mountain, where they were to set up an emergency camp, build a fire, and start preparing warm food.

By sunset, after hours of treatment by their fellow Scouts, Shiner and Kent were bandaged and able to stand. McCarthy and Weal helped them, step by faltering step, down the rock face of the mountain. Lamphier was in better shape but the deep burn to his foot made it impossible for him to walk. So Scout Executive Owen carried him on his back down the vertiginous path, risking both of their lives with every step.

One of the survivors later would describe the next hour with the words: "I am not equal to the task of describing the nightmare and torture of that descent that was made by inches, crawling, sliding. We were forced to zigzag our way across the face of the mountain, for the descent was too steep to go directly down."

Meanwhile, Bradford and Marvin crested Table Mountain and raced down the other side in the near-darkness. The lightning bolt, they had discovered, had ruined their compasses, so that they had to maintain a straight path using line of sight, aligning landscape features to keep from losing their direction – all despite the fact that they were crossing through country neither ever had seen before. Despite everything, they found the ranch house. The entire hike had taken them just one hour and 45 minutes – a pace only possible if they had run most of the 11 miles.

It was well after dark, but after a circuitous trip around the mountain, the hastily assembled group of horse-drawn rescue wagons reached the rendezvous point, loaded up the Scouts and their Scout executive and carried them back to the Ranch. There, a doctor was waiting to help the injured boys.

The next morning, those Scouts who were able returned to Table Mountain to retrieve the body of their friend and fellow Scout Henry Heideman.

Bradford, McCarthy, Marvin, Murray, Weal, and Scout Executive Owen all were awarded Gold Honor Medals for their actions that afternoon on Table Mountain – the largest single group ever to receive the supreme award. Lamphier, Shiner, and Kent received commendations from the National Court of Honor for their coolness in emergency in the face of their serious injuries. Owen earned the distinction of being the first Scout executive to receive a Gold Honor Medal.

But that isn't where the story ends. No one came away from that afternoon on Table Mountain unaffected by what they had experienced. The following story from a single newspaper article reveals a unique and touching tale of what that medal meant to the youngest of those Scouts.

On February 12, 1936, almost 14 years later, an article appeared in the Helena, Montana, *Independent Record*. It told the story of a dying man who had contacted the local Scout executive with a desperate request. He had lost his Gold Honor Medal (presented to him and his fellow troop honorees by President Warren G. Harding himself) and he was anxious to replace it. Could the council help?

The dying man was Wilbur Marvin, the youngest Scout on Table Mountain that day and the boy who had raced for help. Now just 28, he was confined to a Southern California sanitarium, dying from tuberculosis. A second letter accompanied the first; this one from a nurse at the sanitarium. In it, she explained that Mr. Marvin was making his plea because he had a three-year-old daughter who, because of the infectious nature of the disease, barely knew her father. She had, in fact, only seen him "two or three times." Marvin hoped to obtain a duplicate of his medal to give to his daughter to help her remember him and to inspire her with his actions after he was gone.

The nurse finished her letter with the poignant words that "the hopes of receiving a copy of his medal is all that keeps Mr. Marvin alive."

Among all of the events of his comparatively short life, Wilbur Marvin chose this one honor by which his daughter and his descendants would remember him. The article concludes with a promise by the Scout executive to get Marvin his medal.

The President of the United States, Warren G. Harding, decorating six Butte (Mont.) Boy Scouts with the Gold Honor Medal.

A Buckskin Farewell

Dan Beard, whose career working with youth had begun at the turn of the 20th century, who had played a pivotal role in the creation of the largest national youth movement in history, and who had been the friend to the most famous Americans of his era (including presidents of the United States), died just short of his 91st birthday on June 11, 1941.

Born a decade before the Civil War, he had mentored the first generation of young Scouts that had served in World War I; and by his death, he had mentored the two generations of Scouts who soon would both be the soldiers ("the greatest generation") and their leaders in World War II. This last cohort of Scouts Beard would mentor, the boys born in the late 1920s, would lead America to become the most powerful and prosperous nation in history.

Dan Beard in 1910.

Dan Beard celebrating his 90th birthday at the
New York World's Fair in June 1940.

Beard's specific achievements were too numerous to count. Besides creating one of the two organizations that were the foundation of the BSA, he also founded Boy Scout Troop 1 in Flushing, New York. As Scouting's chief operating officer during its early years, he held the fledgling organization together, established its rules and, ultimately, helped give the BSA its overall vision – one that was distinctly different from its British counterpart. His writings, in both *Boys' Life* and a series of books, filled the imaginations of millions of young men in Scouting's first 30 years with dreams of the outdoors. With his close connections to the likes of Theodore Roosevelt and William Hornaday (director of the Bronx Zoo), Beard was a pioneer of American environmentalism and conservation – a philosophy he helped to embed permanently into Scouting.

But perhaps Beard's greatest contribution was to set Scouting's standards at the highest possible level – impossibly high, some critics believed – until Scouts themselves proved those critics wrong. Not least among those standards was the Honor Medal program. Now, each year Scouts would study carefully the annual Honor Medal announcements in BSA publications and wonder how they would handle finding themselves in similar life threatening situations (and maybe the adulation to follow).

A week after his death, newspapers around the country carried a memorial poem for Beard from the "people's poet," Edgar A. Guest. It reads in part:

He'll live wherever boyhood
   pitches tent beside a stream

And fire is made by friction
   and coffee needs no cream.

He'll live where lads go Scouting,
   either landward or afloat,

A great heart dressed in khaki
   with a 'kerchief at his throat,

Oh, I don't know how to say it,
   but somehow it seems to me

His life will flow forever, like
   a river to the sea.

Some write their years in splendors;
   in things of steel and stone

And some as master craftsmen
   their little while are known.

Some break oblivion's silence
   by gaining history's page,

But there's a greater greatness
   than comes to prince or sage,

A majesty of spirit, world-over
   understood

Which guides the lives of others
   to all that's brave and good.

Beard was buried near his home in Spring Valley, New York. E. Urner Goodman, the national program director of the BSA organized his predecessor's funeral. On the day of the funeral, an estimated 2,000 people lined the route to the cemetery in Monsey, New York. There, 127 Boy Scouts formed an honor guard. It would be the largest Scouting funeral until that of fellow Eagle Scout, President Gerald R. Ford, six decades later (Beard had earned his Eagle medal in 1915 at age 64).

In the months and years that followed, Dan Beard was honored by having his name appended to a bridge across the Ohio River near Cincinnati, a junior high school in Flushing, New York, an elementary school in Chicago, numerous Scout camps and programs, and an award for service to Scouting by the Freemasons. His boyhood home in Covington, Kentucky, is a National Historic Landmark. In Alaska's Denali National Park, standing near Mount McKinley is 10,082 foot Mount Dan Beard. A special gold Eagle Medal awarded to Beard in 1922 became the basis for the Distinguished Eagle Scout Award (DESA), the BSA's highest non-Scouting award for lifetime achievement. DESA recipients now include Nobel Prize winners, senators and congressmen, Fortune 500 CEOs, and the first man to walk on the moon.

After 30 years of Dan Beard's support, the BSA Honor Medal program has become a permanent Scouting institution – the embodiment of both the Scout motto of training to "be prepared" for the greatest challenges that life can present, and of the bravery as its highest character trait. The Honor Medal certainly now would survive – especially as the next years of world war would put courage and heroism steadily into the thoughts and dreams of American boyhood.

By war's end, the BSA – in particular, *Boys' Life* magazine – would have in the works for the postwar generation and the Scouts of the Baby Boom era a new institution (of all things, a comic strip) that would capture their imaginations and take the Honor Medal to even greater heights.

It would carry Dan Beard's vision forward into a world he scarcely could have imagined.

HERO'S AWARD
Debbie Rector, 9, plants a kiss on the cheek of her cousin Billy Steber, 10, for saving her life. Debbie, who cannot swim, fell from a raft into 12 feet of water. Billy heard her scream. A Cub Scout, he jumped into the pool and pulled her to safety as he had been taught at the Nashville, Tenn., Y.M.C.A. pool.
(AP Wirephoto)

"A hero is no braver than an ordinary person,
but he is braver five minutes longer." - Ralph Waldo Emerson

A World of Heroes

"I was trying to live up to my Scout Oath and Law."
Scout Harold White in 1920
after diving in front of an oncoming car
to save a little boy.

CHAPTER
4

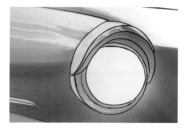

The number of ways that human beings can put themselves in mortal danger almost is endless. Not surprisingly, from the very first days of American Scouting, Boy Scouts were saving lives in the most unexpected and unlikely of ways – a fact largely disguised by the initial biases of Dan Beard and the National Court of Honor.

Nevertheless, beyond the numerous aquatic rescues that the BSA found exemplary, several other types of rescues (such as Dorris Giles and the trolley cable) did manage to earn the Honor Medal – typically because it was impossible to ignore their achievement.

When those original and philosophical restrictions were lifted on Honor Medal recipients in the 1920s, new precedents wer e set that revealed the true magnitude of a Scout's ability to save lives. This was made clear in the total numbers of saves, the heroic nature of the Scouts, and the sheer breadth of the different types of rescues. In the years and decades that followed, not only did Scouts of all ages heroically save the lives of others (often at great risk to themselves) but the nature of those rescues expanded to an astonishing degree.

In the preceeding chapter, we looked at the range of Honor Medal recipients vertically, at members of the different levels and organizations of Scouting. In this chapter, we look horizontally, at the extraordinary *range* of heroic rescues by members of the BSA. It truly can be said that when Americans found themselves in physical danger, Scouts were trained and willing to rescue them.

We begin with the early years, when Scouting was just the Boy Scout program that allowed boys as young as 12 to join its ranks. These heroic Scouts accomplished memorable rescues that attracted the attention of the public, national civic leaders, and the BSA's National Court of Honor:

• **Marcellus Hatcher** was a 13-year-old Tenderfoot in 1915, who told his mother that a nearby house was on fire. Since she didn't fully understand what he intended to do and he had no time to explain it, Marcellus ignored her order to stay put and instead rushed down the street to the burning house. Running through the flames into the structure, he managed to save a child. Mrs. Hatcher only learned what her son had done after his successful rescue act.

• In an important statement of support for the BSA in February 1915, President Woodrow Wilson hosted a ceremony at the White House to recognize five new Eagle Scouts (Clinton Allard, Edward Pardoe, Samuel Hardy, Edward Sheiry, and Frank Watson) and Honor Medal recipient **Howard A. Gatley** (*below, far left side*), all of Washington, DC. The young Gatley had saved the life of 10-year-old Robert Norris of Montgomery County, Maryland, from drowning in the pond at Jackson Mill Dam. Interestingly, Gatley would go on to earn the Eagle award and join the ranks of professional Scouting. While a Scout executive, he completed the requirements for the William T. Hornaday Conservation Award, becoming the first ever to earn Scouting's "Triple Crown" – the Eagle award, the Hornaday award, and the Honor Medal. To date, fewer than 20 individuals ever have done so.

- First Class Scout brothers **Charles H.** and **Horace Krause**, 15- and 13-years-old respectively, were sailing their small skiff on Lake Erie entertaining two young family guests. A gale was blowing on the lake but the two boys were sufficiently experienced to stay in the lee of some nearby tall cliffs. But they spotted another sailboat out in the open water as it scuttled and filled with water. Without time to drop off the two young passengers, the brothers expertly sailed their skiff out through the waves and rescued three men out of the water. Despite the fact there now were seven people in the nearly swamped small sailboat, Charles and Horace sailed them all to safety. When thanked for their efforts, one of the brothers replied, "Oh, that's nothing. I only did my duty as a Boy Scout."[18]

Joseph Kaleiolaa
432—23rd Avenue
Oakland, California
(Troop 33)

*Second Class Scout **Joseph Kaleiolaa**
received the Honor Medal in 1923.*

- 1915: **Harvey Kiederling**, 13, of Plainfield, New Jersey, was watching a circus parade when he saw a child wander out into the street and under a passing team of horses. As the horses reared over him, Kiederling dove under the slashing hoofs and pulled the child out of the way. According to eyewitnesses, "He escaped death by only a fraction of a second."[19]

136

- **Howard Evans**, a Southside Pittsburgh Scout, who had been "decorated with several medals for saving lives and rendering first aid in desperate situations," encountered a group of terrified young girls running from the scene of an accident. As he tended to one of the girl's injuries, he learned from her why they had been running: an accident at the nearby Southside playground.

Running to the playground, Evans quickly took stock of the situation. One of the girls, Ethel Weaver, 11, had been using a "big swing" (probably a large stand-up type) when it broke loose from its cables and crashed to the ground – pinning Ethel beneath it. Evans managed to lift the swing off of the bruised and unconscious girl and applied artificial respiration until she began breathing. Then picking her up, Evans carried Ethel to Southside Hospital, where doctors dressed her wounds and were able to revive her. According to the Hospital, without Evans' quick rescue, Ethel Weaver would not have survived.

- **Willard J. Magavern**, a First Class Scout from Buffalo, New York, saved a girl from burning to death. She was working over an alcohol stove making candy in a pot when she bumped the stove. It tipped over, splattering her with alcohol that ignited instantly. Magavern pulled the burning girl to the floor and rolled her in a rug, smothering the flames.

- Eagle Scout, Knight of Dunamis member, and assistant Scoutmaster **T.J. Ice Jr.**, probably 18, saved his uncle from drowning on a fishing trip to Devil's Canyon, Wyoming, earning him a Letter of Commendation from Dan Beard. For his heroism, Ice was invited, along with three other Scout heroes to attend a congratulatory dinner at the Cosmopolitan Hotel in Denver, Colorado.

The guest of honor for the dinner was the most famous figure of the age: aviator Charles A. Lindbergh, only recently returned from his solo flight across the Atlantic. Lindbergh himself joined Ice and the other Scouts on stage as their honors were announced, shaking their hands, and stopping to talk with each of them. According to the newspaper reports, the applause for these young heroes "was equal to the ovation given to Lindbergh himself."[20]

Huckster Heroism

Unfortunately, the fame and celebrity given Scout Honor Medal recipients also brought out individuals wanting their share of quick and easy glory. Earlier we noted a case of a fraudulent "rescue" that helped lead to the creation of the National Court of Honor in 1911. A second case appeared a few years later. This time in June 1915, when John J. Murray, a 22-year-old Scoutmaster, was arrested by Worcester, Massachusetts, police for setting fire to a barn filled with straw and hay, and assisting with its extinguishment in hopes of being awarded an Honor Medal. Murray was charged with attempted arson and held on a $1,000 bond. He confessed to the crime.

Scout Ralph Beattie
14 Lyceum Street, Geneva, New York
(Troop 6)

Face to Face with Death

But even with this "black eye" on Scouting, hundreds of young men continued their efforts to save people from imminent death.

• February 1932, Mandan, North Dakota. Heavy rains in the nearby hills had swollen the waters of the Heart River as it converged on the mighty Missouri river near town, turning the main stream into a rolling torrent filled with ice and tree debris. Hundreds of locals had come down to the river on a Sunday afternoon to picnic and watch the flooded waters.

They got more than they asked for. A local man decided to take his eight-year-old son out in a boat on one of the quiet backwaters created by the flood. But, as he rowed across a smaller channel he got too close to the main river and the boat was swept into the roaring current. Now racing faster than he could row, there was little the helpless man could do. Within moments, the boat was smashed against a cement viaduct and capsized.

Even worse, the father could not swim. Now tumbled into the water, he made one leap for his son, missed, then grabbed onto a nearby board, and pulled himself out of the river.

As the crowd on the banks watched in horror, the boy was swept downriver at a rate – one observer estimated – faster than a man could run. There seemed to be no chance of rescue.

But two hundred yards downstream stood the bridge of the Northern Pacific railroad with two tracks arrayed in a Y-configuration. Not only was the debris in the river slamming into, and piling up against, the bridge's pilings, but the flooded water itself was just 10 inches under its crossties. In less than a minute the young boy was doomed to hit the bridge.

There were, in fact, several boys on the bridge that day. And when they heard shouting upstream and saw people pointing at the small figure in the water, one boy, the "slight," 14-year-old Tenderfoot Scout **John Dewey**, ran from the bridge and up the bank. There, he kicked off his shoes, shed his heavy winter clothing, and prepared to dive in.

Given the speed of the river, Dewey knew his timing would have to be perfect. And it was. He leapt into the river and surfaced just as the boy went past, grabbing him by the arm. Now a new challenge: there was no time to get back to the bank. They would have to go under the bridge.

*First Class Scout **Ralph Beattie** received the Honor Medal in November 1922 for saving Richard Gasby from drowning.*

So, as they approached the structure, Dewey dove, pulling the boy down with him, disappearing beneath the surface just as they reached the underside of the bridge.

Now the next challenge: how to get from the main channel to the bank. By this point, dozens of onlookers were running down the bank, shouting, and trying to keep up. Some men jumped into their cars and took off in pursuit.

Clearly, they boys weren't going to make it to the side as the current simply was too strong. That's when John saw a separate channel – a sluice way – up ahead. If they got to it they might be able to slow down, but if they missed they likely would be battered to death.

Still holding the boy, John paddled with all of his strength and made it in. The two now raced down the passageway, spinning and turning in the churning water. When they emerged, they were just a few hundred yards from the river's mouth and the giant, half-mile-across Missouri river just beyond. Once there, the two boys could not be rescued.

Desperate, Dewey again hung on to the younger boy and paddled with one arm with all of his strength. It worked: he managed to get them out of the main channel into slower water. By now, the scores of pursuing men caught up with them. John finally reached shallow water. He tried to stand but collapsed. The hero now needed his own rescue.

Taken home and put to bed under a doctor's care, John Dewey recovered after a few hours. The boy he saved was nearly dead from drowning. He was moved to a nearby cabin, where medical personnel worked on him for ninety minutes before he regained consciousness. It wasn't until dawn that he was allowed to return home.

The next day, Dewey's house was surrounded by visitors and well-wishers. Asked to give a speech, the shy boy managed to say only, "Gee, the water was cold!"

It was only later that it was noted that John Dewey had learned to swim at Scout camp only eight months before.

John A. Dewey of Mandan, North Dakota, 1932.

• Scout **Dean Cooke**, of Whitefish, Montana, in late 1924 spotted four young people who had broken through the ice of a pond. Crawling out, he managed to pull out two girls but as he did, he himself broke through into the freezing water. Yet, he still had the presence to ignore his own predicament and focus on saving two more children, a boy and a girl, who still were in the water.

Seeing that the boy was a better swimmer, Cooke focused on saving the girl first. He managed to grab and pull her over to the ice's edge. He then made her climb on his back to lift her out. But by now, Cooke's hands were completely numb and he was unable to lift up the two of them.

At this moment, other rescuers arrived. They pushed a plank out to Cooke, but he couldn't hold on. *Thirty* minutes later, someone arrived with a rope and threw it to an increasingly hypothermic Cooke. Although he still couldn't hold on, the boy had the presence of mind to take the rope in his teeth. Despite the fact that the ice kept breaking every time Cooke and the girl managed to get on the surface, the two finally were pulled out with the rope still in the delirious Cooke's teeth. The girl survived.

At one point in this travail, the other boy in the water came close to Cooke. They reached out to each other, but both of their hands were too frozen to grip – and, tragically, the boy was lost.

• It had taken Star Scout **Joseph Erlenwein**, 17, *(see right)* of Columbus, Ohio, three years to learn how to swim and pass his First Class swimming requirement. But he remained deathly afraid of water and was not a confident swimmer. It was then that he found himself at a river lake campground watching others swim, but happy to be out of the water himself.

Meanwhile, another unsteady new swimmer, Gladys Anderson, was being helped to swim across the channel of the lake by a "Mrs. Lewis." Suddenly, in the middle of the channel, Gladys panicked and, fearful of going under, grabbed Mrs. Lewis around the waist and pulled them both down.

Forgetting his fear, Joseph dove into the lake and swam to the pair. By the time he arrived, Mrs. Lewis already was unconscious and Gladys Anderson was thrashing on the surface and quickly losing her fight. Joseph managed to push Mrs. Lewis' head above the water. Next, he turned to saving Gladys, who tried to grab him as well.

Somehow, this novice swimmer managed to hold Mrs. Lewis above the water with one hand and with the other hold at arm's length a violently thrashing Gladys Anderson. The combined weight of the two women were twice his own but he still swam them to shore.

Depositing the two women safely on the bank, Erlenwein collapsed and was sick from exhaustion for several days. It was months later that his Scoutmaster learned about Joseph's heroism – and only then from other sources. Asked why he had been silent about such an extraordinary achievement, Erlenwein replied that it had been a simple duty and that there was no use in "crowing about it."

• Summer 1939: First Class Scout **Ernest Miner** of Niles Center (now Skokie), Illinois, was hanging out on a quiet street in his neighborhood on a summer day. Nearby, a group of young children were playing. Hearing a noise, Miner glanced down the street to see a speeding automobile hurtling towards them. Miner raced over and, with his arms out, crashed into the group, pushing the children out of the way just as the speeding car ran over the spot where they had just been.

• The third Honor Medal with Crossed Palms, awarded for extreme danger to the rescuer's life, was presented (two decades after its creation) to Star Scout **Norman Putnam**, 15, of Syracuse, New York, for a July 1945 rescue at DeRuyter Lake of a five-year-old girl trapped in a burning motorboat. Putnam not only swam to the boat, but braving the flames, climbed aboard, grabbed the girl, dove with her back into the water, and then swam to shore carrying her.[21]

• The ban against Honor Medals for saving a family member long forgotten, Kokomo, Indiana, Scout **Verlin Bowland**, 17, saved his father's life after discovering him unconscious and lying on the floor of the family garage. It was December 30, 1946, and because it was so cold outside, Mr. Bowland decided to work all day on the car with the garage door closed. Unknowingly, he was inhaling a deadly amount of carbon monoxide. According to the local fire chief, Verland found his father just in time, dragged him out into fresh air, and revived him.[22]

• Even under the new training regime, not every rescue had a happy ending. In 1921, Scout **Thomas H. Robinson** of Camden, New Jersey, dove into the Delaware River to save a friend. He managed to reach the drowning boy and even drag him back to the wharf, where a crowd had gathered. They pulled the boy out and set to work reviving him. But no one noticed that an exhausted Thomas was unable to climb out and now was slipping back into the water. By the time the boy was spotted, it was too late, and he officially became the fifth Boy Scout to die while making a rescue.

Robinson's Honor Medal was presented to his mother, who later wrote: "He was a good Scout and a credit to the organization. I believe it was instilled in his mind to do good through the high standard of the Scout methods. I will always prize the medal and keep it safe."[23]

Eagle Scout Henry Arnold rescued 36-year-old Karl Balinski from drowning in 1929.

Sui Generis

Then there are the singular rescues. Some are firsts, others involve a unique combination of rescuer(s) and rescued, and some are so unusual they are unlikely to be repeated any time soon, if ever:

• Nineteen twenty-nine was an important year for Eagle Scout **Henry Arnold**, 17, from Chewelah, Washington. He not only earned his Eagle, but also the Honor Medal for saving two lives from drowning. Two years later, he also was awarded the annual $300 scholarship (equal in those days to a year's worth of college tuition) from the Veterans of Foreign Wars to the "Outstanding Boy Scout of America" for the year.

• In 1997, the Northcutts, Nathaniel and Carolyn, and their five children, were fishing in a canal in Oakland Park, Florida. Suddenly, Carolyn Northcutt suffered a seizure and fell into the canal. She not only was at risk of drowning but also of being bitten by the numerous poisonous snakes living in the canal. Nathaniel, and 12-year-old son, Nathaniel Jr. – the only two family members able to swim – jumped in to save her.

Meanwhile, the other Northcutt children ran up the canal bank in search of help. They found assistant Scoutmaster **William F. Jones** and his friend John Middlemiss nearby and begged them to save their parents. Jones, who also was a trained Scout lifeguard, quickly dove into the canal and swam the unconscious Mr. Northcutt to the bank, where Middlemiss pulled him out and began a successful CPR routine. Jones, meanwhile, returned to the center of the canal, found a now-conscious Ms. Northcutt, and swam her to shore.

Tragically, only now did the Northcutts realize that their son was missing – no one had told the two rescuers he had entered the water. Jones desperately dove into the canal again but he was too late.

As he received his Honor Medal with Crossed Palms, Jones said sadly, "I'm proud of what I did. But I keep thinking about the boy. If I had just known he was there sooner, I would have been back in the water."[24]

• The following story describes the actions of members of three different Scouting organizations working as a team. In late December, 1980 two father-son pairs – **James Dodds**, the Istrouma Area BSA Council president and his son, Second Class Scout **Jeffrey Dodds**; and David Dansky and his son, Bear Cub Scout **David Dansky Jr.** – were fishing from the Dansky's 21-foot boat on Louisiana's Bayou LaFourche when the boat's engine exploded. The blast flung Jeffrey into the boat's windshield, sent Mr. Dodds to the deck that injured his back, and Mr. Dansky, who suffered from multiple sclerosis, under the boat's dashboard and into the bow compartment.

Keeping calm despite his injury, Mr. Dodds shoved both his son and David Jr. over the windshield, and onto the boat's bow deck. Then he pulled Mr. Dansky to his feet (and with the help of the two boys) managed to get him onto the bow as well. There, as the boat burned and faced the potential of exploding gas tanks, the four hung on, stayed down, and waited for a rescue vessel.

Honor Medals went to the Cub Scout and Boy Scout, and an Honor Medal with Crossed Palms to Scouter Dodds.

• Fourteen-year-old Scout **James Anderson** was working with his troop manning the refreshment stand at local Chautauqua event (a social gathering of public speakers and other events popular in the era) in 1927 in Sidney, Ohio. Unexpectedly, the skies darkened and the camp began to be lashed with rain. The attendees, in the hundreds, rushed for cover beneath the refreshment and rest tents.

Suddenly, to everyone's horror a tornado appeared out of the rain and headed for the campground. It slammed into the big tents ripping out their stakes from the ground and sending the canvas sides flapping, chairs flying, and knocking the visitors off their feet. People who could gain their footing rushed for the exits; others still were stricken motionless.

A Chautauqua tent of a similar size and design to the one in the James Anderson story.

It got worse: now the towering tent poles began to sway dangerously. There was a shout from the crowd to hold the poles and the only person to come running was young Anderson. Though he weighed just one hundred pounds, Jim braced himself against the center pole, fighting to keep it from toppling. His younger brother ran up and tried to pull him away to safety but Jim refused.

A few moments later, his brother again returned and tried to convince him to leave. This time Jim momentarily agreed and joined him. But after taking a couple steps and seeing a large number of people still in the tent, Jim pulled away, muttering "These people's lives are more important than mine." He returned to holding the pole.

He held on long enough to allow almost everyone to escape. Then, as he still struggled to hold on, the pole whipped and snapped near the top. The broken top fell straight down and fractured James Anderson's skull – killing him instantly. He was the ninth heroic Scout to die in the act of saving another.

• Thirteen-year-old First Class Scout **Charles Edward McKnett** of Huntington Park, California, was on a day outing with his parents and two younger brothers at nearby Fish Canyon in 1928. Hiking in, his two brothers, Robert and Francis, went ahead and upon seeing the water, jumped in to cool off.

There was a shout. It was Francis, screaming that Robert was drowning. The boy had taken off his shoes and socks and waded into a pool. But he had slipped on some rocks and skidded into deeper water.

Running up, Charles quickly assessed the situation and ordered Francis to run back up the trail to their father. Then, before the boy could take off, and with odd premonition of his fate, Charles told his brother, "If I don't come out, tell mother I died right."

When the bodies of the boys were recovered, Charles still was holding Robert. He had reached his brother but had failed to get them both to shore. Charles was the first recipient of the Honor Medal with Crossed Palms and the fourteenth Scout to die while saving another.

- Eagle Scout **Charles Magyar**, 23, of New Brunswick, New Jersey, was on duty as a volunteer with the New Jersey State Police in crowd control at the Princeton-Yale baseball game and class reunion.

Just after noon, a crowd of several thousand onlookers gathered on the sidewalk near the stadium in anticipation of a parade by several hundred Princeton alumni heading into the game.

At about 1:30 p.m. the procession came into sight and the crowd cheered wildly. To even more cheers, out of the stadium in the opposite direction and heading towards the parade came two improvised chariots to greet them, each driven by a university graduate, and hooked to a team of "spirited young horses."

Then the unimaginable happened. Spooked for some unknown reason, the second team of horses panicked and broke into a gallop. The inexperienced driver couldn't control them. The chariot began to fishtail wildly, and in the process, one of its wheels crushed in, the chariot tumbled, throwing the driver over the side into the wreckage, and entangling him in the reins.

The horses, now even more terrified, began to pull the wrecked chariot and its driver, dragging him helplessly along the rough asphalt and gravel towards the oncoming parade at an ever-greater speed. Meanwhile, the huge crowd, seeing this emerging threat, began to panic. The police rushed in to try to maintain order.

It was at this moment that Charles Magyar appeared from nowhere. He ran out into the street in pursuit of the chariot and its horses. Timing himself just right, he leaped towards the heads of the charging animals (had he missed he would have been trampled underfoot). He managed to catch the bridles of two of the horses and, being a large man, pulled them to a halt just before they collided with the parade.

The chariot driver, among the many whose lives were saved by Charles Magyar, emerged from the wrecked chariot with only cuts and bruises.

Some stories of Scout Honor Medal rescues are the stuff of ancient nightmares; others are the raw material for new, unwelcome ones.

• Eagle Scout and Council member-at-large **Michael Niederee**, 25, of Great Bend, Kansas, was involved in one of the most memorable rescues in BSA history. In September 1979, Niederee was hunting in the Navajo Canyon near Alamosa, Colorado. His guide, Ed Wiseman, was out of sight a short distance away. Niederee heard a shout, then, the roar of a grizzly bear.

He ran to the sound and encountered the chilling sight of the 350 lb. bear attacking and mauling Wiseman, the latter bleeding shoulder to leg from the bear's claws. At the same time, the guide, who had been carrying only a hunting bow, managed to grab an arrow and began stabbing the bear in the neck.

As Niederee ran up, Wiseman jammed the arrow into the bear's jugular vein. Now bleeding heavily, the beast released its grip, then staggered off to die. Meanwhile, Wiseman himself was in imminent danger of bleeding to death both from his claw wounds and from a broken leg crushed in the bear's jaws.

Niederee went to work to treat for shock and to stop the bleeding, splinting the broken leg, and cleaning and dressing Wiseman's wounds. Then, as darkness fell, he covered the injured man with his own clothing and built a fire nearby to keep Wiseman warm. Then, in t-shirt and jeans, Niederee jumped on his horse and rode down the mountain, making his way in the cold darkness and down a dim trail to the hunting base camp. There, he sent a rider to get help, climbed back on his horse, and rode back to Wiseman. He guarded the man and tended his wounds until dawn, when a rescue helicopter lifted the guide out and flew him to the hospital.

• On a day in August 1926, described at the time as "almost without precedent in the history of life saving exploits by Boy Scouts" (a description that still could stand today) junior assistant Scoutmaster **Howard Peterson** of Boston, Massachusetts, helped save seven individuals from drowning.

Trained in lifesaving, Peterson began the day by aiding a doctor in applying artificial respiration to two individuals who had been pulled "half drowned" from the surf. As he did so, Peterson saw a girl being dragged out by an undertow. He swam out and rescued her.

Next, Peterson saw three men, who had been rowing out a boat to save the girl he had rescued, in the water. Their boat had capsized. Other bathers on the beach were forming a living chain to save them. But as Peterson watched, that chain had broken and several more individuals were seen floundering in the water.

Once again, Peterson ran down the beach and dove in. This time, he saved four individuals from drowning.

After that, an exhausted Peterson went home to get some sleep. After he awoke that evening, Peterson decided to take a walk down the beach and clear his head from the events of the day. That's when he saw two more figures, a man and a girl, struggling in the water, again trapped by the undertow. Too exhausted to attempt yet another rescue, he ran and found help nearby. Both swimmers were saved.

One assumes that after having saved *seven people in a single day*, Howard Peterson got a well-deserved night's sleep.

• Santa Barbara, California, 1924: The father of First Class Scout **Stewart Meigs**, 16, came into the camp where his family was staying to report that he had just seen a sailing skiff capsize at a spot called Arch Rock in the Santa Barbara Channel.

Despite a severe storm, Stewart and his father launched their own skiff from the beach and, after forty minutes of hard rowing, managed to cross the three miles from their camp to where the skiff lay in the water. There they found Mr. W.D. Wilkinson, 50, clinging to a rock, and the body of his drowned wife floating nearby. They soon learned that two more adults were missing.

Second Class Scout **Rex Guinee** *of Tower Hill, Illinois, received the Honor Medal for saving two drowning boys in 1925.*

THE REMINGTON AWARD FOR HEROISM

Because Wilkinson was exhausted and in shock, it took everything father and son had to get him into their boat. He immediately collapsed next to the body of his deceased wife. After righting the capsized skiff, father and son rowed both boats in growing surf through the Arch and, with considerable risk, managed to beach the skiffs "on a steeply shelving cobblestone sand about 10 feet wide, at the base of a high cliff" out of reach of the waves.

Then, as the storm grew in force, Stewart and his father set to work trying to revive Mrs. Wilkinson. They labored for two hours, without success, as the storm mounted into a gale. The tiny beach gave them crucial shelter, as on the other side of the Arch waves and wind flung foam and bits of seaweed 100 feet into the air.

Stewart tried several times to climb the cliff, but the intense wind pelted him with big bits of shale and threatened to toss him into the sea. Ultimately, there was no choice but to huddle in the heavy rain and wait out the storm.

At 5 a.m., the wind died down enough to enable the group to escape. Mr. Wilkinson, who still was partly delirious, refused to leave the beach unless the Meigs brought along his wife's body. They agreed and, wrapping her in a sail, placed her in the bottom of a boat. Then, after loading everyone into the skiff, father and son double-rowed their way out into the sea.

But the storm surge still was too strong. Unable to make forward progress, the Meigs were reduced to rowing just to keep the skiff's bow into the high waves. After several hours, the current finally drew the boat upon the beach at a nearby harbor.

After getting instructions from Mr. Wilkinson, Stewart took off to hike to the camp from where the doomed party had launched. The distance was four miles in a straight line but Stewart soon found himself hiking nearly twice that distance up and down canyons, along slippery sheep trails, and across crumbling rock fields. Making it harder, he had not eaten anything since the previous morning.

It was dark again when he finally stumbled into camp.

Gathering up a single volunteer, food, flashlights, and blankets, Stewart immediately set out again on the return trip. They hiked all night in moonless darkness – facing imminent death if they slipped on dry grass and gravel atop the cliffs above the surf.

They reached the harbor and the two exhausted men at midnight.

ODDS AGAINST HIM
T SCOUT SAVES MAN

SCOUT EXECUTIVE MILBURN L. FAY
Logan County, Ill., Council

*cout Executive **Milburn Fay** of Logan County, llinois, received the Silver Lifesaving Medal in 920 for saving a man from drowning.*

• At about the same time on the other side of the country, Scout **Harold White**, 14, of Lowell, Massachusetts, was crossing a street. He stopped in the middle of the motorway to let a car pass. Suddenly, White saw a small boy running into the path of an oncoming automobile that was less than 10 feet away. With no time to grab the child, White dove and head-butted the child to the curb.

Somehow, both Scout and child survived; the little boy only suffering a scratch on his hand.

In the aftermath, Harold White went on with his day, telling no one of the remarkable feat of heroism he just had performed. It only was made public after the driver of the car wrote to White's Scoutmaster of his heroism.

Asked why he had not spoken of that day, a surprised White explained, "I was trying to live up to my Scout Oath and Law."

- Eagle Scout **Myers Chaires**, 17, of Spring Hope, North Carolina, was standing on a Florida boardwalk in 1920 when he saw a crowd on the beach gesturing out to sea. Looking there, Myers saw three small heads bobbing in the water beyond the breakers.

Despite being an Eagle, Chaires knew he was not a strong swimmer and understood that this distance would be the farthest he ever had attempted. To make matters worse, there also was a strong current. He hesitated for a moment but then steeling himself, Myers grabbed a life preserver and, still wearing his clothes, ran into the water.

His progress was painfully slow, not only due to his weak stroke and life preserver dragging behind, but also because Myers constantly was being knocked over by big waves. Finally, he made it past the line of breakers but only halfway to the children. Now he was so exhausted that he began to sink.

It only was then that Myers realized that his shoes and clothes were dragging him down. He managed to kick off his shoes and keep going. Suddenly, the current began to carry him out to sea – but it also was taking the children with it. There only were two heads visible.

Finally, Myers reached the first child, a four-year-old girl. She grabbed the life preserver in such desperation that she nearly pulled them both under. Myers now was so completely exhausted that he knew the only chance of surviving with this girl was to abandon the second one for now and head to shore. By the time they reached the beach, Myers couldn't walk and had to be helped up the beach.

Happily, another rescuer, this one an expert swimmer, arrived on the scene. He leaped into the water. With a fast crawl stroke he raced to the second girl, grabbed her, and started back in. But then he began to experience difficulty keeping them both afloat. Seeing this, the partially recovered Myers headed back out into the surf with his life preserver. He took the child from the swimmer and brought her in.

Later, Myers Chaires and the other swimmer went out one more time to search for the third child. But they never found her. It was assumed that a large shark seen nearby had taken her.

The Honor Medal presented to Terderfoot Scout Paul Kettner's mother in 1924.

• This next account is a heart-rending reminder of the dangers in undertaking a rescue – especially by someone inadequately trained. On September 15, 1923, in Lehighton, Pennsylvania, Tenderfoot Scout **Paul Kettner**, 14, was hiking at a local reservoir. Lorella Wagner, 10, was wading along the edge of the steep concrete wall of the reservoir when she slipped and fell into the water.

Hearing her cry, Kettner ran to her aid and dove into the water. Unfortunately, while he could swim, he was not well-trained in lifesaving and allowed the frantic girl to get too close. Lorella grabbed him in a death grip. Kettner tried to pull free but wasn't strong enough and they both sank.

They never resurfaced. When their bodies were found, they both were clinging together "indicating that his last conscious thought had been for the safety of the girl." But especially horrifying was the discovery that on the slimy, moss-covered walls of the dam were Kettner's desperate scratches as he tried to find a hand grip.

• In early 1928, Crystal Lake, Iowa, was hit with a devastating winter storm. The air temperature fell to -20F, while the wind rose to 60 miles per hour. Faced with such a blizzard, the local schools shut down, and the students were loaded into the horse-drawn buses and sent home. But by then the snow drifts had piled so high that most of the bus drivers gave up, turned their rigs around, and headed back to the schools.

That's what happened to the bus carrying Second Class Scout **Burtis Juhl**. It nearly had reached the homesteads of the bus's passengers when the driver, approaching an insurmountable drift, chose to turn back. But as he did, two little girls, seeing they were close to home, jumped out of the back of the bus and started out into the storm. Almost from the moment they hit the ground, the blast of wind hit them and spun them around.

That's when Burtis spotted their faces in the howling snow as they receded from the moving bus. Without a second thought, he jumped out as well, and, head down into the wind, made his way to the girls. When he finally reached them, he tucked a girl under each arm and, bent over, and fought his way forward with them.

All-but blinded by the blowing snow, Burtis stumbled his way forward, time after time crashing and falling into drifts taller than his head. But he plunged on.

The girls' mother heard her crying daughters even before they reached the house – and she went out and found the three freezing children and brought them in. Burtis' face and hands already were frozen. But after warming himself for a moment by the stove, he insisted on heading back out into the night. He had realized that his little sister, who had taken a different bus, now probably was back at school. Not wanting her to be alone, Burtis set out again into the storm to find her.

A rescue party found Burtis, now nearly dead from exposure, dragging his way back down the road to the school. He was taken to a nearby house where he was treated for painful frostbite.

*Twelve-year-old Scout **Adolphe Platney** of Asbury Park, New Jersey, received the Honor Medal in 1925 for saving a boy from drowning, who had broken through the ice on a frozen pond.*

THE
REMINGTON
AWARD
FOR
HEROISM

This next story is one of the largest rescues in Scouting history and a testament not only to BSA's lifesaving education but also to teamwork:

- Three Scouts from Cordova, Alaska – Star Scout **Philip Lydick**, 15, and Tenderfoot Scout brothers **Jerry Cochran**, 13, and **Lew Cochran**, 15 – were diving from a raft into the snowy, water-filled Lake Eyak in the summer of 1930.

Less than a hundred feet away a boat launch filled with children taking a pleasure cruise, suddenly and without warning, sank into the freezing water in a matter of seconds. There was no other help around and only a Girl Scout among the group could swim. She grabbed two of the girls in the water and kept them from sinking. But she quickly became exhausted began to lose her own struggle. She was starting to go under when Lydick swam up and took the two girls from her. He started to swim with them, all the while encouraging the Girl Scout to swim with him. Then Lydick spotted a large oil can from the sunken boat and, using it as a flotation device, he managed to get all three girls to shore.

Meanwhile, Lew Cochran had been diving for several other struggling children. Incredibly, he had managed to bring four of them up from the depths and now was fighting to keep them from sinking again. Younger brother Jerry was diving in search of a small child who also had slipped beneath the surface. He found her and started towards the shore as well.

At this point, two other Boy Scouts on the beach of the lake spotted what was happening and they went into the water as well. Shrewdly, they swam to the raft, released it from its anchor and, still in the water, pushed it towards the children and their rescuers. At the same time, a Native American guide, who also had seen the rescue, launched his own skiff and paddled out at full speed.

Between the three Scouts in the water, the Scouts with the raft, and the guide with the skiff, everyone on the launch was saved – a total of seven people who lived to see another day.

- In 1931, an act of Boy Scout heroism was so extraordinary that it was carried by newspapers around the country. Fourteen-year-old **Kenneth Hall** of Brooklyn, New York, was sailing in a yacht with some friends. Hall was in the ship's galley when its oil stove exploded.

Everyone around Hall dove over the rail into the ocean. But, because there were still others on deck, Kenneth chose instead to stay in the galley and try to cut off the fuel line before there was a second explosion. Moments later, that explosion occurred, burning the young man to death.[23]

Monday, June 9, 1931, the Elks Club Hall in Brooklyn saw one of the most poignant scenes in Scouting history. A State Supreme Court Justice James Cropsey presented the Honor Medal to Kenneth's mother, Mrs. Jessica Hall. 1,500 Scouts and friends (including Kenneth's fellow Scouts from Troop 43 Flatbush) stood in complete silence in their Scouting brother's honor.

Beyond Color

Finally, the following story reveals an act of bravery that possibly encapsulates all of the Honor Medal rescues of Scouting's first fifty years. It also is one that offers a glimpse of an American society in the early 20th century with its complex stereotypes. Ultimately, this rescue points to one of the greatest achievements by any Scout of any time:

• **Cesare Zampese**, 13, holder of the rank of Second Class rank from Omaha, Nebraska, told his own story to *Boys' Life* magazine in November 1926:

Two boys and I were swimming at Carter Lake. We noticed two small boys swimming a little ways from us. Upon hearing a noise I looked and one boy was not in sight at all and the other was struggling and sinking. I hurried to him and grabbed him and dragged him to the surface and shook him and told him to grab my shoulders. I took him to the bank and he told me that his brother had gone down to the bottom and not come back.

I dove in having some trouble to get down to the bottom as the water was deep and after clawing around I finally found this other boy whose body had apparently been sucked into a hole in the bottom, and was rapidly being covered by mud. I brought him to the surface, took him to the bank, and worked over him as long as I could.

I was so exhausted that it had to be finished by another Scout. The patrol wagon came with the police doctor and took the boys away. I was rested by this time and went directly home.

An aquatic rescue with a brave Scout who saved two boys from the nightmare of sinking into the mud and slime at the bottom of a lake – and being revived by the same Scout, who collapses from exhaustion – made a remarkable story. Without a doubt, it was an incredible act of bravery and emergency training – all that Scouting in its second decade had come to expect from its boys.

*BSA President Walter Head and
Second Class Scout Cesare Zampese
in 1926.*

But there is more to this story. It may come as a surprise to readers accustomed to segregated life in the early years of the century that these two young boys whom Cesare risked his life to save were African-American. Furthermore, when investigating the facts surrounding this rescue, the BSA discovered that Cesare Zampese had saved at least eight other individuals from drowning before anyone considered nominating him for the Honor Medal.

"*Bravery is the capacity to perform properly even when scared half to death.*" - Gen. Omar Bradley

CHAPTER

5

Heroes of All Types

*"I rejoice to look upon
you as fine examples of
young American manhood."*
– President Warren G. Harding
at the presentation of six Honor Medals
in Butte, Montana, in 1923.

One of American Scouting's greatest – and least celebrated – achievements has been its century-long struggle, both internally and externally, to include *all* American boys. At the heart of this was the recognition from the BSA's earliest days that Scouting (and its rank advancement program in particular) was, more than talent or intelligence or skills, about *character.* And that meant that any Scout, whatever the disabilities or social obstacles he faced, should be able to fully participate in the program – including assuming leadership roles and earning the Eagle Scout rank.

One historic obstacle in American life has, of course, been race. When the BSA was founded, the Civil War was just forty-five years in the past – the equivalent today of the 1960s, a time still remembered well by many, and which still deeply impacts modern life. In 1910, not only were there millions of Americans still alive who had experienced America's most devastating war, but thousands who had *fought* in it – on both sides. Reconstruction still was a vivid memory. Jim Crow laws still dominated the South, lynchings were common with the Ku Klux Klan on the rise and just fourteen years before in 1896, the U.S. Supreme Court had enshrined the "separate but equal" division of races in law for the next six decades through the *Plessy v. Ferguson* decision. In the United States in 1910, the military was segregated, the public schools were segregated, and the government under President Woodrow Wilson soon would be re-segregated.

But not necessarily in the Boy Scouts of America. Scouting played an early and important role in the movement for civil rights. From the day of its founding, the BSA accepted *all* boys in the United States as having an equal right to both membership and to fully participate in the program – albeit often in mono-racial troops for the first few decades. The Boy Scouts played an early and important role in the movement for civil rights.

In spite of the many cultural obstacles placed before them, the number of black Scouts slowly and continuously grew through Scouting's first fifteen years. By June 1926, the BSA celebrated its first African-American Eagle Scout, Edgar Cunningham of Waterloo, Iowa. Less well-known was that the first black Scout to earn the Honor Medal received it three years earlier.

His name was **Damon Bass**, 15, of Kansas City, Missouri. Here's how the wire service, United Press International, carried the story:

Damon Bass, a Negro, saved Sam Cottage, 8, from drowning in May 1922. Damon pulled the youth out of a creek in which they were swimming, and after applying artificial respiration as taught in the Scouts, for 15 minutes, revived him.[26]

The milestone nature of Bass's award went all-but unnoticed, overshadowed by the guest of honor at his medal ceremony – First Lady Florence Harding. Her husband, President Warren G. Harding, was in the midst of a national speaking tour that would end with his sudden death three months hence in San Francisco. For now though, the President was in good health and humor, and had arranged for the First Lady to present Honor Medals and other Scouting awards at this ceremony.

In Kansas City, Bass shared the stage with another Honor Medalist, **Russell Davis** *(see right)*, whose own rescue story even was more compelling – and tragic. Davis had heard the screams of little Margaret Clark, who had been playing with matches and set her clothes on fire. Davis ran to the girl and put out the flames with his bare hands. The girl died three days later; Davis sustained "terrible burns" on his hands.

The ceremony must have been an unforgettable event: the two Scouts, one black and the other white, standing beside the first lady of the United States, earning one of the premiere honors of boyhood – in a city and state that had been all-but destroyed by a Civil War still in the memories of much of the audience, some of whom no doubt were both former slaves and Confederate soldiers.

Certainly Mrs. Harding was moved by the experience. At a similar event a few days later in Butte, Montana, President Harding would declare:

Scouts, I do not know of anything that has occurred on our western journey which has afforded me greater pleasure. The greatest thing in life is to be of service, and if there is any greater thing than being of service, it is the superlatively great thing of being in service in an hour of need. I know how a great trial appeals to the latent manhood of every one of us. I know how somewhere inherent in the nature of every one of us is the strength to respond to a call in a moment of urgent need, and I rejoice to look upon you as fine examples of young American manhood who have made such a response and who have performed such distinctive service. It is a fine index of the part you will play in the life before you. I am proud of you as president of the Republic; I am proud of you as commander-in-chief of the Boy Scout organization because you are a fine example and a fine inspiration to the young manhood of the Republic.[22]

Finding the names of black Scouts who have earned BSA Honor Medals is a difficult task for a very good reason: precisely because Scouting never identified its Scouts by race (finding Asian and other minority honorees is even more difficult). One usually only can identify those recipients through early media coverage of "negro" Scouting heroes, and later, through visual identification in the "Scouts in Action" comics in *Boys' Life* magazine. That said, here are a few examples:

• In 1932, 39-year-old Scoutmaster **Edgar D. Hegamin** of St. Louis, Missouri, was working as an elevator operator in an office building. A fire broke out from an exploding gasoline can in a "hat cleaning" shop on the first floor. The smoke quickly vented up the elevator shaft – alarming workers throughout the building and, incredibly, sending Hegamin down through the enveloping smoke to the first floor to try to put out the flames armed with only a small fire extinguisher.

Quickly realizing that the fire already had grown too big, Hegamin turned instead to rescuing people still trapped inside the building. In all, he made four trips in the elevator – "in spite of blinding smoke and unbearable heat" – and rescued 24 people from the upper floors. Documented in the *1935 BSA Annual Report*: "If it had not been for Hegamin's unselfish thought for others and his calm courage in the face of personal danger, many of the persons in the burning building would have succumbed in the dense smoke."

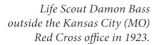

Life Scout Damon Bass outside the Kansas City (MO) Red Cross office in 1923.

• In late December 1934 **Edward Claxton**, 13, of Reno, Nevada, rushed into a nearby burning home to help evacuate the Lomax family. Still missing were two Lomax children, Theda, 4, and Donald, 3. Braving flame and smoke, Claxton searched everywhere – finally finding the two children hiding under a bed. He successfully carried them out of the house without injury.

Claxton's heroic rescue received considerable local media coverage. We reproduce it here as it provides an interesting insight into the mores of that era:

Edward Claxton, 13, Reno colored Boy Scout received the plaudits of a former governor of white men and experienced a thrill rarely accorded white boys.

Edward, with a newsreel camera grinding and klieg lights blazing on his serious ebony face, was given the Boy Scout life-saving medal by former acting Governor Morley Griswold before 145 applauding businessmen at the annual chamber of commerce banquet at the Century club.

There was a catch in Morely Griswold's voice as he grasped Edward's hand and said, 'Young fellow, it's an honor for me to give this to you. You've got as much chance as anybody if you just keep on hitting the ball like you did here.'

Edward, who saved the lives of Theda Lomax, 4, and Donald Lomax, 3, when the Lomax home burned here December 29, saluted the former state leader, the applauding crowd and clicking camera.

Dr. C.E. Piersall, Boy Scout leader, presented Edward's parents, Mr. and Mrs. James Claxton. Claxton works for the sheriff's office now and pitches baseball for Scott Motors during baseball season.

Dorrance Jones, Scoutmaster of Troop 4, to which Edward belongs, and Al Russell assisted in the ceremonies. W.H. Kelly, Universal Newsreel cameraman assisted by Walt Rankin took the pictures, which are expected to be shown in Reno in about two weeks.

It is interesting to note that, by comparison, the BSA had no record of Edward Claxton's race – only that he was a hero. As this is being written, there is only one Theda Lomax living in the United States, an elderly woman who resides in South Carolina – 80 years after Edward Claxton's rescue.

Scout Edward Claxton posing with the two Lomax children he saved outside of their burned out house in Reno, Nevada, in 1934.

• Earlier that year, two Ada, Oklahoma, Scouts, **Leroy Collins**, 16, and **A.D. Gale**, 18, both Tenderfoot Scouts, were standing around and talking with a few of their friends when a girl came running up screaming that a house just up the street was on fire. The two Scouts ran to help and found the house already billowing in smoke. They heard three children crying inside that had been left there by their mother who had gone to work.

Gale ran in first with Collins close behind. In the thick smoke the children almost were impossible to find. Finally, Gale located one of the children in a bedroom. He rushed in to discover the walls already covered in flames and, barely discernible, a child (T.J. Johnson, 1) in a crib in the far corner. The child – just inches from the approaching flames – already was burned in his face and arms. Gale scooped up the child and headed for the door.

At the same time, Collins found a second child (I.V. Johnson, 4) standing near the door of the house's inner-most room. Talking calmly, he took the child's hand and led him out. As they passed the bedroom where Gale was making his own rescue, the boy, seeing the flames but not the figures inside, pulled the door shut. By the time Gale realized what had happened, Collins and the boy already were outside. Try as he might, he couldn't pull the stuck door open.

Outside, Leroy, realizing that his fellow Scout still was inside, left the boy with onlookers and charged back into the house. Braving the flames, he followed Gale's shouts and managed to kick open the door. Collins then helped Gale and the infant out.

There still was one more child screaming inside. Gale and Collins attempted one last rescue, but, according to the BSA report: "by this time the flames were so terrific that it was impossible to enter the house." The two Scouts only could watch in helpless horror as the house burned to the ground.

• Among the scores of newspaper photographs of BSA Honor Medal recipients, one of the most compelling is a wire service image, carried by papers across the country in June 1947 of a young black boy and an old white man holding each others' hands. The boy in a Scout uniform is standing at attention and staring into the distance. The man in a suit wears the BSA's Silver Buffalo medal around his neck, staring with admiration at the boy.

The photo was taken at a BSA national honor ceremony held in New York City. Among the honorees that night, for the Silver Buffalo award, presented for the highest level of "service to American boyhood," were such giants of the era as Joseph Spellman, Cardinal of New York, and financier and presidential advisor Bernard Baruch. The man in the photograph, who just had received the medal and neck ribbon, was Dr. George J. Fisher, National Scout Commissioner.

And the Scout? He was 16-year-old First Class Scout **William Jackson Jr.** He had been invited to the Manhattan ceremony from his home in Columbia, Missouri, to represent all 47 Scouts who had been recognized for saving a life the previous year – 20 of them (including Jackson) had earned the Honor Medal. Jackson was one of four Scouts who had saved five children from a burning home in October 1946. Jackson had been singled out for the extreme risk he took in the rescue.

• April 1958: A group of junior high school students from New Orleans was on a tour of Southern University near Baton Rouge. After lunch in the University cafeteria, a group of the students decided to take a walk down to the nearby river. As they did, 9-year-old Wanda Garibaldi screamed in pain. While walking through some dead leaves she had been bitten by a snake. Frightened and confused, she called for help. Hearing her cries, 17-year-old Explorer Scout **James E. Brooks** ran to her assistance. After assuring her that the snake was gone, he tied a restricting band on Wanda's leg above the bite marks; then sucked out as much venom as he could [the standard first aid technique of the time; now no longer used]. Wanda was taken to the school infirmary, then to the hospital. Thanks to Brooks' prompt and knowledgeable response, she recovered completely.

High Scout Honor— Sixteen - year - old William Jackson Jr., a First Class Scout of Columbia, Mo., receives congratulations from Dr. George J. Fisher, national Scout Commissioner, after receiving the Boy Scout Gold Honor Medal for his part in the heroic rescue of five small children from a burning home in Columbia last October. Young Jackson was one of forty-seven Boy Scouts receiving the high honor.—Wide World Photo.

• Explorer Scout **Nelson Crosby**, 15, of Twin Oaks, Pennsylvania, was dressing for school when a neighbor rushed into his house crying that her house was on fire and her three children still were trapped inside. Crosby ran to the house – only to find that the flames already were so intense that he couldn't enter through either the front or back doors. So he ran to the side of the house, smashed a window and climbed in. The smoke was so thick that he immediately dropped to the floor and crawled. Unable to see anything, Crosby groped his way through two rooms. The second proved to be the nursery. Feeling his way to the crib, he found a three-month-old infant and carried it out the way he came in.

Handing the child to its stricken mother, Crosby headed back into the house in search of the other two children. But nothing more could be done: the house now was completely enveloped in flames. Reluctantly, Nelson Crosby exited the house before he became its third victim.

• On a hot Sunday in June 1986 in Amarillo, Texas, the residents of an apartment complex crowded into its swimming pool to enjoy the day. But the fun stopped the instant a little girl began screaming that her brother was drowning.

Wolf Cub Scout **Brian Anthony**, 10, immediately yelled for someone to call an ambulance and leapt into the pool. He swam to the boy, Torey Mason, 7, pulled him from the bottom and over to the poolside. A bystander pulled both boys out of the water. Then, determining that Mason was both unconscious and had no pulse, Anthony began giving him artificial respiration. Meanwhile, an adult administered chest compression. Within five minutes, the boy revived and later made a full recovery at the hospital.

For such a heroic act that combined bravery, skill, and a cool head (especially by an elementary school student), Cub Scout Brian Anthony was awarded the Honor Medal.

• In October 1983, Scout **Noah Best Jr.**, 12, was babysitting his younger siblings as well as a friend's 5-month-old daughter. Checking on the napping baby, Noah realized that she wasn't breathing and her lips were turning blue.

After telephoning for help, Noah put his Scout first aid training to work by giving the baby mouth-to-mouth resuscitation through both his nose and mouth, while breathing gently. When that failed to revive the baby, he switched to performing an equally gentle cardiac massage.

The baby finally began to breathe on her own just moments before the paramedics arrived.[23]

A 3D image of Hurricane Danny upon making landfall in Alabama in July 1997.

• First Class Scout **Kenneth Young**, 15, and Star Scout **Tyron Allen**, 14, were installing a Boy Scout exhibit in an office building in Washington, DC, in February 1987 when they heard a man's voice crying for help.

Following the sound down a hallway, they found themselves in the building's snack bar. There, they discovered that the blind man who ran the place had caught his hand between the wall and a vending machine. To make matters worse, the machine still was operating and mashing his hand. Together, the two Scouts freed the man and applied pressure to stop the heavy bleeding. Then they tended to the man's wounds and called the paramedics.[24]

• Chatham, Virginia, June 1990. Henri Fitzgerald, 11, was dancing on the front porch of the family home, as older brother, Tenderfoot Scout **Jermaine Fitzgerald**, 13, watched from the other side of the glass front door.

Then, as Henri practiced a spin, his left arm crashed through the door, slicing open his wrist and spraying glass shards in Jermaine's eyes. Though the vision in his injured eyes was blurred, Jermaine still could see that his brother's wound was life-threatening. He grabbed some paper towels and applied direct pressure to the jagged tear in Henri's left wrist. Then, finding a clean towel, he wrapped it around his brother's wrist to hold the pad in place – continuing to apply pressure. When he considered the situation sufficiently stable, Jermaine grabbed the phone and called his aunt, who called the local paramedics.

When emergency personnel arrived, they bandaged Henri's arm and rushed him to the hospital, where he required more than five hours of surgery to repair his damaged nerves, tendons, and blood vessels. At the same time, they flushed out Jermaine's eyes with a saline solution. Fortunately, he suffered no permanent damage.[25]

• The roaring eye wall of Hurricane Danny was just twenty miles away and approaching fast towards Daphne, Alabama, on July 19, 1997. Sixteen-year-old Star Scout **Andre Mitchell** was among a group of adults and children who had gathered to hunker down before the storm arrived.

Suddenly, four-week-old Nicholas Bolton stopped breathing. And though there were two adults present trained in first aid, both panicked and only Andre had the presence of mind to step in and treat the baby. Remembering his First Aid merit badge training, Andre twice revived the baby using CPR.

With the hurricane bearing down, they now were almost out of time and had to get the baby to the hospital. The adults decided to go but there only was room for four in the car with the baby. That meant that Andre had to stay behind. It was then that he made his most important decision of that unforgettable day. He insisted that he be allowed to teach the adults how to perform CPR.

In the end, that lesson proved decisive. On the way to the hospital, the baby stopped breathing and it only was through their newly learned skills that the adults were able to revive him.

Little Nicholas survived to celebrate his one month birthday the next day – and, with good fortune, will live a long and healthy life.

¡Vale la Pena!

Identifying Hispanic Honor Scouts presents an even greater challenge. That's because, especially in the Southwest, they rarely were described as being Hispanic in newspaper stories – and, again, never in BSA reports. However, it generally is agreed (and thanks to a photo with the newspaper story, *see right*) that the first Boy Scout of Hispanic heritage to earn the Honor Medal was Manuel Camarillo, 16, a Life Scout in Troop 11, El Paso, Texas. We also know that he was an assistant patrol leader in the Wildcat Patrol that was led by Scout Salvador Guillen. In August 1922, Camarillo rescued Simon Arozco, age 5, after the boy had fallen into the Franklin canal and gone under "for the fourth time." A full-length photo of Camarillo, in his Scout uniform tunic with a sleeve full of merit badges, a white shirt and bow tie, and the Honor Medal on his chest, appeared that December in the *El Paso Herald*.[31]

• Less than a year after Camarillo's rescue, three more El Paso Scouts, all likely of Hispanic heritage, were honored for another pair of rescues at that same Franklin Canal. In the first case, Refugia Flores, 13, and a fellow student at the adjoining Bowie school, were crossing the canal via a wooden bridge. She stumbled and grabbed the bridge's railing – which collapsed and dropped her in the water. Her classmate, Scout **Carlos Fiquierros**, 13, saw her fall and immediately leapt into the water but he soon became exhausted trying to both grab and ward off the frantic girl. Furthermore, due to the weight of his school uniform and shoes, he also was on the brink of drowning.

At that moment, two other Scouts (and fellow classmates) dove into the canal: **Frank Acosta**, 14, and **Mered Velez**, also 14. By now, the four figures had been swept 75 yards downstream. Acosta and Velez managed to grab Refugia and Carlos and swim them to the bank where they were rescued by witnesses. At that point, Refugia was unconscious but was revived by a city health officer who had rushed to the scene with the right equipment.

The same *El Paso Herald* story also related yet another Franklin Canal drowning case (also involving a Scout) with this one coming a few weeks before Camarillo's. The rescuer this time was Cleafas Calleros, who had saved a small boy from the dangerous waters. Once the rescue was completed the saved boy took off running. The story relates that Cleafas searched for the boy for nearly a year in the hope he could obtain an Honor Medal nomination. There is no indication he ever found the child.

Meanwhile, the article reported, workmen already were busy building a sturdier new railing for the bridge and installing fencing along the canal's banks.[26]

El Paso Boy Scout Given a Medal For Saving Lad's Life

ANUEL CAMARILLO, a member of troop No. 11, Boy Scouts of Amer-

• Ninety years later, another remarkable rescue story occurred in El Paso. In January 2010, 17-year-old Eagle Scout **Fernando Espinosa** was walking his Franklin High School teacher and publications advisor, Glenda Tanner, to her car. As they stepped out on the crosswalk in front of the school, an automobile appeared out of nowhere. Spotting the car, Espinosa shoved Tanner out of the way and in doing so took the full brunt of the car's impact. He rolled up the hood of the car, injuring his left knee, then crashed his skull into the windshield before rolling off and landing on the curb.

Somehow, after regaining consciousness, Espinosa dragged himself over to help Tanner. "It was complete instinct because it was so quick," Espinosa recalled later, "I think all of the experiences I've had helped me. I remember, after being hit, checking on Mrs. Tanner and telling myself to just breathe and stay calm."

Tanner's foot was broken in three places. As she told the *El Paso Times*, the injury meant that she wouldn't be able to dance at her daughter's impending wedding and that she would set off airport metal detectors for the rest of her life, but at least she was alive.

Espinosa, a varsity swimmer, was unable to participate in an important meet after the accident and seven months later still was being treated for blood clots in his left leg. However, he had no regrets. "I am glad to have been there that night," Espinosa told the paper, "And I am grateful to all the people who helped me during and after the accident – the doctors, nurses, and firemen."

Embarrassed at being called a "hero" and at all of the attention he was receiving, Espinosa said he merely hoped that his act would be an example for all younger Scouts: "The main thing I want them to know is to always be a gentleman and try to help people ... and to really love what you have at the moment because you never know what is going to happen."[27]

Fernando Espinosa at his Honor Medal presentation ceremony in 2010.

Above and Beyond

There are other challenges faced by Scouts that directly affect their ability to enjoy the full Scouting experience. It can be said that the greatest achievement in the Boy Scouts of America is not the boy who stays with the program and earns his Eagle Scout medal. It's that *any* boy can pursue that goal. Once again, if Scouting ultimately is about character, no cultural, physical or mental impairment ever can be allowed to stand in a boy's path.

As shown by the records of the earliest meetings of the National Court of Honor, Scouting's founders have been concerned from its beginnings about the ability of all boys to participate in what is, to a large part, an outdoor, learning-based program. As early as 1913, the National Court of Honor discussed how to enable "handicapped" boys to become Scouts and achieve rank advancement goals in Scouting. That discussion – which only has widened over the decades to include the entire spectrum of human challenges from physical disabilities to diminished intelligence to mental illness; to geographic isolation to non-traditional education to racial and religious prejudice, poverty, and (most recently), sexual orientation – still continues after more than a century.

Scouting has responded (sometimes promptly and other times tardily) to these challenges with an equally wide range of solutions. Within the BSA's first decade, it already had developed a second set of rank requirements – equally difficult, but also recognizing that some Scouts simply could not participate in the program's more strenuous outdoor experiences – for physically disabled Scouts. Scout summer camps also developed programs and facilities for these Scouts – perhaps more slowly than it should have, but certainly faster than the rest of American society.

For Scouts living on the frontier or later in isolated rural communities, it supported and then absorbed the Lone Scout program. Today, Scouting has been adopted by many home schooling families.

The BSA also attacked religious prejudice early: it not only barred it from Scouting altogether but with its religious medals, it honored many different faiths. Between 1939 and 1945, Scouting introduced religious medals, not just for the Catholic Church and the Protestant denominations, but also for Jewish and Buddhist Scouts. Today, Scouting offers nearly two hundred religious awards for Cubs, Scouts, and Adults of every faith, alphabetically, from the African Methodist Episcopal Church through Zoroastrianism.

From the beginning, Scouting also has provided uniforms, equipment, camp scholarships, and, through the National Eagle Scout Association, college scholarships to Scouts in need. And, drawing con-siderable public attention in the 21st century, the BSA's managers voted to accept homosexual boys of Boy Scout age as well.

But, in terms of living up to both its charter and its commitment to keep character-building as its first priority, Scouting's finest achievement has been not only to accept Scouts of diminished mental capacity, but also to hold them to the program's standard rank requirements, while allowing them unlimited time to earn those ranks. Those boys who earn Scouting's highest rank (sometimes well into their thirties) are some of Scouting's most honored Eagles.

As with the rest of Scouting, these "challenged" Scouts have shown the courage to save the lives of others. In some cases, are those very disabilities that have taken those rescues to a higher level than many others.

• Although other Scouts may have faced greater dangers, in terms of the sheer magnitude of his achievements and against such great odds, Eagle Scout **Howard B. Rote** of Vineland, New Jersey, may be the greatest of all BSA Honor Scouts – and one of its finest young Eagles.

Certainly Chief Scout Executive James E. West thought so. He wrote in *Boys' Life* in February 1922: "I hardly know of a more striking example of Scout courage and scorn of obstacles."[28]

The year before, Rote looked down from the upper deck of a berthed yacht and saw a child below him the water having fallen off the public pier. The child not only was struggling to keep from drowning, but also was at great risk of being crushed to death between the boat and the pilings. Without hesitation, Rote jumped over the side, falling the twenty feet and just managing to hit the water in the gap of the boards on the dock's surface. He then swam to the child, grabbed her and towed her to safety.

This little girl was, in fact, the *third* person to date that Rote had rescued from drowning. On a previous case, Rote revived the unconscious and non-breathing victim through artificial respiration.

This would be impressive enough – but Rote also accomplished these rescues

… despite having just one arm.

As West asked: "Think it over, you boys, with your eyes that see, ears that hear, your sound bodies. Any reason why you shouldn't do at least as well?"[29]

• While on a camping trip at Charming Forge, Pennsylvania, in the summer of 1922, the Scouts of Troop 11 heard screams of distress from a nearby millrace. They ran to the rescue. The first Scout to arrive at the scene – remarkable because he had an artificial leg – was senior patrol leader **Dawson Wolfe**. Just as remarkable was that Wolfe was an excellent swimmer – apparently the best in the troop. He quickly dove into the moving water.

Seeing the figure of a sinking man's head, Wolfe swam over and caught him just as he went under. According to the *New York Times*, Wolfe then held the man's head above the surface long enough for some of the Scouts to reach them. Pulling the man to shore, the Scouts worked on him for more than an hour until he finally revived.[30]

• On an April morning in 1974, Star Scout **Tony McWilliams**, 25, of Louisville, Kentucky, was watching a pick-up baseball game in the trailer park where he lived. Suddenly, one of the players noticed that the shed behind one of the house trailers was burning and that the flames were leaping toward the trailer itself.

One of the boys ran home to call the fire department. Another ran to the park office and fetched the manager, who broke through the trailer's glass door and called to see if anyone was inside.

McWilliams, who had been watching the frantic scene, noticed that there were two 55-gallon drums filled with fuel oil near the burning trailer. Realizing that if they exploded the spattered and burning fuel might ignite four other nearby trailers, he rushed to them, kicked them over, and rolled the drums across the street and out of harm's way.

Then, not convinced that the trailer yet was empty, McWilliams went inside, crawling under the thick smoke. There he found a small dog cowering in a corner of the living room. He carried her to safety.

What made McWilliams' act of bravery especially impressive was that the young man suffered from cerebral palsy. Moreover, when over-excited, he was subject to seizures. And yet he didn't ponder those risks for a moment as he made his way toward the flames.

- In July 2013, while on a kayaking and canoeing trip on the Current River in Missouri, the Scouts of Troop 320 of Springfield decided to take a short snack break on the river's bank. After a brief respite, the older boys in the troop decided to cross the river under the guidance of an assistant Scoutmaster and swim in a nearby alcove of still water. The younger, less experienced Scouts stayed on the near bank with the rest of the adults.

One young, inexperienced Scout who, had been trying out his underwater goggles near the adults, on the spur of the moment decided he wanted to cross the river and join the older Scouts. Without telling anyone (and also not wearing a life-jacket) he took off. As he crossed the middle of the stream, the faster water in the main channel swept him off his feet and began to carry him downriver.

Spotting the boy, Scoutmaster Don Fotheringhame, shouted for one of the older Scouts on the other side of the river to take off in pursuit. He did, but couldn't catch the boy, who was heading directly for a pile of fallen trees. Two people already had drowned in the swollen river that year, with one of them being snagged by a tree branch and pulled underwater.

That's when Fotheringhame saw Life Scout **Bryce Mulhall** standing in the river further downstream. At his Scoutmaster's shout, Mulhall made his way out into the young Scout's path and caught him by the hand as he passed.

After asking the boy if he was okay, Mulhall went into lifesaving mode and performed a "perfect case-book rescue" in the words of one witness. By now, the Scoutmaster had thrown a lifejacket into the current; Mulhall caught it and put it

on the boy, then pulled him across and out of the river.

"I acted quickly and my mind was straight on him," Bryce later would say. "I decided I had to spring into action, and that's what I did."

One person who didn't witness Bryce's rescue was his father, Mike Mulhall. At the advice of Fotheringhame, who said that Bryce was "doing fine," this was the first camping trip on which father had not accompanied his son. An Eagle Scout, Mr. Mulhall always had gone on campouts with his son in part to share the Scouting experience, but also because Bryce is autistic.

During the months waiting for his Honor Medal application to be investigated and approved, Bryce Mulhall also completed the re quirements for Eagle Scout.

*In the 12-month span from September 1921 to September 1922, First Class Scout **Louis Matthews** of Dallas, Texas, saved three children from downing.*

Mind over Body

Not all disabilities are permanent. Illness and injury also can temporarily place an individual in the predicament where being called upon to save another's life can require an almost superhuman effort. In these cases, a rescue may look similar on paper to many others but may in fact have demanded far greater reservoirs of courage and strength.

• In December 1926, **Ralph C. Raughley Jr.** earned an Honor Medal (and a Carnegie Award) for saving a boy from drowning in a pond. What made this rescue particularly remarkable was not just that the boy was older and heavier than Raughley (who had to carry the boy all of the way to shore and then apply artificial respiration to revive him) but that Raughley accomplished this heroic act while convalescing from a bout of *malaria*. Reportedly, Raughley was so exhausted by the rescue that he needed medical attention himself.

• Life Scout **Robert E. Howe** of Waterloo, Iowa, was 16-years-old in 1926. He was recuperating from a hand injury with it wrapped in a bandage soaked in an alcohol solution when he heard the screams of a little girl in the street outside. Rushing there, he saw the girl screeching and running around in confusion, her clothes and hair in flames. Running, Howe tackled the girl on some grass. He held her down with his bad hand and beat out the flames with the other. Emergency personnel noted that had the fire reached Howe's bandaged hand, it likely would have ignited as well and Robert Howe would have lost his arm.[31]

185

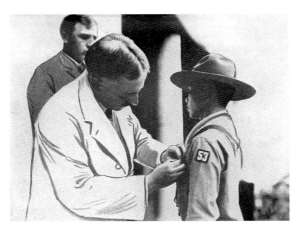

*Scout **Theodorico Casipit** is presented with the Honor Medal by Governor of the Philippines Henry L. Stimson in Manila in 1928. He is the first Philippine Scout to receive the recognition.*

After all of his efforts over the previous decades to prepare Scouts to save lives, Dan Beard must have been gratified by the rest of the newspaper story about Raughley's award:

Each year the record of lives saved by Boy Scouts grows longer because Scouts are trained in life-saving. Most of the rescues are made with small risk to the rescuer because of this training. There are many instances of life-saving by Scouts where the facts are never revealed by the brave but modest Scouts.

It is a tribute to Scout Training that more than 21,000 boys were taught to swim at Boy Scout camps last summer. A score of Honor Medals for life-saving awarded last year tell the story of some of the Scouts who risked their lives to save others.

This is in keeping with the tenth Scout Law, 'A Scout is Brave.'[32]

Heroes has no Boundaries

Sometimes forgotten is the fact that the Boy Scouts of America is not confined, strictly speaking, to the borders of the United States. From the beginning, Scout troops also have operated in U.S. Territories (including Alaska and Hawaii before they became states) and Protectorates, and at U.S. military bases around the world. Not surprisingly, over the decades Scouts and Scouters at these remote locations have found themselves in the same lifesaving situations just like their brothers back in the States:

• On New Year's Day 1936, the *S.S. Bolinao* was anchored at the municipal wharf of Butuan in the Philippines. Being a holiday, the wharf was crowded with locals to meet folks disembarking from the ship. The instant the gangplank was let down, a crowd rushed to get on the boat. In the rush, 9-year-old Teopista Sevilla was shoved aside, stumbled, and fell into the rushing water of the Agusan River below. There were screams and shouts for help but no one made an effort to help – one reason being that the river was at flood stage; another that it was known to be infested with crocodiles. Someone called for the rescue crew to man a lifeboat but before anyone could react, 16-year-old **Julito Semine**, a Tenderfoot Scout, dove into the 30-foot-deep water. Little Teopista did not know how to swim and already had sunk to the bottom. Julito clawed his way down into the dark, silted water and caught hold of the boy's hair. Julito surfaced with a limp Teopisto on his arm and now had fight to keep the strong current from dragging them both away. Luckily, someone on the wharf had located a rope and threw it toward them. Julito caught it and the two were pulled to safety.

• In 1915, Tenderfoot Scout **George Summers Brownell**, 13, was at Gatun Lake on the Panama Canal when he spotted a 3-year-old child falling down the face of the lake's dam. Brownell leapt into the water fully dressed, and though the water was twenty feet deep, he dove down and saved the child.

• Honolulu 1912, at the dawn of American Scouting: A young "Porto Rican lady" living in Alewa Heights was chopping kindling for the stove when she missed her swing with the axe and nearly split her foot in two; in the process, she severed an artery. Her family attempted to stop the massive bleeding but failed. In desperation, they sent for a local boy whom they knew was a Boy Scout: Second Class Scout **Victor Boyd**.

Boyd arrived to find the young woman in severe straits and in imminent risk of bleeding to death. Making brilliant use of the objects he found nearby, Boyd managed to construct a tourniquet out of a scarf a pebble (to create a pressure point), a stick, and some first aid cotton He managed to stop the bleeding. For years thereafter, young Boyd was known by his nickname, "Tourniquet Vic." As for the young woman three weeks later, having fully recovered, she presented herself at the Boyd house and offered to work for the family for the rest of her life – for free. The Boyd's thanked her for the offer but told her that Boy Scouts never took payment for their service.[33]

• In March 1924, six Scouts hiked out of the town of Rio Piedras, Puerto Rico, to buy flowers for a funeral. On their return, they were invited to ride onboard a passing truck carrying a load of crushed stone.

As the truck was crossing a bridge a half-mile outside of town, it was hit head-on by a fast-moving car. The car was destroyed by the crash. The truck was deflected into the side of the bridge, demolishing the concrete railing. This left the truck's cab and front wheels hanging over the stream fifteen feet below. The rock load began to pour rapidly out of the truck's rear bed.

The force of the impact had flung open the truck's passenger door and catapulted Scout R. William Ramierez over the railing. He now lay unconscious in the water Scout **William Chabert** instantly leapt from the truck, ran down the embankment at one end of the bridge and to his friend's aid.

To do so, Chabert not only had to run under the dangling and increasingly unsteady truck, but also under a dangerous shower of falling rocks. Despite this, he managed to wade into the stream, gather up Ramierez, and carry him to safety

• In June 1981, Webelos Scout **Brian O'Sullivan**, just 10-years-old and the member of Cub Pack 114 based in New Ulm, West Germany, was rafting down the Danube River with a large group that included his father, Capt. John P. O'Sullivan. As the party floated through an area of fast water, one man fell from his raft into the water. As Capt. O'Sullivan jumped into the river to rescue the man, he accidentally also knocked his son into the water. The other riders on the inflatable raft desperately tried to pull Brian out of the water, but as they did, the life jacket the boy was wearing tore loose and the fast current pulled Brian underwater.

When Brian resurfaced downstream, the life rafts now were in the distance. Flailing in the water and on the brink of slipping under again, he was relieved to see another life jacket floating nearby. He lunged for it and to his astonishment discovered that it already was being worn – by his father, who was floating face down and unconscious. Clinging to the life jacket as well, Brian held his father's head above the surface and pulled him towards the bank. There he was met by his fellow crew members, who had spotted the pair, and were wading in the river to help. They pulled father and son to shore, while others ran to get help. Brian's father survived.[34]

• August 1973 at the Rotary Scout Camp in Leala Village, American Samoa: Fourteen-year-old Faitala Iose was playing with some friends on the nearby reef, when Faitala accidentally was bumped off the slippery reef's edge into deep water. He quickly was hit by a succession of large waves that crashed him back into the reef, injuring his arm, and nearly knocking him unconscious.

Swimming nearby in a reef pool, 14-year-old Scout **Vili Asaivau** heard shouts, jumped out and ran to help. Faitala, who was a non-swimmer, was losing his fight against the waves to stay on the surface. Vili dove into the ocean and holding the other boy's head up, used the waves themselves to drive them ever-closer to the reef. As the two approached, the other Scouts who had been in the pool grabbed them and dragged them up onto the reef's top. At this point, Vili, who was exhausted by the rescue, had to be held on his feet. Meanwhile, Faitala, still breathing, was raced to a hospital in nearby Pago Pago.

• Four classmates at London Central High School in High Wycombe, England, that included three Scouts from a troop at the local U.S. Air Force base, were invited to the home of a friend, Dodd Haldeman, 16, to witness the detonation of an explosive he'd created from directions found in a newsstand magazine he'd just purchased. When they arrived, Haldeman invited them to follow him into the nearby woods. Carrying the bottle filled with the volatile explosive in his hands, he took the lead. The rest followed him in a single file line down the trail.

Suddenly, there was a tremendous explosion. Because he was in front, Haldeman took most of the blast. He was knocked to the ground and lay screaming, holding his left hand that had been blown to ribbons, and bleeding from glass wounds to his face and left thigh.

While two of the Scouts ran for help, the third Scout assisted the injured boy. Eagle Scout **Cletus Thiebeau** stripped the lace out of one of his shoes and made a makeshift tourniquet to stop the heaving bleeding from what remained of Haldeman's hand. Together, the two Scouts helped get their friend to the base's infirmary.

The Scout World

By James West

The Honor Medal, highest and rarest award of the Boy Scouts of America

Jesse W. Dees

Henry Abbott

(Left) David Bunch
(Above) James E. Rowland
(Right) Elwood Langdon

George Barnes

Frank Cada

Seven recipients of the 38 Honor Medals presented in the year 1927 from the pages of Boys' Life *magazine.*

• In October 1997, Life Scout **Talal Cocker**, 14, and another student from the International School in Nairobi, Kenya, were riding with Talal's mother and younger brother Zarek on their way to a troop meeting. Suddenly, they encountered a violent, nearly head-on, crash between a car and a truck. Running to help, Talal was astonished to discover that the victims in the crashed car were his assistant Scoutmaster Paul Beckingham, his wife, son, and his son's friend. While Zarek stayed in the car, Talal and his mother rendered first aid.

Mrs. Beckingham, who managed to crawl out of the car's passenger window, was suffering from a broken collarbone. Talal quickly made a sling out of his neckerchief and led her to his mother's car. Mrs. Cocker then raced Mrs. Beckingham to the hospital. Meanwhile, other passers-by stopped, gathered up the two boys from the wrecked car, and drove them to the hospital as well.

Talal stayed behind to continue first aid on his assistant Scout-master. Mr. Beckingham not only was unconscious but also suffered from several wounds to his face and head. The impact had driven his car's motor into the passenger compartment pinning him beneath.

While other bystanders helped pull the man out of the car, Talal tended to Mr. Beckingham's wounds, treated him for shock, and kept his neck stabilized. Then, when the emergency crew arrived, Talal ran out and directed traffic until the ambulance left the scene.

• Louisiana Eagle Scout **Thomas Veade**, 16, was sleeping in a van taking part of a Venture Crew to their hiking and camping trip near Banff, Alberta, Canada. Suddenly, he was awakened by the sound of the vehicle coming to a skidding stop. A second van, carrying the rest of the Venture crew, had blown a tire and flipped over three times.

Running to the crashed vehicle, Thomas found his younger sister, Christine, and a second girl in the wreckage. He pulled them clear and determined that neither was hurt seriously.

Next, he climbed into the van and found Kathleen Moore, 14, with a large section of her scalp torn back from her skull and the wound bleeding heavily. Her hand was bleeding as well. Using both hands, Veade applied direct pressure to the wounds. As he did so, he noticed that Moore was slipping into shock, so he also covered her with his own body to keep her warm.

Since it took 30 minutes for the paramedics to arrive, Thomas stayed with Moore the entire time. Once at the hospital, her injuries were treated and she was moved to a trauma center where she remained for seven days.

Heroines

Women always have been a part of Scouting in one way or another. For the first twenty years that participation mostly was on the periphery, such as serving as nurses at Scout camps. But unofficially, women (in the role of mothers) have been central to the Scouting experience from its founding. Anyone who ever has been a Scout owes a debt of gratitude to the moms who buy the uniforms and the food for campouts, who wash the filthy clothes after camp or a 50-mile hike (and get poison oak or ivy in the process), sew the badges on uniforms, and most of all, wait at home, quietly worrying, and then welcoming their sons back to civilization. To date, these women number in excess of 115 million.

With the creation of Cubbing (Cub Scouts) in 1930, women found a new, integral, role in Scouting. Given the youth of the Cubs—now ranging in age from six- to ten-years-old (first through fifth grade)—as well as the fact that the program was designed to take place largely in homes, BSA's managers determined that the best leadership for packs and dens should be mothers.

These "den mothers" officially were volunteer Scouters, fully the equal of Scoutmasters and Sea Scout Crew Chiefs. By the Baby Boom era of the 1950s that swelled the ranks of Cub Scouts into the millions, there were tens of thousands of den mothers leading them.

But it wasn't until 1969 that the BSA allowed young women to participate more fully in the Boy Scout program. After six decades, the impetus was the Exploring program's shift in its focus away from strictly outdoor and sports themed posts to career experience posts affiliated with police departments, ambulance companies, hospitals, and other professional occupations. The BSA had long kept its distance from American girls – not least to

Den mothers assist their Cubs at the Circle Ten Council's Scout Exposition in Dallas, Texas, in 1939.

keep from imposing on the Girl Scouts – which had, after all, been founded as the Girl Guides in England by Baden-Powell's wife, Olave, and his sister, Agnes.

However, with the new Exploring program (and the soon-to-be-created, non-traditional Scouting Learning for Life program in local school systems) there was no overlap, and thus no reason to keep membership from young women. Today, there are over 133,000 female Scouts in the Exploring and Venturing programs making up about 45 percent of their membership. And being part of Boy Scouting, they also are eligible to earn many of its ranks and awards – not the least of which is the Honor Medal.

• In May 1975, Robert Bartell and his sister Carol were standing by their car, parked near Patton's Bridge facing St. George Island, Florida, admiring the view. At that moment, a fisherman came running up the bridge yelling that his friend was drowning. Grabbing a rope from their car, Robert and Carol ran to the embankment and threw one end to the figure in the water. But James Horne didn't respond: he already was unconscious and floating face-up in the water.

Seconds later, Horne sank beneath the waves.

As they desperately tried to come up with a new strategy, Robert's 17-year-old daughter, **Rosa Linda Bartell**, an ROTC Explorer at Florida State University, dove into the deep and choppy water and swam to where Horne was last seen. She found the figure several feet underneath the surface, took him in a cross-chest carry, and pulled him to the surface. Without waiting to reach land, Linda turned Horne over in the water and punched him hard between the shoulder blades. The shock not only brought Horne back to consciousness but set him coughing that helped clear the water from his lungs.

Linda then pulled Horne to a safe spot on the embankment, where her father and another bystander lifted them both to safety. Other than some cuts from shells on the embankment, both the rescuer and the rescued were unharmed.[35]

- Explorer **Vernona Marie Faith**, 18, was fishing off Balboa Pier in Newport Beach, California, when she heard a loud splash followed by screams. Vernona ran toward the gathering crowd. Once there, she saw that Pete Milsonovich, 30, apparently had fallen off the pier and hit his head on a piling below. He now was floating face down in the water.

Realizing there was no time to waste, Vernona jumped fully clothed over the railing and down the 20 feet to the crashing waves below. There she grabbed Milsonovich, checked his pulse, turned him over, and opened his airway to help him breathe.

Vernona was so busy tending to the victim that she scarcely noticed that the waves were moving the two of them ever-nearer to the pilings. That's when a bystander jumped into the water. He braced himself against the nearest piling and, while Vernona kept Milsonovich afloat, kept them from slamming into the pier. Together, they kept the victim alive until a rescue boat arrived.[36]

- In March 2012, while driving to a council leadership conference in a caravan of cars, **Brandi Tena**, 18, of El Paso, Texas, was witness to an accident. A car drove off the road and down into a ravine, rolling over several times before it finally came to rest. Tena ran down the hillside to the car, to find its doors crushed and unopenable. The female driver was trapped inside. Through the broken window Brandi talked to the woman to keep her from slipping into shock, telling her everything would be fine. As she did, Brandi, who was preparing to head off to college to study kinesiology, used her training to conduct a medial assessment. She gave her evaluation to the rescue team when they arrived.

During the awarding of her medal, Texas Governor Rick Perry noted, "Brandi Tena (see right) is a good example that this (honor) is not just for boys – it's also for young ladies that are involved in the Venture programs and that are part of making the state better."[37]

Making the Varsity Team

Varsity Scouting was created in 1984 in Salt Lake City, Utah, as an alternative program (like Venturing and Exploring) for older Scouts. It largely was founded by the Mormon church and still has strong roots among members of that faith. As envisioned, the goal of Varsity Scouting was to keep older teen boys attracted to Scouting through sports activities. It retains much of traditional Scouting, including the Scout Oath and Law. Venture Scouts also can continue to pursue the traditional Scout ranks up through Eagle; though members wear a slightly different uniform and are organized into "teams" rather than troops.

Varsity Scouting never has been a large program (in 2015, there only were about 63,000 Varsity Scouts and 23,000 adult volunteers organized into 8,300 teams). Yet, despite their comparatively small numbers, Varsity members are outsized in their representation among Honor Medal recipients:

• Awakened by a noise at 4:30 a.m. in his Sandy, Utah, home, Ted Phillips, 44, climbed out of bed and headed downstairs. Phillips assumed it was one of his children but as he stepped off the stairs onto the first floor he suddenly was attacked out of the darkness by an intruder waving a large hunting knife.

The intruder lashed out, stabbing Mr. Phillips in the chest. Phillips, keeping his head, shouted out to his wife, "Get the gun!" even as he fell to his knees in pain. The intruder dropped the knife and fled from the house.

Following his mother down the stairs, 14-year-old Varsity Scout **Scott Phillips** found his father on his hands and knees, blood soaking his shirt and the carpet under him. As his mother called the police, Scott retrieved the family first aid kit. Using multiple bandages and direct pressure on his father's wounds, he managed to control the bleeding until emergency personnel arrived ten minutes later. It took hours of surgery but Mr. Phillips survived.

• **Jade Terry**, a 14-year-old Varsity Scout from Enterprise, Utah, was outside of town horseback riding with a friend, when they stopped at a house to talk with the Truman family, a couple with four-year-old son, Truce. Asked by Truce if he might ride a horse around the yard, Jade's friend offered his.

When the little boy finished his ride, he pulled the horse up beside Jade and his horse. Hoping to get closer, Truce backed up his horse and unintentionally bumped Jade's horse. The collision frightened Truce's horse so that it bolted, still with the little boy on its back. Seeing the horse storming up an icy hill, Jade took off in hot pursuit. He caught the stampeding horse near the top of the hill and reaching over, he grabbed Truce by the waist and pulled him over and onto his own saddle. The runaway horse raced on, down a hill covered with trees and boulders – a likely fatal path if Truce had fallen off.

• Fourteen-year-old Life Scout and Varsity team member Matt Hall of Provo, Utah, was walking with two friends when, to their disbelief, they encountered one teenager – Stephen Hall, 14 – being stabbed by another. The attacker fled, leaving Hall (no relation) with deep wounds in each thigh. Victim Hall yelled to another boy to call the paramedics, then, in shock and panic began to run.

Matt Hall and his friends finally managed to catch up with the teenager and convinced him to lie on the grass on an incline so that his legs were elevated. Matt covered Stephen with his jacket and treated for shock. Then, taking a t-shirt from a bystander, Matt set to work on Stephen's right thigh, which was pumping blood. He tried pressure on the wound but that failed as the boy's main leg artery had been severed and he was in imminent threat of bleeding to death. So, Matt switched to direct pressure, tourniquet-like, on Stephen's femoral artery.

He managed to keep Stephen alive until the paramedics arrived. The injured boy required major surgery – and three quarts of blood – to restore the severed artery and cut muscles.

Men of Honor

Even today, not every act of heroic lifesaving by a Scout or adult Scouter is recognized with an Honor Medal. Though eligibility for the Medal has been expanded over the decades to surviving rescuers, adults, Cub Scouts, Senior Scouts, family members, and women, it still is the general rule that the Honor Medal should not be awarded for actions made in the course of an individual's duty. Thus, doctors, paramedics, nurses, and others aren't honored for lives saved while doing their jobs.

While understandable, this rule does mean that BSA never has formally recognized a number of extraordinary acts of bravery in saving a life – including one of the most famous military rescues of the 20th century:

- On March 10, 1966, **Major Bernard F. Fisher** led a flight of A-1E Skyraiders on a bombing mission in defense of a small U.S. Special Forces camp at A Shau under attack by 2,000 North Vietnamese regulars.

The Skyraiders assault on the attackers faced several huge obstacles. For one thing, the camp was surrounded by 1,000 foot tall hills, and the one entrance gap to the valley was heavily defended with enemy anti-aircraft guns and other weapons. Moreover, that day the cloud ceiling had dropped to less than 800 feet, which meant that in crossing the gap, the fighter-bombers would have to fly just a few meters off the ground, through a burning jungle, all the while being fired upon by scores of guns on both sides of the valley.

As one veteran of that day described it:

Congressional Medal of Honor recipient Major Bernard F. Fisher in 1966 & 1970.

'It was like flying inside Yankee Stadium with the people in the bleachers firing at you with machine guns."

On the first pass, the plane piloted by Major Dafford Myers, was chewed up by this fire and was forced to crash land on the camp's runaway – not an easy task given that this runaway was damaged heavily with mortar craters and the debris from wrecked planes. As it crashed and skidded on this runway, the plane burst into flames. Somehow, Major Myers managed to climb out of the cockpit, jump down off the wing, and then, under heavy fire, crawl, and run for cover.

Seeing what had happened below him, Major Fisher radioed in a request for a rescue helicopter – only to be told that none was available. So Fisher decided to make the rescue himself; despite warnings from his fellow pilots not to try it, and even though with an airplane it meant almost impossible odds.

Calling the rest of his flight to strafe the side hills, Fisher banked and ran the gauntlet of fire through the entrance into the valley. But now he was flying too fast to land as the runway was 1,000 feet shorter than the length usually used with this aircraft. So he pulled up – damaging the plane's tail – in preparation to make the run a *second* time. Once again supported by his fellow pilots strafing the hills, Fisher made his run. Again, his plane was shot up heavily, but it still was flying and he still was alive. He landed somehow between the craters, shell casings, and rocket tubes, and evaded the burning wreckage of Myers' burning plane. As automatic weapon fire kicked up dust around him, Fisher rolled to the end of the strip. Then he turned the plane around and taxied slowly back, searching everywhere for his fellow pilot.

That's when Myers burst out from his hiding place and ran for the plane and forced the single most dangerous moment of the rescue. Fisher stopped the plane – making it a huge, motionless target – and opened the cockpit for Myers to climb on board. Needless to say, Myers didn't waste any time, clambering up the wing and diving in head-first (with Fisher's help) into the cockpit.

Bernard Fisher and Dafford Myers after Myers' rescue from behind enemy lines on March 10, 1966.

Although he had made the rescue, now Fisher had one last life-threatening challenge before him: he had to fly the plane out of the valley. To do so, he had to spin the plane around a second time to face the wind, and then go full power to escape the gunfire, which only had intensified. He made it, arriving safely with his battered passenger at Pleiku air base. The ground crew there found 19 bullet holes in his plane.

For the rescue, Major Fisher was awarded the Congressional Medal of Honor, the first awarded to a member of the Air Force in the Vietnam War. Before his adventure, Fisher had long been involved with Scouting: first as a Boy Scout in Clearfield, Utah, then later while at various postings in the U.S. Air Force as a Cubmaster and Scoutmaster. Following his tour in Vietnam, Major Fisher continued his involvement as a Scouter with a troop at Hahn Air Base in Germany. [38]

After retiring from the Air Force as a colonel, Fisher returned to Idaho, where he farmed and was active as a Boy Scout leader. He also helped train Scouts in the wilderness survival skills he had learned in the Air Force.

Major Fisher barely had known Major Myers before that day. After that, Myers called Fisher every year on the anniversary of the rescue – a tradition that continued for 22 years by his daughter after Myers' death in 1992, until Fisher's own death in 2014.

Looking back on the rescue, Fisher told the *New York Times*, "It's important that you respond to your feelings when the time comes for it."

• The acting chairman of the National Court of Honor after the passing of Dan Beard in 1941 (and at the outbreak of World War II), soon would distinguish himself as a national military hero—one whose action would well represent the ideals of Scouting heroism.

Theodore ("Ted") Roosevelt Jr. was the oldest son of the former president of the United States. He was in high school by the time his father became the nation's chief executive and graduated Harvard near the end of his father's second term, Ted was the least impacted (and least noticed) of Theodore Roosevelt's children through his presidency. Brother Kermit became famous as his father's hunting partner on an African safari and

Brig. Gen. Ted Roosevelt's arrival on the island of Sicily in 1943 during World War II.

an expedition into the Brazilian wilderness. Sister Alice became the doyenne of Washington society and Brother Archie was wounded in combat in both world wars. Brother Quentin died heroically as a fighter pilot in WWI. Ted – who had his father's wide grin but not his barrel physique – served in a number of political roles (including New York State assemblyman, governor general of the Philippines, governor of Puerto Rico and assistant secretary of the Navy) and in commercial positions (chairman of American Express and vice president of Doubleday Books). He also helped convince Irving Berlin to donate the royalties of "God Bless America" to the Boy Scouts of America.

Ted, having distinguished himself in World War I (he led a regiment in several key battles and was awarded the Distinguished Service Cross and the French Legion of Honor) returned home to help found the American Legion in 1919.

With the outbreak of World War II, Ted Roosevelt returned to the Army, this time as a brigadier general, reporting to Major General Terry Allen. Though honored for bravery in North Africa after the defeat at Kasserine Pass, Roosevelt – reporting direct to Gen. Allen – was relieved of command.

Gen. George S. Patton, who assumed command, would write of Roosevelt: "There will be a kick over Teddy, but he has to go, brave but otherwise, no soldier." Patton would live to change his mind.

Ted Roosevelt then saw action in Sicily but little thereafter. In February 1944 he was called back to England to serve on the staff of the Normandy invasion. He repeatedly requested a combat command, but was denied one by his commander Major General "Tubby" Barton, who, in a scene made famous by the movie *The Longest Day*, told Roosevelt that he was too old, too stricken with arthritis, and too valuable to send into battle.

In the end, Roosevelt prevailed. Barton approved his petition with grave misgivings, saying he didn't believe he ever would see Roosevelt alive again.

On D-Day, June 6, 1944, Brig. General Theodore Roosevelt Jr. commanded the allied forces on Utah Beach. At fifty-six-years-old, he was the oldest man taking part in the invasion, the only officer whose son (Captain Quentin Roosevelt II) was landing on neighboring Omaha Beach, the only general leading his troops out of the first landing craft, and very likely the first American to step foot on the sand that day.

Gen. Roosevelt quickly discovered that his landing crafts had drifted more than a mile south of their objective. And in one of the most indelible images of that day – made immortal by Henry Fonda playing him in the movie – Ted, armed only with a cane and a pistol, personally reconnoitered the beach (sometimes fully exposed and under fire), calmed his troops by telling them anecdotes about his famous father, and even hiked to the rear of the beach looking for access causeways.

When satisfied he'd made the right decision, Ted returned and called together his two battalion commanders, showed them their location on the map, pointed out lines of attack, and announced: "We'll start the war from right here."

Those words earned Ted Roosevelt, like his father before him, the Congressional Medal of Honor on September 28, 1944 (one of only two pairs of father-son Medal of Honor recipients; the other being Arthur and Douglas MacArthur). By attacking from their current position, instead

of pulling off the beach, Roosevelt's 4th Infantry Division was able to reassert the momentum being lost by the American troops pinned down on neighboring Omaha Beach. Roosevelt's decision may well have saved the Normandy Invasion.

As the first wave moved inland, Ted stayed on the beach, meeting each arriving regiment with stories and jokes and directing them forward into the right position – doing all of this while bullets screamed around him. Using his cane, he also served as traffic cop, directing traffic jams of arriving trucks and tanks.

Brig. Gen. Ted Roosevelt in his jeep in France after the successful D-Day invasion in June 1944.

One soldier later would say that seeing General Roosevelt walking around, ignoring enemy rifle and artillery fire – even as he was being showered by clods of dirt – gave him the courage to go on. If the general is that unafraid, he said, it can't be that bad.

After the war, General Omar Bradley, in charge of the invasion and the commander of U.S. combat forces in Europe, was asked about the most heroic action he'd ever seen in combat. He replied, "Ted Roosevelt on Utah Beach."

For his heroic actions, six days later on July 12, 1944, Roosevelt was named by Bradley as commander of the 90th Infantry Division and promoted to major general. Earlier that day, he had spent several hours in happy conversation with his son, Cpt. Quentin Roosevelt, as they sat in a truck. Then, at 10 pm, he suffered a major heart attack and died about midnight. When General Dwight D. Eisenhower, supreme allied commander, called in the morning to inform Ted of his promotion, the general was told that Roosevelt had died during the night.

George Patton, who long since had changed his mind about Roosevelt, served as one of his pallbearers and wrote in his diary, "[Ted] was one of the bravest men I've ever known."

Super Heroes

Most of the Honor Medal rescues among the 13,000+ meritorious action citations to date are clustered around just a handful of rescue types: thus, of the first 1,000 Honor Medal recipients, which takes the list through 1935, about 80 percent are water and ice rescues. We've already noted the large number of these types of rescues during Scouting's first decade, but the trend continued almost unchanged through the second.

The Butte, Montana, lightning strike of August 21, 1922, was a rare exception that also seems to have set a precedent for a much wider definition of heroism in the decades that followed. By the 1940s, that standard now encompassed almost every imaginable scenario in which a Scout could save the life of another human being. Given the unpredictability and perversity of the natural world and of human behavior in the years that followed, it appeared that Scouts found themselves in just about every one of those situations. Some were expected: the growing number of automobiles, airplanes, motorized machines, and extensive electrification, all-but guaranteed that there would be a growing number of emergencies involving these inventions.

*First Class Scout **Lyman E. Boyle** of Frankfort, Indiana, saved two girls from drowning after their boat tipped over in 1926.*

But other types of life-threatening emergencies simply couldn't be imagined. Indeed, they were – and remain – the stuff of nightmares. The fact that Boy Scouts, still mostly teenagers, continue to rise to these occasions is astounding. It is a lesson both in human creativity and the almost unlimited capacity of a trained Boy Scout to heroically and successfully take on the most extreme situations and risks.

Here's a rescue story from 1919 that, if it was not thoroughly authenticated, would read like a scene from an Eagle Scout Steven Spielberg movie:

• **George O. Noble**, 19-year-old assistant Scoutmaster from Chariton, Iowa, was driving down a lonely country road when he saw smoke in the distance. He decided to drive toward it and within minutes realized that it was a house engulfed in flames. Leaping out of his car, Noble was met by a pair of hysterical parents saying their two children were trapped in the house.

After wrapping his head in a wet cloth, Noble ran into the house and up the burning stairs to the second floor bedrooms. There, in one bedroom, he found the little Calder girl lying unconscious from smoke inhalation. He wrapped her in some nearby bedclothes and raced her to safety down the stairs and out onto the front lawn. Handing the girl to her parents, Noble barely took a breath before he spun around and raced back into the house.

But he couldn't find the boy, James Calder, age 8. So Noble ran back outside for air and more details from the boy's parents. They told him that little George was indeed on the second floor and explained how to locate his bedroom. And so, for the third time, George Noble ran back into the burning house. The flames now were higher than ever. As he ran up the stairs, they collapsed under him but George was able to grab an exposed beam and pull himself up to the second floor.

He finally located James' room but the walls already were curtained in flames. He looked everywhere but there was no sign of the boy. Then, on a hunch, Noble ran over to a large trunk and flung up the lid. There was little James, having taken refuge from the fire. But, just as he reached down to pull out the boy, the floor collapsed.

The next thing George Noble knew was that he was sitting astride the closed and upside down trunk in the house's burning *cellar*, having somehow survived the two story fall. Flames were all around him – so hot that his hands and legs were blistering from the superheated metal bands on the trunk.

Somehow, George managed to tip over the trunk and extricate little James. The two managed to escape the collapsing house through a small window at the far end of the cellar.

Finally, out of the inferno, Noble retrieved his Scout first aid kit from his car and treated the childrens' burns. He then ordered the traumatized parents to put the children in his own car and get them to the doctor. After they left, George Noble (it's hard to imagine a more appropriate name) tried to dress his own wounds…but fainted. That's how the doctor found him an hour later.

Once George recovered and received treatment, he went on his way. Eventually returning home, miles away from the scene of that rescue, he didn't even tell his parents of his experience. It was months later when the Noble family learned of George Noble's heroic action when the Calder parents finally encountered some friends of George and expressed their thanks to him for what he had done. When asked why he hadn't mentioned it before, Noble replied, "Being a Scout, I simply did my duty."

George Noble was the fifth recipient of the Gold Lifesaving Medal and the first living Scout to receive it.

Thanks to the advance of technology, some acts of bravery in Scouting's first decades only now seem so if we remember the context in which they took place. A classic example:

• The story of Gold Honor Medal recipient **Richard L. Weaver**, 12, of San Francisco, California, stands out as perhaps the most unusual reason for an award in Scouting history.

Similar to the story of **Leigh Elmer Garver**, who donated 50 square inches of his own skin to his badly burned uncle in 1913 and received the fifth Silver Lifesaving Medal for doing so, Weaver donated a whopping 100 square inches of his leg skin – an area of flesh about the size of the entire top of a person's thigh – as a graft for his cousin, Vernon Garnett, 8. Vernon had been severely burned, and after three months his doctors agreed that without a skin graft the boy was certain to die.

The Silver Lifesaving Medal presented to Leigh Elmer Garver in June 1913.

Though grisly to modern eyes, this hardly seems an act of great heroism or risk. Not so to the people of Weaver's time (1924) who nominated him for the award. Nor for the National Court of Honor that decided to give the boy its highest award for a living hero. In that pre-antibiotic age of haphazard sterilization and limited choices in anesthetics and pain relief, a sacrifice like Weaver's would have been painful and extremely risky. In fact, the surgery took three hours and afterward the young man was at great risk of blood poisoning. That both cousins survived the process was far from preordained. In the end, they both lived.

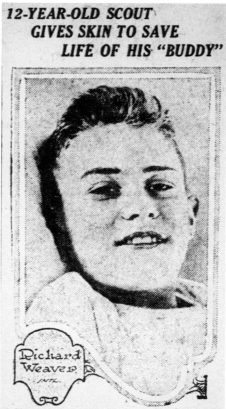

12-YEAR-OLD SCOUT GIVES SKIN TO SAVE LIFE OF HIS "BUDDY"

Richard Weaver

The Boy Scout pledge to "help others when possible" was exemplified in San Francisco when Richard Weaver, 12-year-old scout, gave up 100 square inches of skin from his back and legs to be grafted onto the back of 8-year-old Vernon Garnett, his playmate, who was burned by hot tar. The cuticle transfer saved young Garnett's life.

Happily, thanks to other technologies – smoke detectors, automatic sprinkler systems, alarms, non-flammable computerized emergency dispatching systems, Doppler radar, etc. – a number of potential fatal scenarios that were common a century ago have become increasingly less common, if not altogether disappearing. As a result, few modern Honor Medals are being given for rescues like this one:

• 1926: Eagle Scout **Francis W. Wayland**, 16, of Washington, DC, was sleeping in his dorm room on the third floor at Randolph-Macon Academy near Winchester, Virginia. He and his two roommates were awakened in the early hours of the morning by shouts of "Fire!"

By the time the three heard the warning and rushed out of their room, the fire already had blocked their exit hallway. At this point, one of the other boys panicked and – despite being warned by Wayland – tried to run through the fire. Wayland grabbed him and dragged him back but not before inhaling a lot of smoke. He fainted – but luckily, after a moment, revived in the clearer air near the floor.

Then Wayland asserted his leadership. He ordered his roommates to accompany him back to their room and closed the door. Then he organized them into tying together sheets and bedding to make an escape rope. The first to climb out the window was the panicked boy. He made it down. Then the second boy made the attempt. When halfway down flames burst out of a lower window that ignited and severed the makeshift rope. He fell to the ground, luckily unhurt.

Dizzy from the smoke filling his room and flames filling his floor, Francis Wayland realized he had no choice and jumped three stories to the pavement below. Although seriously injured, he survived.

• In a rare, but not unprecedented event, a tornado touched down in southeast Washington, DC, in 1927 tearing off the roofs and upper floors of a block of row houses. First Class Scout **Cyprian Haithman**, 15, who lived nearby, heard the screams of a woman in one of those houses. Haithman broke through the front door and picked his way through the debris to find Rosa Thomas with her young child in her arms – both partly pinned by fallen bricks, beams, and plaster. Both mother and child were injured. Cyprian dug them out and helped them out of the house and across the street to safety.

Only then did he learn that there were two more children in the house. So, ignoring the risk of the rickety building falling on him, Cyprian grabbed another boy and, together, they went back into the house and saved them.

The Stuff of Nightmares

Some acts of bravery by Scouts almost are too disturbing to contemplate:

- A group of boys were playing in the swimming pool at the Baptist Hill Assembly in Mount Vernon, Missouri, in August 1977. They began to challenge each other to dive to the bottom of the pool and touch the drain cover. Terry Beuterbaugh, 14, took up the challenge but just as he touched the drain the pool's circulation system kicked on. The resulting vacuum grabbed Terry's arm and locked him into the drain pipe twelve feet under water.

The boy's predicament was spotted by the pool's lifeguard, Eagle Scout **Steven Vaughan**, 18, who dove into the pool to help. It took him three trips to bottom, each time coming up for air, before he could finally pull Beuterbaugh free and drag him to the surface. He then performed mouth-to-mouth on the unconscious boy until he revived.

- April 1977: The Fix family – mother Donna and three sons, Chris, 6, Eric, 12, and Start Scout **Gregory Fix** – drove to the family cabin at Buffalo Lake, Montello, Wisconsin. As they always had done, the family built a fire and then lit the pilot lights on the stove and refrigerator. Then, exhausted from the trip, they went to bed early.

At 3 a.m., cold and with a severe headache, Greg awoke and told his mother he wasn't feeling well. She got up to get him an aspirin but as she started across the room, she collapsed to the floor, unconscious.

Splashing water on her face, Greg managed to revive her. But now he sensed that something was terribly wrong. Grabbing Eric, Greg told him to run for help. But even as he gave the order, his brother also began to slump to the floor unconscious. Greg managed to revive him too. He made both of his brothers go outside.

Now, suspecting a gas leak, Greg and his mother found the liquid propane tanks and shut them off. As he helped his mother out of the house, Greg's own legs began to buckle. It took a few minutes of fresh air before he revived fully himself.

The next day, a careful search found that it was indeed a gas leak in the cabin's refrigerator. Another hour of sleep would have killed the entire family.

• On a windy April evening in 1974, Matt Golle and Jerrard Hine, both 13, were flying a kite on the shore of Lake Zurich, Illinois, when the kite string broke, sending the kite fluttering down onto some mud on the edge of the water.

As the two boys made their way out into the sticky mud they were terrified to find themselves stuck fast and sinking. The more they tried to pull themselves out, the more they began to sink, until they were up to their chests and unable to move.

Scout **Carl Vrba** was riding past on his paper route when he heard their cries for help and made his way out into the mud to help. He grabbed one of the boy's wrists, but finding himself also sinking into what was, in fact, mud *ten feet deep*, he backed off and searched for another solution.

Vrba found it in some boards lying nearby. Standing on one of the boards, he slid two others to Matt and Jarrard, who clung to them to stop their sinking. Talking to the boys to calm them, Carl then used another board as a wedge, driving it down beneath Jerrard's feet to break the suction and pull him out.

By now, another group of boys had arrived on the scene and, assisting Carl, managed to pull Matt out. Both boys left their shoes behind, torn off by the suction and buried deep in the mud, fortunate that it could have been their fate as well.[39]

- Early on an October morning in 1973, Eagle Scout **Arthur Scott**, 18, was driving his father to work in Syracuse, New York, when he saw a car on the rain-soaked highway go into a skid and crash into a nearby gas station. The sliding car hit all three pumps on the center island, tearing them off their bases and bursting into flames.

Stopping his car, Scott raced to assist the driver, even as the flames began to engulf the crashed car. He reached the driver's side door to find Edward Sanderson, 52, unconscious, trapped inside with a bleeding head wound, and with his clothing on fire.

Turning around, Arthur yelled to the gas station attendant to shut off the pumps and call for help. He then set to rescuing Sanderson. Scott yanked open the jammed door and patted out the flames on the man's jacket. Stabilizing Sanderson's head wound, he managed to pull the 230 lb. man out of the car and drag him away from the flames – even as the gas station attendant was using a fire extinguisher around him to put out the fire.

By the time an ambulance arrived, Arthur had moved Sanderson to safety and stabilized him. After a hospital stay, Sanderson recovered.[40]

- Heavy June rains in North Benbrook, Texas, near Ft. Worth, had turned a local concrete drainage ditch into a roaring torrent. Seeing the two-foot-deep jet of water as an opportunity rather than a threat, Clay Yandell, 10, climbed in and quickly was knocked off his feet and carried down the ditch. An instant later, the boy's legs were dragged under a broken piece of concrete and pinned with a buried pile of brush.

Scout **Rudd Long**, 16, saw Clay being carried down the ditch and then trapped underwater. At the risk of his own life, he jumped into the ditch and as he did, called to a friend to get help.

Fourteen-year-old **Nicholas Carone** *of New Haven, Connecticut, saved William Coletta from drowning in February 1941.*

Unable to pull the boy free, and fighting the pressure of the roaring water, Rudd lifted Clay's head momentarily above the surface and gave him mouth-to-mouth resuscitation. He continued to do so, often having to go under the surface himself to give Clay the breath of life – all while the water pounded against them. A neighbor arrived and, with Rudd, tried to divert the water away from Clay, but with little success. Meanwhile, young Clay began to drift into unconsciousness.

About this time, the boy's mother arrived. Seeing her son drowning, she too jumped into the canal only to be swept off her feet. She had to be dragged out.

After a half-hour, a group of local men reached the scene. Tying a rope around Clay, they managed to pull the boy out of the trap. The men despaired that they were too late – that Clay already had drowned.

But Rudd refused to give up, he continued his artificial respiration until Clay was loaded in the ambulance and put on a mechanical respirator. He made the right choice: young Clay Yandell survived.[41]

• The parents of Scout **Keith Clement**, 13, of Ashfield, Massachusetts, were working together mowing a hay field on their farm in June 1976. While Ms. Clement drove the tractor-mower, her husband walked ahead of her and clearing branches out of her path.

Suddenly, Mr. Clement lost his balance and slipped onto the ground. Ms. Clement, unable to stop the mower in time, crashed into and over him. The mower's blades slashed at her husband's leg – cutting flesh and muscle to the bone and severing the man's femoral artery.

Running to his screams for help, Keith found his father not only severely injured, but rapidly bleeding to death. In an instant, he took what likely would be a fateful choice: he put a tourniquet on his father's leg – fully knowing that, in saving his father's life, it also might cost him his leg.

Loading Mr. Clement into the family pick-up truck, Keith and his mom raced for the hospital only to spend agonizing minutes waiting at a crossing for an endlessly long freight train to pass. While they waited, Keith tended to his father's tourniquet, alternately loosening and tightening it (not recommended by Boy Scouts) to keep a little blood flowing into Mr. Clement's leg.

It worked. Mr. Clement not only lived, but his leg later was saved.[42]

• This is a nightmare that never seemed to end: it began at four o'clock in the morning at the Higgins' family two-story house in Woodbourne, New York, February 1953. The entire family was asleep, when an explosion rocked the house.

Tenderfoot Scout **Joseph Higgins**, 11, awakened by the noise, ran downstairs to find his father and mother rounding up his seven brothers and sisters to evacuate the house. The oil heater had exploded and the house already was aflame.

Joseph's father told him to run back upstairs and help get the rest of the kids out. Joseph did just that. But as he led three of his siblings down the stairs, he realized that two more, the twins, still were missing. Sending the three out into the snow, Joseph raced back up the burning stairs, severely burning his bare feet.

The second floor landing was filled with smoke but Joseph pushed his way into the twins' bedrooms. He found his brother first. Smashing that bedroom's window with a chair, he grabbed the boy and dropped him into a snowbank ten feet below. He then searched blindly across the room and found the other twin, Cathy.

By the time he found her, the room already was partially engulfed in flames. Joseph carried Cathy to the window and helped her jump. He followed her out the window into the same snow bank.

But Joseph Higgins' act of bravery wasn't over. Gathering the family on the driveway, Joseph realized that his parents weren't there. An instant later he heard their calls for help – they were trapped on the house's enclosed back porch.

So Joseph ran back into the house one more time and helped find a path for his parents to escape. With them in tow, the house now completely engulfed in flames, and with his brothers and sisters freezing in the snow, Joseph yelled for everyone to follow him and run to the family car. No sooner did they make it (with his parents and Joseph carrying the youngest children), the house exploded from the second oil heater – turning the structure into a huge fireball. Had he been a few seconds slower in any of his rescues, Joseph, his parents, and perhaps several of his siblings would have died in the blast.

It took two weeks in the hospital for Joseph Higgins and his sister Cathy to recover from their severe burns. The rest of the family was unhurt.

• Eagle Scout **James Koonce Jr.** was enjoying a day of surfing at New Topsail Beach, North Carolina, in July 1967 when he saw a group of people on the beach, waving and gesturing down the shore.

Upon learning that a person was drowning, Koonce paddled to the beach and ran down to where the man was last seen. Another person already had tried and failed to rescue the swimmer, who now had dis appeared under the waves. Following his directions, Koonce swam out and dove for the bottom. There he found the explanation for the failed rescue.

Lying on the bottom, unconscious, was Dewey Thompson, 29, a very large man weighing 230 pounds. James knew in an instant that he had neither the swimming strength nor the buoyancy to get Thompson to the surface.

So, James did the next best thing: he grabbed Thompson's arm and *dragged* him along the ocean bottom for fifteen feet until he could stand in the shallows and get the larger man to the beach.

By this point, James Koonce was utterly exhausted by the rescue effort and barely could stand. Yet, he still performed mouth-to-mouth resuscitation on Thompson. Luckily, within minutes a vacationing nurse ran up to help.

But their efforts were to no avail. Thompson was so large that neither James nor the nurse could get their mouths around his to create a seal. Minutes passed and finally, in desperation, Koonce turned Thompson over and used a back-up technique – the back-pressure method – he had learned in Scout lifesaving.

By the time a rescue team arrived, Thompson already had begun to revive.[43]

• In the early hours of a Sunday morning in April 1976, Eagle Scout **Carl Gawart**, 17, was driving his sleeping brothers, Chris, Clint, and Craig, home to Battle Creek, Michigan, from their vacation. That's when an oncoming car lost control, turned at a high speed up the dividing median and went airborne, directly at the Gawart car. The flying automobile crashed onto the highway just in front – and Carl, hitting the brakes, had no time to stop before crashing into the smashed vehicle. The two cars locked together, spun around spewing gasoline as they went, and ended up sideways and blocking the highway.

Though nearly knocked out himself, a bruised Carl pulled all three of his injured brothers out of the car and carried them away to a safe place in case there was an explosion. He then treated their injuries.

By now, other vehicles had arrived on the scene. And while they checked on the passengers of the other car, Carl borrowed the use of one driver's CB radio to call for help. As he did, other arriving cars crashed into the Gawart car. Had he not gotten his brothers out promptly, they might have been killed.[44]

• At the end of the harvest in early November 1983, Wolf Cub **Scott Bohman**, 8, and his brother Webelos Cub **Brian Bohman**, 10, along with two other boys were helping the boy's father unload corn at their Mishicot, Wisconsin, farm.

Mr. Bohman had backed his truck up to a top-feed "gravity box" – a large container that feeds corn cobs into a blower that lifts the corn through a long tube to the top of a silo.

The work was going well until one of the other boys, Darin Breunig, 10, leaned over too far and fell into the gravity box. Head down and buried up to his waist in the moving corn, Breunig was in imminent danger of being pulled into the blades of the blower, or being trapped and suffocating in the tube.

Just in time, Scott managed to grab Darin's legs and hold him, but he quickly began to lose his fight against the weight of the still dumping corn. He yelled for help. Brian and his friend Matt Heyroth, 12, jumped into action. Brian turned off the blower and opened the blower's gates in hopes of getting more air. Then the three boys tried to pull Darin out of the box. But now there simply was too much weight on top of the boy. So while Matt kept Darin from slipping in deeper, Scott ran to find his uncle and Brian ran to get his father.

Upon their arrival, the two men climbed into the bottom of the gravity box and pushed Darin *upwards* through the corn. By now, his lips had turned blue from lack of oxygen but he soon recovered.

• January 1978: First Class Scout **Duane Masonheimer** and his friend Tracy Tacker, both 14, were skiing near Waterhal Township, Pennsylvania. Tracy raced ahead down a 50-foot hill and, unknowingly, set off an avalanche. At the top of the hill, Duane only could look down and watch as his friend disappeared under the pile of rolling snow.

The instant the slide stopped, he raced down in search of his buried friend. But there was no sign – the fresh snow had covered any track or mark. Duane continued his desperate search until he spotted a tiny movement. It was Tracy' fingers just above the surface of the snow.

Rushing over, Duane began to dig with his bare hands exposing first Tracy's hand, then arm, and finally his head. By now, Duane's hands were starting to freeze. He kept digging, until he exposed his friend's face. Tracy still was alive. Unable to work his hands any more, Duane made sure his friend was conscious and breathing – then ran to Tracy' nearby house and got help. He then was pulled from his snowy tomb, unscathed.[45]

*Tenderfoot **Richard Young** of Northumberland (PA) and his mother receive his Honor Medal certificate from Rev. C.P. Lewis, while Scoutmaster Leon Quick looks on.*

*Thirteen-year-old **Don Clardy Jr.** of Cockrell Hill, Texas, saved an infant girl from inside a burning two-story house in October 1925.*

For at least one Scout, the act of heroism proved merely a prelude to perhaps an even greater act of bravery:

• **John Alden Daniels**, 14, of Buffalo, New York, in 1912 earned one of the very first Lifesaving Medals for saving the life of William Simmons, who had been caught in the fast current of the Niagara River just north of Fort Erie. Daniels and a friend were in a boat fishing on the river when they heard Simmons' calls for help. They quickly weighed anchor and rowed to Simmons, pulling him to the surface just as he began to disappear.

But that's just the beginning of the story. Just weeks later, Alden was standing with a crowd on the bank of the same river, this time in Buffalo's Riverside Park, to watch a run by of the world's then-fastest motorboat, the Dixie IV.

Then the unthinkable happened: the pilot of the boat lost control and the Dixie IV careened out of the water, ran up the bank, and slammed into the crowd. Alden Daniels was the worst among those hit and was pinned under the motorboat for fifteen minutes, conscious the entire time, before rescuers could extricate him. By this point Alden's leg was so badly crushed that amputation was inevitable.

Nevertheless, after being loaded into an automobile and while being raced to the hospital, Alden insisted that the driver stop at his home so that he could tell his mother that he was not badly hurt – and to ask her to tell another boy to temporarily take over his newspaper route.

Ultimately, surgeons did have to remove Alden Daniels' leg below the knee. While in the hospital, true to his undeniable character, he asked his mother to tell his fellow Scouts not to send him any flowers, but rather to keep their money. Asked how he could possibly be cheerful after what he'd just been through, Alden replied that Boy Scouts should smile even in suffering.[46]

Finally, in another rescue that seems like a scene out of a movie – this is the rare case of father/son medal recipients.

- Late 1940s: location unrecorded, but likely in Central California. The Cromar family, Leonard, Gladys, and 3-year-old Richard, were standing near the edge of an irrigation ditch. Richard, playing, lost his balance and fell in. The moving water quickly pulled him through an underground pipe. Seeing this, Leonard Cromar dove in and swam to the pipe. Though he barely could fit, he finally managed to squeeze part-way through. He was able to grab Richard and hold him above the surface. Leonard also was acting as a partial plug and soon found himself half-into a dimly lit stone vault with a heavy grate on top that was filling rapidly with water and threatening to drown them both.

Above, Gladys Cromar's screams caught the attention of Life Scout **Jimmy Walker** and his Eagle Scout father. Quickly surveying the situation, Mr. Walker ran up the canal to open its headgate and divert the onrushing water from the vault. Jimmy, meanwhile, dove into the canal and, being smaller, managed to fit through the opposite end of the pipe. He found father and son near death.

Bracing Mr. Cromar against the side of the tank – and praying that his father would stop the water in time – Jimmy took little Richard, shoved him through the open pipe and then swam with him to the surface of the canal. There his father, who had returned, pulled the child out of the water and saved him with artificial respiration.

Meanwhile, others now had arrived, and with a crowbar managed to lift the grating. Using a ladder, Jimmy climbed down and helped bring up an exhausted, but alive, Leonard Cromar.

The "Scouts in Action" illustration published in the June 1948 issue of Boys' Life *magazine that depicts the save of Leonard Cromar by Life Scout Jimmy Waker and his father.*

For their actions, Jim received the Honor Medal and his father, the Medal of Merit.

"Those who say that we're in a time when there are no heroes, they just don't know where to look." - Ronald Reagan

CHAPTER

Scouts in Action

*"I appreciate these boys and men
even more than when I started [at Boys' Life].
I've become their biggest admirer.
They really are true heroes."*

– Aaron Derr, Senior Writer, *Boy's Life* magazine.

Every six months for the last dozen years, Aaron Derr has sat down with a list of about 300 names, along with brief summaries of their stories.

As senior writer of *Boys' Life* magazine, it has been Derr's job, since not long after he joined the magazine, to search through this semi-annual list of new Honor Medal and Medal of Merit recipients and look for likely candidates for a comic page in the magazine entitled "Scouts in Action."

Each month in the pages of the magazine, "Scouts in Action" celebrates the most compelling of these lifesaving medal winners by telling the story of their heroics in suitably action-packed comic book style. This is not a minor matter, either for *Boys' Life* or for the Boy Scouts of America, because "Scouts in Action" is, in fact, the most popular, most read, and most venerable youth feature in American publishing.

"When I was offered the job," he recalls, "I didn't realize what a big deal it was. I sort of lucked into it. My boss asked if I wanted to do it."

"All I really knew that it was a popular part of the magazine. I can remember once, before I took the job, there was an error in one of the stories. My boss said, '*Hey, no big deal, it's only the first page kids read.*' It was only after I accepted the job that I realized just how important 'Scouts in Action' really is to Scouting – or how many inspiring stories there would be. Every person I've met, young or old, with any connection to Scouting has some anecdote for me about 'Scouts in Action.'"

A National Institution

Since its introduction in the January 1947 issue of *Boys' Life*, "Scouts in Action" consistently has been the page most of the magazine's youth readers turn to first and the feature they list as most important each month. That still is true today, as the magazine's subscribers number 1.2 million and total readership exceeds four million.

It goes without saying that today's America is radically different from post-World War II United States. One need only peruse an issue from that era – thanks to *Boys' Life's* own nine decade archival on-line "Wayback Machine" – to see a very different reality. The pages of the monthly 1947 issues are filled with many advertisements for bicycle speedometers, do-it-yourself taxidermy, wing-tip shoes, Remington rifles, and Wildroot hair oil. The "Movie of the Month" is *The Song of the South* – a film now considered so controversial for its racial attitudes that Disney no longer shows it. The main feature describes winged bombs, missiles, and other innovative new ordinance "that were some of the fantastic weapons loosed on the Japs near the war's end which have their peacetime uses."

The cover photo, showing a senior patrol leader in his campaign hat - sled and pack nearby - cooking sausages in the snow, is comparatively benign. But just a month before, the cover shows a Scout and Scoutmaster delivering Christmas presents to three soldiers – one in a leg cast, another with an eye patch, and a third in a hospital bed in the "paralyzed veterans" ward at Halloran General Hospital in Staten Island, New York: "These men will come in a for a lot of attention this year and rightly so because some of them, disabled for life, need all of the assistance that can be given them." It is a reminder that the country had just emerged from a global war that had cost the lives of tens of millions of people.

Sixty-five years later, the October 2012 issue of *Boys' Life* has as its cover a look at the new electric supercars and in its pages could be found stories about a new software app that enables users to tour world historic sites using 3D glasses, and includes plans for balloon tours to the edge of space, combat uniform exoskeletons, and the latest designs in titanium mountain bikes.

Seen side-by-side, it not only is hard to imagine that these are the same magazine but that they even came from the same planet. And yet, surprisingly, featured on page 46 of the 2012 magazine (as well as on page 48), and on page 51 of its 1947 predecessor is a full page, multi-panel comic telling the stories of Scouts saving lives – both under the same banner of "Scouts in Action."

Not surprisingly, the styles of illustration are different, with the older in the inked black-and-white chiaroscuro (light and dark contrasts) of Golden Age comic books and the younger in bright colors and computer shading. But the message of both is the same: Scouting combines bravery with training to save the lives of helpless victims in desperate straits. It seems incredible that such a simple topic and format not only could survive for seven decades but remain at a zenith of popularity.

And yet, the enduring popularity of "Scouts in Action" is not that surprising. The comic format always has tapped into something elemental about being young – indeed, in being human.

Boys' Life *magazine, October 2012.*

Young people, far more than adults, continually ask themselves how they will behave when challenged by life's greatest tests. It is the old story of young men, found everywhere from the *Iliad* to the latest reports from 21st century war zones, asking themselves if they'll have the fortitude and the courage to not run and fight when the bullets start flying. Life threatening situations – for others, and for oneself – is another such test. We ask ourselves: if there was an a automobile crash, or a struggling figure slipping beneath the waves, or a burning house . . . would we swallow our fears and run to help even if it meant a high chance of losing our own life?

As we all know, the most frustrating part of that question is that we truly cannot answer it until we find ourselves in just such a situation and facing just such danger. That is the attraction of real-life stories of heroism: they show us that other people have faced similar dangers and found it in themselves not only to run to the rescue, but to do the correct thing once they get there – even under unimaginable stress.

That's why humanity always has had an insatiable appetite for stories about heroes – they show us the best of what we can be. They push out the boundaries of what brave human beings can do. And they give us hope that we could accomplish similar feats if given the chance.

The founders of Scouting – Baden-Powell, Seton, and most importantly for heroism, Beard – understood this. They knew the self-doubt found in all boys, the power of stories of heroism, and the need to find role models for doing the right thing. They also recognized the vital importance of matching this Call to Glory with a body of skills, taught at a young age, to increase the odds of those acts of bravery being successful for both the rescuer and the rescued.

These combinations of doubt and desire, bravery and competence, and promotion and celebration, were with the Boy Scouts of America from the beginning, and they informed the content of every issue of *Boys' Life* from its very first number of January 1, 1911.

Often forgotten is that, at its founding, *Boys' Life* was not affiliated with the Boy Scouts of America. Publisher George S. Barton, who founded, largely wrote, edited, and published that eight-page broadside, newspaper-sized first edition (it had a print run of just 5,000 copies) called it the "Boys' and Boy Scouts' Magazine." He was covering his bets by appealing to the three biggest competing Scout movements of the era: the BSA, the New England Boy Scouts, and the American Boy Scouts.

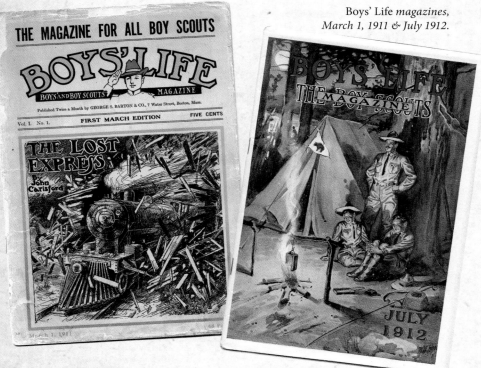

It worked, apparently, because when the commonly acknowledged "first" issue of the restyled *Boys' Life* appeared two months later on March 1, it had shrunk in size but ballooned to 48 pages with a two color cover. It also had caught the eye of the BSA's Chief Scout Executive James E. West, who by early 1912 entered into negotiations to buy the magazine exclusively for the BSA. On June 10, 1912, he purchased *Boys' Life* for $6,000 and named himself as its new editor-in-chief.

West appears to have had three motives for the purchase. One was to keep it out of the hands of the competing Scouting programs that might be thinking of the purchase themselves and to remove the biggest existing platform for promoting them. Second, as the stated reason, West was committing the BSA to a high-profile national initiative – "Learning to Read" – and wanted the magazine as a vehicle to disseminate it. Finally (and at the heart of West's strategy) BSA needed to win the race for national membership and obtain a Congressional charter for a national media campaign to do so – and *Boys' Life* was the perfect instrument.

As with many such plans, if the purchase of *Boys' Life* was as cynical as it was idealistic, the reality was that it succeeded even beyond West's dreams. It did so not just for the goals that West planned for the publication but even more so for a fourth factor: institutional culture.

From the very first BSA-owned issue – thanks to such formidable writers as Beard and Seton (as well as guest celebrities such as Theodore Roosevelt, famed baseball pitcher Christy Mathewson and environmentalist Gifford Pinchot) – the founders, of Scouting used the magazine as a vehicle to elaborate on the meaning of Scouting, from outdoor skills to patriotism to honor and duty. While much of this may seem overwrought to modern readers, it certainly wasn't so to boys and their parents in the early years of the 20th century. One of the reason the BSA succeeded was that, while still a very small organization in terms of membership, in vision it already was presenting itself as an important new institution in American life. And within a decade it managed to live up to that image.

Inaugural Announcements

The notion of heroism absolutely was central to early Scouting and also, not surprisingly, to *Boys' Life* magazine from the start. The July 1912 offering, being the first issue of *Boys' Life* as the "Official Organ of the Boy Scouts of America," carries the announcement of BSA's first recipients of the Silver and Bronze Lifesaving Medals for heroism. For example, the following individuals received the latter:

- **George Turner** of River Edge, New Jersey, for saving the life of a fellow Scout who fell through the ice on the Hackensack River,
- **Leman Conrad** of Watkins, New York, for saving a woman from drowning in Seneca Lake, and most atypically,
- **Jack Fred Sheetz** of Wyncote, Pennsylvania, for staying at the wireless station on the steamship *Lexington* after it ran aground.

This same issue carried a short story about a young man who, after realizing he is the descendent of Continental soldiers who fought at Bunker Hill, rises above the teasing and agrees to a boxing match with a bully. There also are short news items about a Scout who saved an almshouse and barn in Burlington, New Jersey, and other Scouts that helped flood victims in Florence, South Carolina, and Monroe, Louisiana.

Wireless Operator, Hero of Wreck of the Steamer Lexington

Jack Sheetz.

Beaufort, S. C., Sept. 7.—Jack Sheetz is only 16, but when the passenger steamer Lexington was wrecked near Beaufort, he stuck to the wireless key and sent out calls for help until the revenue cutter, Yamacraw, went to the rescue. His father, Henry F. Sheetz, is head of the manufacturing department of the Presbyterian Board of Publication at Philadelphia. He declares himself very proud of Jack, who is soon to take up the work of his last year in the high school in Philadelphia.

Dan Beard makes his appearance in this issue as well via an open letter to all Scouts. It is a curious mixture of high and low; on the one hand, trying to sell the nation's boys on subscribing to the magazine ("And remember that the bigger the circulation of this magazine is, the greater influence we will exert") and on the other, that ascribing to Scouting the loftiest of goals (the sentence just before the sales pitch ends with: ". . . you are working to make this nation greater, bigger, more powerful, and more noble than it has ever been, by making it a nation of splendid, honorable, efficient men").

Indeed, the concepts of "honor," being the third word of the Scout Oath, and "duty," being central to the core Scouting ideals, suffuses the early issues of *Boys' Life*. This especially is true after Edward Cave took over as editor-in-chief of the magazine and began to systematize its contents. The August 1912 issue features "Play Clean Ball" written by New York Giant pitcher Christy Mathewson, the figure most admired for his integrity in Major League Baseball history. The October 1912 issue offers something similar, this time "Honor in Football" by legendary Yale football coach Walter Camp; while the December offering features Mabel Boardman, who just had re-organized the American Red Cross. She tells the story of the "Death of King Arthur" that equates Boy Scouts with the noble knights of old.

Meanwhile, every issue carries the hugely popular feature: an "Honor Roll" of Bronze, Silver, and any Gold Lifesaving Medal recipients.

Boys' Life promotional ad, 192

On The BOYS

$1.00

BOYS' LIFE BOYS' LIFE BO

8 MONTHS' T

Three years later, the ever-competitive Beard and Seton each successfully added "associate editor" to their by-lines within the magazine's pages. At the same time, the "Honor Roll" moved from the back of the publication to the very center within the multi-page section on official Scouting news. One reason probably was to attract readers to this less-exciting section, the other because the number of Honor Medal recipients was growing too large to give each one extended coverage.

The year 1919 was the *annus horibilis* of the Lifesaving Medal, and it fell to the March issue of *Boys' Life* under the heading "Honor Medal Winners" to include the names of Eicher, Goodnow, Grimes, and Seyfried as the first recipients of the Gold Lifesaving Medal. Each boy had an asterisk after his name – and below: "NOTE – The boys whose names are starred gave their lives in the heroic effort to save another life. The Gold Lifesaving Medal in these cases was sent to the next of kin of the dead Scout."

There was no celebration of the first Gold Lifesaving Medalists and no discussion of their heroic deeds. In fact, the listing continues with the list of Bronze and Silver Lifesaving Medal winners. Nearby, as if clearing the decks, there is a separate story about the National Court of Honor and its new members, including Belmore Brown, Major David Abercrombie, Fredrick Vreeland, and Dr. William T. Hornaday being the key figures in the renaissance of the Honor Medal Program. The next issue contains one final list of medalists missed in the previous issue – then silence.

LIFE SPECIAL!

?—ONLY $1.00

Every Scout a Swimmer ad in Boys' Life, *circa 1920.*

In the May 1919 issue, the spot that usually is reserved for Honor Medal recipients has been replaced, tellingly, by an article about the BSA's new "Every Scout a Swimmer" initiative. The December issue tells the story of "Scout Candidate" Verne Joseph, who helps stop a lynch mob by intervening as a traffic cop; and of "Scout McCaferty" who is out hunting with his father (a Rio Grande secret service agent) when the latter accidently blows his hand off. Scout McCaferty, trained in first aid, saves his father's life. And yet, there is no mention of either boy receiving an award from the BSA. It is as if *Boys' Life* editors, knowing great stories when they saw them, were desperate to get them into the magazine but were restrained by a moratorium imposed from above.

By the February 1920 issue, *Boys' Life* had become such a force in American life (and such a lucrative employer of freelancers) that it was able to attract the two biggest figures in American journalism, war correspondent Richard Harding Davis and muckraker Ida Tarbell, to write, respectively, a surprisingly tough-minded parable about a troubled businessman and "good turns," as well as an admiring piece on Abraham Lincoln as a proto-Scout. The illustrations by some of the best magazine artists of the era are stunning. Yet, there is almost no mention of Scouts and their acts of bravery.

Nor is there still in July 1920 – though the notion of noble sacrifice and heroism crop up again in a brief news item about the death of former Scout Carl Newberry, who had been part of the rescue team of the British steamship *Wellington* that had sunk while Newbury tried to bring it to port. Through *Boys' Life*, Scouting seemed to be inching its way back into the heroism business.

Finally, that return is signaled in the June 1922 issue. In the "National Council News" section, officially edited by Chief Scout Executive James E. West, the lead story is about the National Council meeting held the previous March in Chicago. There, the story says, "Commissioner Beard enthusiastically praised the remarkable record of Scout achievement in Life Saving for the year, as well he might. There having been 147 medals for conspicuous service in the saving of life at the risk of a Scout's own life." That's it. But, with the new medals in place, training programs underway at Scout camps around the country, and new rank requirements in the *Scout Handbook*, Dan Beard was ready to bring the Honor Medal back into the public eye.

Indeed, the next issue of *Boys' Life* (August 1922) devotes most of its first editorial page to Scout lifesaving stories; and West gives over his entire page to telling even more Honor Medal stories. Scouting never would again hide its heroes.

Industry Standard

For the next twenty years, the BSA through *Boys' Life* regularly would celebrate its life-saving award winners through this same format – usually embedded in James West's national Scouting news section (now called "The Scout World") in the form of two or three multi-paragraph award stories, followed by lists of winners of Honor Medals and Certificates of Merit. These sections seemed to wax and wane less because of the qualities of the stories rather than by the size of the editorial space that month.

There were variations, of course, especially it seemed right after meetings of the National Court of Honor and the confirmation of a whole new cohort of award recipients. Thus, the *Boys' Life* issue of January 1937 not only featured a photo at the top of "The Scout World" of Star Scout **Robert Armstrong** of Spokane, Washington, receiving his Honor Medal, but continues with two more pages later in the magazine describing other Honor award rescues.

Obviously, letters to the editor and whatever survey tools *Boys' Life* had at the time continued to convince its editors and BSA leadership of the ongoing popularity of these stories.

And yet, it also should be noted that after thirty years, this coverage of Scouting's heroes had become pretty stale and formulaic. The awarding and reporting still was being managed by many of the same figures (notably Beard and West) who had created this format. But they now were getting old – with Beard in his eighties and West in his sixties – and they seemed quite content with the status quo. Since they essentially were beyond challenge, nothing was going to change.

By comparison, the rest of the world (and the world of Scouting and *Boys' Life*) *had* changed – in some cases, radically so. The stories of brave marines at Belleau Wood during World War I were long gone, as were stories about that exciting new technology known as *radio*. The biplanes that filled the pages of the magazine in 1919 now were supplanted by images of sleek new bombers and fighters. The boys in the pages of those early issues who had grown up in the optimism and excitement of the Roaring '20s now were raising a new generation of Scouts in the dark days of the Great Depression and under the growing threat of another world war.

There had been technological innovations as well, along with the rise of hugely influential new cultural institutions. Leaps in the quality of printing quickly made themselves known in the pages of *Boys' Life*: three color printing (though still used sparingly and mostly in ads); a huge increase in the use of photographs – which themselves were far sharper than the soft focus images in the early magazines; a much greater emphasis on graphics and design; and most importantly, an explosion in comic strips and cartoons.

The latter should not be surprising. Today, the 1930s are considered the Golden Age of Comics among collectors with good reason. All-but unknown the decade before, comics exploded on the scene in the 1930s with the creation of such iconic publications as *Superman, Batman* and the whole panoply of DC comic heroes. It also was the era of the first great Disney movie cartoons, culminating in *Snow White* and *Pinocchio*. Meanwhile, daily newspapers across the country carried pages of comic strips, from already ancient comics like *Mutt and Jeff* to *Blondie* to the iconic *Little Orphan Annie* and *Krazy Kat*. As much as an artistic form, comics defined the '30s.

As a magazine dedicated to reflecting the interests of its 300,000 juvenile readers, there was no way that *Boys' Life* could not become increasingly populated with this new art form. And thus, by that same January 1937 issue, with its single concession of a photograph of one Honor Medal recipient, the magazine featured a cartoon or line drawing with at least 50 percent of it being advertisements.

And that was just the beginning. The magazine also now had added a panoply of its own proprietary comic strips scattered throughout its pages. They bore forgettable names like "Danny Dimdawn's Diary," "Killo Watt in 3037" by "Stratos Phere," "Good Turn Bobby," and "Brainy Bill and Beefy Ben" – and featured equally forgettable storylines.

This new and dynamic visual look obviously appealed to the Boy Scouts of the Thirties, because in the years that followed it consumed more and more of the magazine – leaving little space for narratives about the latest Scout Honor Medalists. By the February 1940 issue, with its famous Norman Rockwell cover painting of a Scout praying in a pew with his grandfather titled "A Scout is Reverent," almost all BSA news (including West's "The Scout World") consisted of photographs with extended captions. Dan Beard's page was devoted to a memorial to his old friend Douglas Fairbanks Sr., a silent film star who was popular to the grandparents of the magazine's current readers.

Clearly the world was moving on and at least one part of traditional Scouting was being left behind – and the most remarkable part of the program with it. Scouts still were saving lives (in fact in record numbers) and their stories still were being carried in local papers and distributed by wire services around the country. But on the ground, at the level of the Scouts themselves, their presence was shrinking. Something had to give.

Rethinking the Past

As it did with many features of modern life, World War II changed almost everything. The United States entered the war an industrial country; it emerged at the dawn of the atomic/space/information age headed into the greatest period of prosperity it ever had known. It faced a new and implacable foe in a Cold War and was about to experience the greatest demographic bulge in human history: the Baby Boom Generation.

All of these forces would transform Scouting as well. The BSA soon would enjoy record membership; first in Cub Scouts and then, by the 1960s, in Scouting. But the organization also would have to compete with a whole host of new distractions, starting with television and the rise of other youth programs (such as the Little League) and concluding with the computer, smartphone, and Internet. The GI Bill and the Interstate Highway system brought Scouting's next generation of youth to the suburbs. Although a better site for recruitment, it also put America on the road in endless moves – taking away the continuity crucial for the six or seven years it took most Scouts to complete the program and earn their Eagle.

Babe Ruth bat ad, Boys' Life, August 1923.

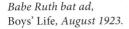

Taxidermy ad,
Boys' Life, *November 1960.*

Before it was done, with Boomers aging into adulthood, Scouting would radically change its image, if not its philosophy. The old emphasis upon the outdoors, camping, and hiking would remain, but they would be matched by career and leadership training, tech skills, high adventure, and a host of other programs designed to prepare youth for the complexities of the new global economy. And it all culminated in what would be considered by many to be Scouting's greatest creation, the Eagle Scout service project – not only the largest youth service initiative in history, but also the crowning touch on the Eagle award, the so-called "PhD of Boyhood."

With such a multitude of advertising distractions and peripheral influences, it would have been easy for the Honor Medal to fade into obscurity – especially since its greatest supporters either were dead by the end of the war (Beard, Seton, and Roosevelt by 1946) or retired (West). But in the face of everything, Scouts still were saving people – and the stories of those rescues remained compelling as ever. No part of Scouting understood this better than *Boys' Life*. It already had been the public's arbiter of the most important Honor Medal rescue stories for three decades. Now, unfettered by any requirement to embed those stories in the news section, the magazine was free to look for a more compelling way to tell that story.

Thus, in the February 1945 issue of *Boys' Life*, Westinghouse published a full-page comic telling the story of wireless communications. Elsewhere in the publication, Royal Crown Cola ran an equally elaborate comic – *"The Adventures of R.C and Quickie"* – that featured our heroes rescuing a circus crowd from a runaway lion. Remington Arms offered a full-page comic of a boy using his rifle to shoot a troublesome fox. It is entitled "ACTION with a Remington .22"

Meanwhile, through the war, the magazine also had run a pair of on-going comic strip-style features; one explaining different modern technologies (such as how helicopters work), the other providing short biographies of famous figures in aviation, from airplane designers to aces.

Boys' Life *magazine, February 1945.*

It all came together, fitfully, in a full page comic on the inside back page of the January 1947 issue of the magazine. It is entitled "Scouts in Action" and credits to Bob Brent and Fred Kida. Featuring all of the dynamic comic ink work of the era, it opens with the image of a late 1930s coupe in forced perspective rushing through debris-choked flood waters and surrounded by storm winds that toppled power poles and crashed a rowboat into a house. The corner box reads: "On a late summer evening some years ago, near the port of Noank, Connecticut." From inside the coupe, the radio is crackles, "Attention all! The storm is getting worse! Abandon all homes near the coast!" and a voice balloon reads "A fine time for a Sea Scout skipper to be away on business! Wonder how the Scouts are doing without me?"

The comic continues through a total of ten panels, telling the story of this Sea Scout skipper as he meets with his Scouts and learns that they have stood guard over the community awaiting his return. One already has been cut in the forehead by flying glass (and tended to by the Skipper's wife – always in the exact same profile indoors and out). Together, man and boys go back out into the storm on patrol guarding the neighborhood from looters. At the dock, where the exploding waves more resemble flames than water, the Skipper is informed that the crew's ship has gone to take a doctor and medicine to a nearby island.

"Scouts In Action" illustration,
Boys' Life, *January 1947.*

Then two panels are shown of the Sea Scouts at work. In the first, the banner reads: "And so it went – this spectacular tale of Sea Scout courage! Sea Scouts standing duty at the fire alarm boxes for days! Distributing hundreds of telegrams!" The next panel shows two of the Scouts in trench coats carrying a little girl on a stretcher, under the banner: "Rescuing the injured!"

The penultimate panel shows the crew, all in uniform, meeting at the Skipper's house after the experience. Boards nailed over the windows are a reminder of the disaster. The Skipper's wife stands to the left, holding the baby. The Skipper stands to the right. As he is saluted aboard the meeting, he says to the Scouts, "Boys, I've got nothing to say to you except this." It is the first complete sentence so far in the comic that doesn't end with an exclamation mark. ". . . I want to shake hands with each man, humbly, and with admiration!"

Then the final panel: a close-up of the handsome, rawboned Skipper, in suit and tie, standing before an American flag that has apparently been strung up for the meeting. He says: "I was afraid you Scouts would be hog-tied without my leadership. But I was **dead wrong!** I learned that leadership takes care of itself, because **Scouting** is leadership!"

Perhaps, a bit over-the-top by modern tastes, but what the comic may lack in narrative and dialog it more than makes up for in its dynamic, slashing illustration. Moreover, partly due to the subject matter, it is distinctly more exciting than the many other editorial comics and advertisements found elsewhere in the magazine. Even the comic adventure serials that *Boys' Life* had attempted over the previous decade – including ones with crashing airplanes and other motifs designed to goose up the action – lack the visual excitement of this first "Scouts in Action," mainly because they lack the authenticity of a real-life location.

It's easy to see why the initial "Scouts in Action" would earn a strong enough response from readers to justify making it a regular entry. And yet, after seven decades of subsequent entries of this comic feature, there also are some disturbing elements in this premiere entry.

The most important is this: Did the events portrayed in the comic *actually happen?*

At first glance, the story seems real. There is, after all, a precise location; not to mention a key figure, the Skipper, who seems to be derived from real life; most of all there are the details of the storm, the phone boxes, the name of the Crew's boat, the Sea Scouts Carl, Lloyd, and Ken, the wife and baby. And yet, the closer you look, the less substantial the story becomes. For example, there is no precise date, just "some years ago." The Skipper also has no name, nor do we ever learn the last names of the boys. But most of all, other than the meeting after the storm, we never learn the *consequences* of the event portrayed. In particular, were the boys honored in some way for their sacrifices? Did they earn any BSA honor or merit medals that would validate this story?

The result, after the initial thrill from the story, is a disquieting doubt about the whole thing. If it is real, why is *Boys' Life* being so cagey about crucial facts? If it is fictional, the decision by the magazine to include so many phony details almost constitutes editorial fraud on its young readers.

This editorial confusion reached a zenith later that year in the September 1947 issue that tells a (literally) incredible story of two Air Cadet Scouts. This "Scouts in Action" stretches across the upper half of two pages near the back of the magazine and claims to tell the story of Tom Naylor, age 17, and "Huddy" E. Hudson, squadron leader in a training flight "from Wickersham at

SCOUTS IN ACTION by BOB BRENT and

I'LL NEVER FORGET THE AFTERNOON OF OCTOBER 30, 1946. I CAME *THAT* CLOSE TO NOT REMEMBERING *ANYTHING* I CAN STILL SEE AN OBITUARY COLUMN READING : "DARN FOOL AIR SCOUT TOM NAYLOR, (THAT'S ME), AGED 17, AND "HUDDY" E. HUDSON, SQUADRON LEADER AND TOP-RANKING PILOT OF LONG EXPERIENCE, TOOK OFF FROM WICKERSHAM AT SAFFORD, ARIZONA, WHEN ... "

Safford, Arizona" on October 30, 1946.

So far, so realistic. But then the story-line quickly heads into territory that beggars belief. Young Naylor wants to attempt some aerobatic moves in their double open cockpit monoplane, but Huddy warns him off, saying that, with only two lessons, he is not sufficiently trained for such hijinks. But Tom ignores him and, as soon as he gets the stick, throws the plane into "chandelles and Immelmann turns" and other looping and spinning stunt maneuvers.

That's when the flight – and the narrative – spins out of control. In the course of a spin, an unprepared Huddy is flung about in such a way that his sleeve releases the catch on his seatbelt and he is tossed out of the plane into the open air at 5,000 feet. Luckily, Huddy is wearing his parachute (thought balloon: "Yipe! – Where's the r-ripcord?").

Happily, the chute opens.

As he parachutes down, his concern turns to Tom, who is in a full dive towards the ground. Cut to Tom, who looks back and realizes that Huddy is missing and that, with his limited skills, he must save the plane…and himself. He manages to pull the plane out of its dive and make a nearly perfect three-point landing.

Talking to a farmer who has come up to investigate, Tom admits that he is less relieved about surviving the landing than he is scared of Huddy's wrath. But, in the final panel, Huddy is nowhere to be seen (presumably he survived his own landing), but rather, Tom is at the next Air Cadet meeting, where he is explaining: ". . . and that's how Huddy made the Caterpillar Club [for parachuting out of a plane] and I got my solo certificate instead of an obit[uary]!" The flight commander has

his arm around the boy's shoulders, saying, "To put it mildly, fellers – a happy ending that almost wasn't!"

Really? Can this story possibly be true? On the one hand, it must be: *Boys' Life* has provided us with names, ages, dates and location. And yet: an insufficiently trained teenaged pilot decides to go rogue and attempt maneuvers beyond his abilities – an action that *ejects* a passenger nearly a mile up in the air . . . and he is honored for his actions with a solo piloting certificate? Not arrested, not the subject of an FAA investigation, not stripped of his certification and thrown out of Air Cadets, but honored by his adult leader and subjected to good-natured ribbing. How could this scenario have possibly occurred in this manner? Neither *Boys' Life* nor Brent and Kida are saying.

"Scouts In Action" illustration,
Boys' Life, *September 1947.*

This problematic approach continues through the end of 1947. Then, in December, something happens – "Scouts in Action" is gone – replaced by another comic by Brent and Kida entitled "The Eagle Trailer" featuring Eagle Scout Mickey Merritt. Adding to the confusion, "The Eagle Trailer" looks just like "Scouts in Action." The rescue of a little girl off a rock projecting from a cliff in the face of rattlesnakes is suitably thrilling with a resemblance to what we saw with Air Cadets falling out of airplanes . . . and yet it is obviously fictional. The one real difference is that this comic contains a brief explanation of how to create a stretcher from two poles and Scout shirts – a real-life tutorial that only adds to the confusion (and is a first glimpse of many such tutorials to appear in "Scouts in Action" in the years to come).

Clearly, something was happening at *Boys' Life* – a debate over whether to tell true stories or fictional ones; and if non-fiction, how much information to provide on the under-aged participants and what the selection criteria should be.

The result of that debate was unveiled in January 1948 – "Scouts in Action" was back with no question as to whether the comic was based on real events. The individuals in the story (including the two Scout rescuers) are named, as is the precise location, and the chain of events leading up to the save – including, shockingly, the death of two of the victims. There simply is no precedent for this in the 35-year history of *Boys' Life*.

Brent and Kida have returned in style. Perhaps it is the resolution of their doubts (or more likely the extra couple months they had to work on the strip) but this particular entry is a noir masterpiece, perhaps the best drawn "Scouts in Action" ever. The doomed women in the boat in the opening panel are given individual features. The water images are all impressive – none more than the stunning presentation of water streaming off Scout LeRoy Camp's elbow as he swims toward one of the women. Every stone in the bridge over the water is detailed, and the silhouettes of the Scouts atop that bridge are carefully articulated. But perhaps most impressive of all is the image of Scout Camp as he races towards the water, stripping off his shirt with his campaign hat flying off his head. It is a textbook lesson on how to capture motion.

The Heroes of To-day

Scout Harold Pullen

Scout Harold Pullen of Atlantic City and Scout W. LeRoy Camp, Jr., were on a bridge over a dam when they saw a boat containing several girls drift over the dam and smash on the rocks below.

Totally disregarding their own safety, Pullen and Camp jumped into the swirling waters and with great difficulty brought the girls to shore.

 The Remington Arms Company presents the Remington Award for Heroism—a Scout Knife with shield engraved as shown—to each winner of the Heroism Medal.

Look for another hero next month!

The image in the final panel is indelible: a long shot of the two Scouts coming ashore to meet other Scouts, holding between them the limp body of one of the women. Is she one of the rescued? Or one of the dead? Her limp legs offer no clue.

The box at the bottom of the final panel reads:

A few months later, as befitting their bravery, Scout Pullen and Scout Camp received Gold Honor Medals!

All the pieces now had come together – and on the first try. This second attempt, the one in which *Boys' Life* editors finally decided what they truly wanted to do with the comic, should be considered the true beginning. In the years to come, "Scouts in Action" sometimes would be as good as this inaugural strip but it never would be better. And though the comic would evolve over time – notably with the dedication of the final panel to a portrait of the hero(es) and the image of the medal earned – "Scouts in Action" never would stray far from the design of that January 1948 entry.

As for the young readers of *Boys' Life* in January 1948, "Scouts in Action" must have struck like a thunderbolt. Not only was this definitely *not* the kind of content they associated with the magazine but, astonishingly, it was *true*. These were real Scouts in these stories; young men their age whom they might well meet at some future Jamboree or other Scouting event. These weren't supermen, just well-trained Boy Scouts who stepped up to apply those skills in life-threatening situations. And it was this ability to *identify* with Scouting's heroes (thus the increasing use of close-up portraits through the years) that proved the critical step in quickly giving "Scouts in Action" the pre-eminence it has held in *Boys' Life* and youth publishing ever since.

"Scouts In Action" illustration,
Boys' Life, *January 1948.*

Production Standards

Though the feature has changed little since Aaron Derr took over the job, the nature of his work has evolved with the technology revolution. It used to be that, on his request, Aaron would receive a computer print-out of all of the recent award winners, in batches of six months. To that list of names, "someone from the National Court of Honor would append one or two sentences of descriptions of rescues involved.

"From that list, I'd pick twenty or thirty candidates I liked," he says. "That is, which had the greatest potential for the comic book high-style treatment." When selected, the National Court of Honor would send him the complete medal applications for those selected and he'd winnow the list down to six narratives.

"These days, all of that information is on the BSA headquarters server. I just call up the list" – it's usually about 150 to 200 nominations over the previous month. Of these, now that we've expanded our 'Scouts in Action' coverage to three stories per month, I still pick twenty to thirty: three per month, or eighteen, plus a cushion of a few more in case some stories drop out because of legal issues or some families don't want to participate."

"There's no real magic to it," Derr continues. "I just go through the list and pick out the ones that seem most worthy and that lend themselves to visual treatment."

Aaron also is constantly vigilant to the need to vary the content of these stories; to display the remarkable range of rescues made by today's Scouts. "I try to balance the most compelling stories," he says. "I constantly worry about stories of people caught in rip currents. It seems like I get more of those stories than any other, so I'm always wary of using another one."

"I want to keep things varied – ice rescues, fire rescues, water rescues...all while trying to find the most worthy stories." Whenever possible, Derr tries to mix up the entries geographically: "I don't want two or three stories in a row from the Pacific Northwest or New England or anywhere else."

Age, too, is a variable that Aaron keeps an eye on. He tries to include Cub Scouts whenever possible, though he knows that the criteria for medalists at that age (ten and under) is not as high as for Boy Scouts, Venturers, and adults. The most astonishing stories, he admits, typically involve the oldest Scouts and adult Scouters.

Ironically, the one form of diversity that Derr says he never applies in his selection process is ethnicity. That's because Scouting (continuing the century-long precedent) still has no entries in its paperwork for a Scout's race or ethnic background. "The result," says Aaron, "is that I usually am as surprised as the readers by the race of the young hero in the latest edition of 'Scouts in Action.'"

A final criteria Aaron employs in his section is the sensitive nature of many of the rescues. Not only do visually static or low-key rescues – overdoses, Heimlich maneuvers, allergic reactions – rarely make the magazine's pages; but neither, in most cases,

do especially gory scenarios, such as traumatic amputations, extreme burns, or deaths along with those saved. "I want nothing too heartbreaking for the kids," says Derr.

He recalls one story that featured the spectacular visuals of a mountain climbing team. But the actual event – a mother falling into a crevasse, being rescued, but dying afterwards – "was just too much for our readers." Similarly, the story of two Scouts driving off a man who was attacking their mother was deemed too much the stuff of nightmares.

By the same token, when an extreme story *does* make the pages of *Boys' Life*, its visual presentation usually is muted. Many of the Honor Medal stories in this book – such as Scouts saving people who have lost limbs or been severely burned or are suffering from spurting arterial wounds – are presented differently in "Scouts in Action" (like a severed arm being tucked under the victim or blood as added shading), to represent the actual event from a more genteel angle.

The ultimate example of this is the story of the Scout hit in the side by a model rocket that appears in the next chapter. Recognized as an appropriate topic for a "Scouts in Action" comic, the image of the impaling rocket is as sanitized as possible – far from the reality of the actual smoke, blood, and flames that happened in real life.

That isn't to say that the images that remain aren't compelling. For example, the shark attack rescue by Brookner W. Brady Jr. in Chapter 3, that ranks as one of the greatest acts of Scouting heroism of all time, is presented with the most powerful imagery imaginable, but there are no visible bite marks or clouds of spilled blood in the water.

Some stories simply are too complex to be presented in "Scouts in Action." The ultimate example of this during Derr's tenure was the Little Sioux disaster. The details of the tornado attack were so horrendous, the stories of injury and heroism so numerous, and the immediate aftermath so moving that they simply could not properly be encompassed into a single (or even multiple)

page comic. Rather, it was a story that screamed to be told as an oral history, over numerous pages, by its participants.

That is exactly what Aaron Derr decided to do and he also chose to draw upon his extensive journalism skills to report it himself. The result was one of the most moving Honor Medal stories in the history of the magazine, made even more touching as it was told in the simple words of the Scouts themselves.

Afterward, it was back to work, finding stories for the six months of the magazine.

N CAMP

From Life to Art

When creating a single "Scouts in Action" entry, Derr and illustrator Grant Miehm conduct a series of pass-offs to each other over the course of several months. It begins with Aaron following up on his selection of stories and names, contacting the prospective subjects or, more properly in most cases, their parents.

Given that there typically are more than 300 Honor Medal and Medal of Merit recipients each year, the fewer than 50 that ultimately are selected represent only small part of the total pool – which inevitably leads to disappoint from those Scouts (or, more accurately, their parents) who believe themselves deserving.

Among those medalists who actually are selected, the problem can be just the opposite. "You would be surprised by how many subjects – and their parents – initially say 'no,'" says Derr. "Some are shy; others are embarrassed. Still others have already had so much attention – newspapers, TV crews, honors ceremonies – that they just don't want anymore."

"What I tell them is that their stories are inspirational to other Scouts. That the message to those Scouts is: 'You too can do this, you have the training,' and that they may help in the future to save more lives."

Most, in the end, agree. Next, Aaron asks them for any visual materials they may have for the story – a portrait of the heroic Scout, newspaper photographs, etc. – as well as a precise factual description of the actual rescue event, including details of the location, the clothing everyone was wearing, the types of automobiles, and so on. Some of this is available from the official statement made by the Scout in the medal application.

Finally, Aaron prepares the Scout and his or her family for the result. "I tell them that 'Scouts in Action' is like watching a movie based on your favorite book and that we can't put in every detail; but rather, we try to capture the *spirit* of the event. We don't change the story but sometimes we have to fast forward through the details."

Often, the most delicate matter that Derr must deal with relates not to the heroic Scout but rather to the behavior of others (sometimes friends of the hero) during the rescue.

"In many stories, there is a group that is swimming when someone starts to drown. All of the rest bail, while that one Scout stays in and does the rescue. We usually reduce that to 'while others panicked …' and we don't show that group. In several stories, it's actually adults – even law enforcement personnel and EMT's – who freeze and don't know what to do. And, in a surprising number of cases, it's a Scout that gets into trouble and his fellow patrol members think it's a joke – with only one Scout realizing the gravity of the situation.

"In those delicate stories, we try to keep the focus on the hero and minimize the lack of contribution by the others. That seems to satisfy the Scout and his or her family."

With subject approval in hand, the story next is packaged, bundled with two dozen others, and sent off to illustrator Grant Miehm.

When he receives the packet in Canada, Miehm says, "The process of creating 'Scouts in Action' begins with my reading through the profiles … I distill that material down to produce a brief, written summary of all the rescues. Then Aaron and I confer to make sure we both understand the important details of each event."

"Next, I'll write the scripts – all captions and dialogue, and a description of the action for each panel. Aaron then will edit those and tweak anything that he feels may need to be adjusted.

"I then do a detailed layout for each page with the edited copy and all the page elements in place, to give the editors a solid idea of how the final page will look and how the story is going to be told visually. And again, Aaron and all concerned will review that and may request any changes they feel are necessary."

"We try to be as accurate as we can be," says Derr. Both he and Miehm conduct endless Internet searches, looking up locations, vehicles, equipment, uniforms and so forth in order to "convey the spirit of the event" as precisely as possible. "It is important for us to know if it was a Ford Explorer or a Honda SUV. If a lifeguard throws a flotation device, we try to find out if it was shaped like a life preserver or a lozenge. That kind of detail may not seem important, but for some reason it really is.

"We also want to make sure that the young readers understand what the proper procedure is for a particular rescue – even if the Scout in the story didn't follow it. That's why we always put a disclaimer at the bottom of the page noting that fact. We don't want to teach wrong techniques."

To make sure they haven't missed anything, Derr says, "I pass the drafts around to other people at the magazine and BSA for their opinions. It's a useful double check."

"The finished pencil stage comes next," says Miehm. "Each of the panels is drawn out as a fully finished illustration without color. The expertise of the *Boys' Life* editors then comes into play once more, to make sure all the details are correct and that the rescue is being portrayed properly."

"Finally, I execute the ink and color stage. The page is inked on traditional 'Bristol'[white paper]board using a brush and / or a pen, scanned into the computer, and colored in Adobe Photoshop. The text is created using Adobe Illustrator. All of the files for each page are uploaded via an online file transfer site after editorial approval, to appear in print several months later."

It's a busy life – especially beginning in January 2015 with the addition of "Scouters in Action," an adult version of the comic in *Scouting* magazine. Miehm adds: "Handling the workload is time-consuming but that doesn't lessen my enthusiasm for doing it. Coordinating with Aaron on scheduling and keeping things up to speed is crucial to maintaining the high standard of art and writing on 'Scouting in Action' and its sister pages, and to getting them done on time."

Approximately four months after Derr's original selection, Miehm puts the finishing touches on the last of the "Scouts in Action," "More Scouts in Action," or "Scouters in Action" pages in the packet. Given the long lead times of the magazine, the first of these entries will appear in *Boys' Life* and *Scouting* four to six months after completion.

Drawing the Story

Grant Miehm joined *Boys' Life* at the end of 1999 to be the freelance artist on "Scouts in Action" – that is, he worked on the initial drawings for the page. Once he proved himself, Miehm was given the added duties of writer, designer, and colorist, eventually packaging all of the "Scouts in Action" related material.

Like Derr, he was comparatively new to Scouting and to "Scouts in Action." "I'd seen 'Scouts in Action,'" he remembers, "but I wasn't aware of its importance among readers."

By the time he came to the magazine, Grant already had a memorable career. "I was born and raised in Canada. My parents were average, working people and were not involved in doing creative work at all."

"I've drawn for as long as I can remember. As a kid, I even drew on the walls of some of the houses we lived in as my folks redecorated. There are large drawings I did buried under the wallpaper of those houses to this day, I'd imagine."

Miehm admits to having been a "comics nut" since childhood, heavily influenced by comic art and television and movie animation, as well as being a voracious reader." He also was, albeit briefly, a Scout: "I was a Cub Scout and I guess it's no surprise that I [earned] my artist's badge."

"After high school, I studied broadcasting but it wasn't for me. I toured all over central and eastern Canada as a professional musician for a few years after that, before leaving to study art in the New York City area. I subsequently graduated from an intense course dealing with illustration, design, narrative art, and comics."

To the comics world, Miehm is best known – indeed he remains something of a legend for having revived the popular 1940s comic book hero, the "Shield" for the DC Comics' Impact imprint.

"I created a contemporary version of that character from the ground up, writing the series' bible, plotting the book and providing the art. It's nice too, that *Legend of the Shield* seems to be fondly remembered."

At DC Comics from 1988 to 1992, Miehm worked on a number of well-known comics, including the *Flash, Justice Society, Green Arrow,* and *Starman.* He subsequently worked on Marvel's *Namor: The Sub-Mariner* and *The Avengers* For television, he drew for Disney's *Gargoyles* and Saban Entertainment's *Mighty Morphin' Power Rangers.*

Asked if it is different working for, say, Marvel versus the Boy Scouts of America, Grant answers like a true artist: "I don't feel there's a difference between working for one publisher versus another when it comes to producing work, because for me, my focus is on storytelling, first and foremost. An artist has to bear in mind the needs and instructions of the editor, of course, but telling the story always is the most important thing. My approach to

doing that, in regards to 'Scouts in Action,' is very different from the approach I took to doing the mainstream superhero work I did for Marvel and DC comics, for example."

Miehm diplomatically adds that "'Scouts in Action' has had no shortage of talented craftsman working on it over the years, to be sure." But asked to pick the predecessor he admires the most, he picks a *Boys' Life* illustrator who never worked on "Scouts in Action," but rather on a 40s comic in the magazine called "Space Conquerors" as well as a number of features. His name is Lou Fine (1914-1971).

Fine, who drew *The Spirit,* is considered one of the greatest illustrators of the Golden Age of Comics. "I think Lou Fine did great work at *Boys' Life,*" Says Miehm.

Today, Grant Miehm lives in the area where he grew up. Over the years "Scouts in Action" has consumed ever more of his career; first with the increase of his duties on the comic, and then with the expansion of the comic itself up to three times monthly.

Rather than be intimidated by the added work, Miehm seems more enthusiastic than ever: "'Scouts in Action,' 'More Scouts in Action,' and 'Scouters in Action' are among the most creatively intense projects I've ever worked on. It's always an exciting challenge, and far more than something that merely pays the bills. Handling the workload is time-consuming but that doesn't lessen my enthusiasm for doing it."

Looking back, Grant Miehm seems surprised about the unlikely path his career has taken. "I knew about the awards a Scout could earn," he says, "but the Honor Medal wasn't something I was familiar with. I quickly became aware of its great significance though, after taking over the creative duties on 'Scouts in Action.'"

That understanding also has grown with the years and with it Grant Miehm's emotional commitment to his work . . .and to its subjects:

"It's difficult to express what I feel regarding the importance of 'Scouts in Action' as something that inspires readers," he says. "Whether a Scout is motivated to rescue someone or to follow the ideals of Scouting more closely, that's a huge thing. I bear that in mind with great reverence as I work on the feature."

"As I read through the various rescues, I'm deeply humbled by the courage that Scouts constantly display. These boys – these young men – are incredibly brave. I'd never be able to muster the courage they do or take on the extreme risk that can be endemic to saving someone's life. One of the greatest blessings God ever gave me was to be allowed to work on 'Scouts in Action' and its companion pages. If providing a positive influence for millions of boys is part of my legacy as an artist, that's something I'm very, very proud of indeed."

Iver Johnson Bicycles ad, Boys' Life, October 1925.

Telling the Images

Aaron Derr now is 44-years-old. Running "Scouts in Action" has consumed a quarter of his life and, for now, he has no intention of leaving it or *Boys' Life* magazine. Like Grant Miehm, he never intended to wind up in this job but now he can't let it go.

Growing up in Dallas, Derr graduated from Louisiana State University in Baton Rouge with dreams of becoming a sports journalist. He took his first step along that path landing a job at the *Lake Charles (LA) American* as a sportswriter. From there, he jumped to magazines, working for the annual *Beckett Price Guide to Baseball Cards*, an excellent way-station for an ambitious young man wanting to the learn the long form of sports writing and gaining a deeper knowledge of a particular sport.

From there, like every young person in his profession, Derr dreamed of working at the national level – and at the supreme American publication in his world: *Sports Illustrated.* So, when a headhunter called to say that *SI* was looking for editors in New York City, he jumped at the opportunity. His fiancée, who had relatives in the Big Apple, went with him, and they were married in Morristown, New Jersey, in 2001.

Buescher Saxophones ad, Boys' Life, *February 1924.*

The job turned out to be with *Sports Illustrated for Kids*…not quite the Big Leagues but certainly Triple-A. But then something unexpected happened: Aaron discovered he *loved* the job. There was something wonderful about writing for young people – of awakening them to the possibilities of the world, of inspiring them to emulate their heroes, of showing them the path to greatness. To his own astonishment, Derr realized that it was young people he wanted to write about; sports was secondary. It wasn't

long before he jumped to an even bigger youth publication: *Time Magazine for Kids*. He was happy.

But it wasn't to last. On September 11, 2001, Aaron was working at Time Inc. His wife, Karen, was in the Empire State Building when the airliners hit the Twin Towers. The Empire State, they later learned, was the secondary target. In the days and weeks that followed, New Yorkers were reduced to shell-shocked zombies as the news carried endless stories of horror and death (but also featured staggering acts of heroism). The couple remained in the Big Apple for only a short time after the attack as the area's high cost of living made it difficult to raise a young family. So they made the move to sunny North Texas.

There, he knew, besides being his home was the headquarters of the country's largest magazine for boys, the *Sports Illustrated* of youth publications: *Boys' Life*. If only he could find work there. But there was one very big problem (or at least he thought it was): Aaron Derr never had been a Boy Scout and *Boys' Life* was the official organ of Scouting.

It was the measure of Derr's talent that he not only was hired by the magazine but within two years was offered ownership of the crown jewel of *Boys' Life magazine*: "Scouts in Action."

In the years since, Aaron has presided over more than 250 entries of "Scouts in Action." What began as a sporadic, half-page panel now has grown to a full-page panel, a second full-pager containing two lifesaving stories and (beginning at the start of 2015) yet another full-pager, "Scouters in Action."

"It strictly was the product of demand," he says. "We kept hearing from readers that they wanted to read more heroism

stories about folks involved in Scouting that were older than the typical teenaged Scout. And because the subjects are adults, these can be some of the most compelling stories."

Needless to say, this expansion is both a credit to Derr's work and a near-tripling of his workload. Yet, he still manages to make time at least twice a year to get out into the field to work on other features. There is another motive to get out as well:

Aaron's eight-year-old son. As he was being interviewed for this book, Derr had just completed a week of afternoons spent at Cub Scout camp. And thus, like many of his adult readers, the boy who was never a Scout now has become a Scouting volunteer.

"My son is just starting to read 'Scouts in Action,'" he says. "And I'm beginning to appreciate more than ever the role it plays in enabling kids to see their own peers as true heroes...and dreaming they might become one themselves."

It may surprise many readers of "Scouts in Action" that Aaron Derr has *never* met Grant Miehm in person. He only can remember talking to the man on the phone a couple times. But it's a long ways from Dallas to Ontario, Canada, and illustrators are notoriously reclusive.

What may shock those same readers is that Derr also never has met one of his Scout heroes face to face. "I know that a few recipients have attended the BSA Annual Meetings over the years; but no, I can't say I've ever met one of my 'Scouts in Action' subjects in person."

There is a reason for Derr's odd reticence: objectivity. The same obsession with getting the details of the story right also drives him to keep his distance from his stories for fear that their intense emotional content will affect his decision-making. "I want to do the best I can for my readers," he says. "When I go through the selection process I always try to keep in mind that the story is not for that one person but for the 1.2 million *Boys' Life* readers out there. I want *them* to be inspired."

And yet, for all of his efforts to keep his distance, Aaron Derr has come to realize that it is impossible not to be affected by the stories he tells: "The honor of doing this work only grows on me by the year," he says.

Boys' Life *promotional ad, January 1925.*

"I appreciate these boys and men even more than when I started. I've become their biggest admirer. They really are true heroes."

"The ultimate measure of a person is not where one stands in moments of comfort and convenience, but where one stands in times of challenge and controversy." – Dr. Martin Luther King Jr.

CHAPTER

7

A New Century of Heroes

*"I knew we needed
to get up there because
I was pretty sure it was bad."*
- Life Scout Jesse Rothgeb,
immediately following the tornado that hit
the Little Sioux Scout Ranch in 2008.

The *Western World* is the weekly newspaper serving the small town of Bandon, Oregon, (population 3,066) a former logging and fishing village, now a tourist town with a famous set of golf courses nearby.

The paper's front page photo on May 14, 2015, over the title "Earning their Badges," shows a group of Scouts from Troop 31, in the classic 21st century half uniforms of Scout shirts (only one wears a neckerchief) and baggy black shorts, sitting or kneeling in a circle in what appears to be the waiting room of a doctor's office. One Scout (according to the story his name is Timmy Merriam) is lying on his back on the carpet with papers and medical bags on his chest.

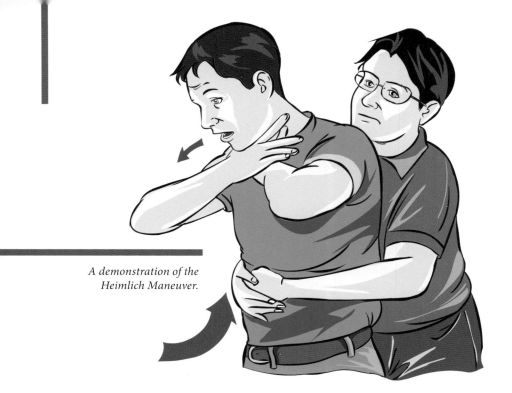

A demonstration of the Heimlich Maneuver.

Kneeling beside him, and obviously instructing the boys, is gray-haired Dr. Hank Holmes of the Coast Community Health Center. Dr. Holmes, an Eagle Scout, is in the words of a troop volunteer, "… giving back and doing a good turn daily."

On this day, Dr. Holmes is doing that good turn by instructing the Scouts on the use of an automated external defibrillator, using young Merriam as the "unconscious" victim lacking a pulse. The Scouts are watching intently, no doubt because the doctor has warned them that they may have to use the device to save a life one day.

Welcome to lifesaving in the 21st century, a new world in which 15-year-olds are being taught to use a sophisticated piece of medical technology that didn't exist eighty years ago – and until the past decade would have cost thousands of dollars and only be used by professional medical personnel in a hospital.[47]

It goes without saying that Scouting has evolved over the last century: from boys in campaign hats and puttees hiking from their homes to the nearby woods to set up their canvas pup tents and chopping down trees for fires; to merit badges in computer gaming and sustainability; to a separate STEM awards (science, technology, engineering, and math) program; and to the Scouting *Handbook* available as smartphone app with lifesaving, first aid, and safety programs at one's fingertip. And much of that change has been the result of an even more radical advances in technology over those decades.

Today, the most influential lifesaving technology, one that has transformed the nature of rescues, was unknown fifty years ago. It is the Heimlich Maneuver (now officially called "the abdominal thrust" though the old name endures in daily language), first described by American thoracic surgeon Dr. Henry Heimlich in 1974. Though the Maneuver remains somewhat controversial (not for its effectiveness, but on the range of its application – coughing and backslapping now are the prescribed first steps before abdominal thrusts), there is little question about its effectiveness in saving the lives of choking victims. Today, it is hard to believe that for many past generations, people regularly died from choking on a piece of partially swallowed food when backslapping failed.

Part of the appeal of the Heimlich Maneuver is its simplicity – both in concept and in application. For Boy Scouts, even Cubs, it still can be performed with considerable likelihood of success, even on large adults. Indeed, by ramming their abdominal diaphragm into the nearest table edge or chair, Scouts and Scouters even have been known to save themselves.

The impact of the Heimlich Maneuver on Scout rescues cannot be underestimated. One obvious reason for this is that whereas drowning is both comparatively rare and requires a distinct scenario (skating on lake ice, swimming in the ocean, canoeing down a river), the potential for a choking incident appears with every meal, and in every location from a picnic to a restaurant to the family dining room or kitchen. Another is that while CPR is only rarely successful (despite the myth), and wounds, poisoning, and broken bones are complicated to treat, the Heimlich Maneuver has a very high likelihood of success even for the untrained.

The widespread adoption of the Maneuver, especially in Scouting, can be seen as a watershed moment in the story of the Honor Medal. In Scouting's first six decades, one witnessed the gradual evolution of lifesaving and first aid techniques. After 1974, technology – especially with the rise of digital technology and its underlying "Moore's Law" of packing exponential degrees of innovation into a powerfully small size – begins to regularly present brand new emergency tools, while at the same time making existing hospital equipment affordable to everyday consumers.

That's not to say that innovative techniques and tools weren't available to early Scouts. Note that a large number of drowning rescues successfully concluded in Scouting's early years were due to the use of "artificial respiration/resuscitation" or its predecessor – chest compression. By the 1920s one sees the first mechanical resuscitators used by ambulance crews. But the reality (at least in some cases until the 1950s) was that nearly all a Scout or Scouter could do was to stop the bleeding, treat for shock, immobilize the broken bone or get the victim breathing, and then keep that person stabilized long enough to load him or her into a wagon – or later an ambulance – sometimes after a long human carry out of the mountains or woods, and to a doctor or hospital. We have noted already the number of occasions in the early Honor Medal stories where the victim (and sometimes the injured rescuer) merely was taken to a nearby house and made comfortable while a doctor was fetched.

The great turning point in the story of emergency medicine cer-tainly was World War II. For the first time, field emergency hospitals were set up close to the front lines (sometimes too close) that were capable of performing sufficient emergency surgery to keep GIs alive and stabilized long enough to be evacuated to full-service hospitals. The result was that the lives of thousands of wounded soldiers were saved.

This process continued to evolve during the Korean War, most famously portrayed in the movie, *M*A*S*H*, and its companion television series. The crucial improvement in medicine during this war was the advent of the helicopters that replaced ambulance trucks. Next, add jet transport aircraft – and by the Vietnam War, the Medical Corps could set as its goal that of saving every soldier who was still alive when he arrived at the field hospital.

By the new century and during the wars in Iraq and Afghanistan, this emergency process continued to accelerate. Many of the sophisticated surgical and diagnostic tools that had existed only at major stateside hospitals forty years before could now – miniaturized and computer-controlled – be moved right up to the battle zone. Combat doctors in these mobile laboratories now were able to achieve extraordinary levels of patient care – to the point that if a soldier wasn't killed outright in combat or during an ambush, he or she almost was guaranteed to survive. Again, thanks to Moore's Law, the costs for this equipment rapidly decreased while being redesigned and simplified for a new life on the consumer market. This widespread distribution was accelerated by a growing demand by institutions (schools, offices, etc.) for such emergency equipment as portable defibrillators and oxygen masks.

Life Scout Alex Huggins of Cape Girardeau, Missouri, received the Heroism Medal in January 2012.

Meanwhile, another medical revolution was taking place out on the battlefield – medics found themselves armed with a new generation of antibiotics, field dressings, splints, intravenous injection devices, coagulating powder, and shock treatments. These migrated to public hospitals almost immediately, and soon thereafter, thanks to the survivalist movement at the turn of the century, into the retail market.

But the biggest breakthrough in lifesaving in the 21st century didn't come from the world of medicine but instead from Silicon Valley and the high tech world. The 1990s saw the appearance (and the global adoption in the 2000s) of three major electronics technologies all invented in the miracle year of 1969: the microprocessor, the Internet, and the cell phone. The microprocessor, the so-called "computer on a chip" not only made the other two possible, but also with 20 billion of them now in use, made them the most ubiquitous products in human history.

These chips brought digital intelligence to every corner of daily life. The Internet not only gave individual consumers access to the world's accumulated knowledge, but also linked together 3 billion "Internet surfers" in a global economy. As for the cell phone, it evolved into the "smart" phone of today with access to hundreds of thousands of software applications ("apps"), many of them designed to help users contact emergency personnel, locate themselves in the wild, and instruct in first aid.

It is a rare Scout today who, faced with an emergency rescue, finds himself truly alone in the world. With global wireless coverage combined with GPS, Scouts now can explore the remotest places in the country – safe in the knowledge that should an emergency occur, emergency rescue personnel not only can be contacted almost instantly but they will know where to go within the distance of a few feet.

But there is more. Dan Beard's greatest fear was that of brave Scouts dying in a rescue because they were insufficiently trained. The Internet offered the answer. Now any Scout that is armed with a smartphone, laptop, tablet or even smart watch instantaneously can find instructions, even videos, on how to deal successfully with almost any medical emergency. Better yet, while awaiting the emergency rescue personnel, the Scout rescuer can even use the camera on one of these devices to transmit live images of the victim's injury to a doctor possibly hundreds (even thousands) of miles away. By 2010, these devices were beginning to add mobile health features and apps ranging from blood pressure, oxygenation, and pulse rate monitors to actual electrocardiographs. And more was to come.

Sometimes technology revolutionizes the very heart of traditional institutions, but just as often its impact is around the edges. A Boy Scout may replace his dirty, dog-eared copy of the *Handbook* with a digital version on a tablet but the Scout Oath and Law remain unchanged. Scouts still hike, camp, cook over campfires, learn to tie knots, and perform first aid – though the instructions now may sometimes come via an on-line video and the hike be tracked by satellite.

And Scouts still save lives – more than ever. But the *nature* of both the crisis and the responses have changed subtly since the beginning of the 21st century. Choking rescues are only the most obvious example – a crisis that wasn't even seen as a rescue situation until the last forty years. Drowning still is a source of many rescues, of course, not least because swimming, kayaking, and sailing still are central to the Scouting experience. But modern kids are far less likely (and thanks to industrial fencing, less able) to find their way to dangerous swimming holes and other sites. By the same token, in northern States, both kids and adults now are far more likely to skate at a local rink than to make their way onto a frozen lake. And, needless to say, street car, horse cart, railroad, and wagon accidents are exceedingly rare these days.

By the same token, with the rise of electric cars and the replacement of other gasoline-powered motors, we likely will see fewer solvent fume and gasoline fire rescues.

That said, the burdens of modern life have brought a whole new set of problems – not least cardiac arrests. The training that those Bandon, Oregon, Scouts received was not coincidental – three of the most likely lethal rescue situations that a 21st century Scout or Scouter is likely to encounter are

choking, an automobile accident, and a heart attack – rare scenarios in the Honor Medal's first half-century.

The second transformation the technology revolution has had upon 21st century lifesaving has been *temporal*. It is unlikely we ever will again see a repeat of the Scouts on Table Mountain in 1922, a story that unfolded over 24 hours – from the lightning strike to the encampment and first aid treatment, to the race over and down the mountain, to the wagon rescue to the transfer of the injured. In a similar situation today, emergency assistance would have been called by cell phone within minutes after the hikers recovered their senses. A rescue helicopter would have arrived within the hour – and the injured Scouts would have been wheeled into

a hospital emergency room minutes later.

In other words, the duration of modern Honor Medal lifesaving rescue is likely to be shorter today than in the past, and (in theory) more likely to be successful. But that doesn't make it any less intense or worthy of honor. On the contrary, now it is the expectation that any victim still alive at the time of the rescue (and certainly upon the arrival of emergency personnel) is likely to survive. The onus now is on the Scout or Scouter to devote an almost superhuman effort to make sure that this is the case. By the same token, if there even is the remotest chance that a victim caught in a dangerous situation still might be alive, the pressure to make the rescue – even at the risk of one's own life – may even be greater.

Equally, in the shortened interval during which a life must be saved, it is incumbent on the Scout rescuer to make the best use of any technology at hand, from a ventilator to a defibrillator to on-line videos to Skype... skills not even imagined by Scouting a century ago.

Not surprisingly, then, many of the Honor Medal and Medal of Merit recipients of recent years reflect the changing nature of life – and sometimes death – in the 21st century:

• A glimpse of the future: Within just six days in August 1977, Life Scout **Mahlon Ozmun**, 17, of Denver, Colorado, saved *two* lives using the Heimlich Maneuver he'd learned in Scouts. Ozmun was working as a busboy at a restaurant in nearby Arvada when, on August 21, diner Daisy Lord began choking. Mahlon ran to her assistance, and using the Heimlich, dislodged a piece of food caught in her throat. On August 26, Mahlon's skills again were called upon, this time to save diner Ivan Thompson, similarly choking on a piece of food.[48]

Eagle Scout Lawrence Sellers and his mother, Tanya, prior to the presentation of his Honor Medal in 2013.

• The students at King College Prep High School had just finished their final exams and headed over to the nearby Vivian Gordon Harsh Park to talk and celebrate. It was a late January day in 2013 and a cold rain drove them under the cover of a nearby awning. There, they huddled, talked, and laughed … until there was a burst of gunfire.

Driving past the park, two young gang members had spotted the group of students, mistook them for rival gang members, and opened fire. Hadiya Pendleton, fifteen-year-old, was hit in the back by a bullet and killed.

The story stunned the nation. Just one week before, the beautiful young Hadiya had performed in front of President Barack Obama (whose home was just blocks away from King College Prep) at his second inauguration. Now she was dead and a shocked nation mourned. The First Lady attended Hadiya's funeral; the President mentioned her in his State of the Union Address; and Harsh Park was renamed Hadiya Pendleton Park. Her name has become a symbol of senseless gang violence.

Almost unnoticed in the press coverage of the tragedy was an act of remarkable heroism. In that same class group gathered out of the rain in Harsh Park was Eagle Scout **Lawrence Sellers**, 16. When the gunfire erupted, Sellers, not concerned for his own safety, instead used his body to shield a friend from the attack. It cost him a bullet in the leg.

"I did what I needed to do," said Sellers. "I didn't think I would receive an award, but I'm honored."

Asked what he would do about gang violence, Sellers replied that there was no simple solution, but "if most of the children that are out there now were in Scouting, they would know right from wrong better than they do now."[49]

A quartet of modern Cub Scout rescues:

• March 1999; Shirley, New York: Webelos Scout **Jason Nappi**, 10, was riding the school bus home with his classmates. Out the back of the bus, the students saw two helmeted teenagers appear on motorcycles. When the bus stopped at an intersection, the two motorcyclists raced up, yanked open the bus's back

For his quick response to a dangerous situation, Webelos Scout Jason Nappi earned a Medal of Merit. Jason is a member of Pack 551, chartered to St. Judes Catholic Church of Mastic Beach, N.Y.

door, and grabbed Nicole Fusco, 11. As they tried to drag her out by her feet, Jason grabbed Nicole under the arms and held on. Frustrated in their attempt, and seeing the bus driver now on the radio to the police, the kidnappers let go and roared off. Jason held onto Fusco until they were gone.

• On a family snowmobiling trip to the mountains near Monte Cristo, Utah, in December 1973, **Scott Folger**, 8, was riding with an adult family friend when their snowmobile got stuck. When the woman climbed off to push the still-running snowmobile, she slipped…catching her leg in the tractor mechanism and breaking her ankle. Young Scott, seeing her distress, quickly turned off the ignition and jumped off to the woman's aid. Once he saw her predicament and made sure the woman was safe, Folger ran for help. He ran the mile through the snow back to the main road, where he flagged down assistance.

The doctor who treated the woman later said that, given the nature of the accident (the wound and the cold), Scott probably had saved her life.

• On a January afternoon in 1993, Bobcat Cub Scout **Gregory Carney**, 7, and his sister Erica, 9, were dropped off by their school bus in front of their house in Indianapolis, Indiana. Discovering that their grandmother still was at work, the brother and sister used their key to let themselves into the kitchen.

Hearing a noise in the living room, they went together to investigate but found nothing. They were returning to the kitchen when a large man wearing a ski mask and gloves suddenly appeared. He grabbed Erica and pushed her down into a chair.

Then he grabbed Gregory and began to drag him toward the back door. There, he used one hand to pin the boy against the door while he reached for a bag and a shoestring and prepared to put it over Gregory's head. At that moment, the boy knew he only had one chance. As the man temporarily released him to free both hands to apply the suffocation bag, Gregory kneed him as hard as he could in the groin. At the same moment, Erica screamed at the top of her lungs.

Doubled over in pain and fearful of being discovered, the ski masked man grabbed both kids and pushed them out the back door. Instead of running away, brother and sister made their way around the house to the door outside of their grandmother's bedroom. Finding it unlocked, they ran in and used the phone to call the beauty shop where she worked.

But their grandmother was just arriving at the house. She called the police but the ski masked man already had run away.

• In August 2000, in Springfield, Virginia, **Kevan Olsen**, an 8-year-old Bear Cub Scout was out in-line skating with friends when he glanced into a yard and to his shock saw a boy hanging by his neck from a tree. It was Andrew Cunningham, 3, who had been climbing in the tree. He had slipped and fallen with the chin strap of his bicycle helmet catching in the v-branch of the tree – and now was strangling slowly. Beneath Cunningham, the little boy's friends stood watching, too terrified to help.

Kevan skated up, planted his skates in the grass, grabbed Andrew's legs and lifted him up, thereby taking the weight off his neck. With considerable effort, Kevan carried Andrew out of the tree, set him down against the trunk, and removed his helmet. He treated the boy for shock and waited for help. When Andrew's mother ran up, the boy told her that Kevan had saved him. In the end, little Andres suffered no injuries beyond a few scrapes and bruises to his face.

Life Scout Christopher Ortiz, a member of Troop 100, chartered to Lackland Air Force Base, San Antonio, Tex., received a Medal of Merit for the rescue.

Stories of bravery and competence from the dawn of a new millennium:

- September 1999, Life Scout **Christopher Ortiz**, 17, was at a family birthday pool party in San Antonio, Texas. His young cousin, Daniela Franco, 8, the birthday girl, was practicing her diving skills.

But as she came up from one dive, in the 9-foot-deep end, Daniela's t-shirt became tangled over her head. She panicked and sank beneath the surface. Seeing what was happening, Christopher dove and caught her as she neared the bottom. He then swam with his cousin to the surface, where Daniela's frightened parents helped the girl out of the pool. For Daniela, her birthday present from Christopher was her life.

• On the eve of Independence Day in 2004, Life Scout **Emanuel Meloul**, 15, was heading home from a fireworks show in Addison, Texas. Shockingly, directly in front of them, a pickup truck ran a red light and instantly was hit by an SUV legally driving through the intersection. No one in the SUV was hurt but the pick-up truck was flipped and skidded to the curb.

Emanuel already was on his cell phone to 911 reporting the emergency as he jumped out of the car and ran to the truck. When he saw blood dripping out of the shattered driver's side window onto the street, Emanuel knew he didn't have time to wait for an ambulance.

Joining others from his car, Emanuel lifted and tipped the truck back over onto its wheels. That done, he ran back to his car and pulled towels out of the trunk. Then, joining an adult at the truck, he found its driver, Eric Laxo, 21, in deep pain from two broken legs and a major neck wound. Instructing the man to use the towel to put pressure on Laxo's wound, Emanuel treated him for shock and kept the agonized man from moving and aggravating his broken limbs.

When police and emergency medical personnel arrived, Emanuel briefed them on the situation before they raced Laxo to the hospital.

• 2007: Eagle Scout **Roarke Baldwin**, 19, was shopping at a mall in Annapolis, Maryland, when he heard gunshots. While other patrons ran in panic to the exits, Roarke instead ran *toward* the source of the gunfire.

There, he found it – an off-duty Secret Service agent had intervened to stop a fight and now he was shot and lying in a pool of blood with a life-threatening wound to the hip.

Roarke applied direct pressure to slow the bleeding and treated the agent for shock. Paramedics and police soon arrived and Roarke gave them a complete report. The Secret Service agent made a full recovery.

• Star Scout **William Kent**, 16, was playing in shallow water at Sunset Beach, North Carolina, while on a family vacation in 2014, when he heard a cry for help.

It came from a man in deeper water. William swam towards him. As he did, he could feel a riptide forming around him – the same one that was dragging the man up ahead out to sea. Nevertheless, in the face of enormous danger, William swam on.

When he finally caught up with the struggling man, he grabbed him and swam to the side, parallel with the beach. That got them both out of the riptide and into calmer water. Although the man barely could speak, he managed to tell William that there were others still caught in the current.

Once back on the beach, William grabbed another boy and a boogie board and took off into the ocean. There, they found a woman on the brink of drowning. Putting her on his boogie board, they swam her back to the beach. William was about to head out a third time, when his mother called to him that two other swimmers had just been rescued and were on the beach and in need of CPR.

So William ran down the beach to where a crowd had gathered and found the two drowned swimmers lying on the sand. As he knelt beside one of them, a nurse ran out of the crowd and joined him at the other victim. They continued administering CPR until the paramedics arrived. Then William trotted down the beach warning others of the riptide danger and helping other swimmers out of the water.

• Life Scout **Reid Vaenuku**, 18, of Euless, Texas, was getting ready for bed when the cell phone charger he kept on his bedside table burst into flames.

Reid rushed into the bathroom for a glass of water to extinguish the flames. But by the time he returned the fire already had jumped to his bed and was out of control.

There was no time to waste. Reid ran down the hallway and shouted for everyone to get out of the house. His family made haste and Mrs. Vaenuku called 911 on the way out of the front door.

With his family safely outside, Mr. Vaenuku tried unsuccessfully to use a garden hose to spray through the broken window of Reid's room and put out the fire. However, a quick head count determined that Reid's younger brother wasn't with them.

Without hesitation, Reid ran back into the house. He found his little brother still asleep in his bed. Awakening him, Reid led the boy out, making him bend low to get below the heavy smoke.

Now with the entire family outside and safe, there was nothing left to do but watch. By the time the fire department arrived, the Vaenuku house was engulfed in flames. It soon burned to the ground. Although the family had lost everything; thanks to Reid, they did not lose each other.[50]

By the time the fire department arrived, the house was engulfed in flames. It was eventually lost, but thanks to Reid's actions no one was hurt.

Former Life Scout Gerald Christian "Reid" Vaenuku was a member of Varsity Team 273, chartered to Euless 1st Ward, LDS Church, Euless, Texas. He received an Honor Medal for his actions.

BOY SCOUTS OF AMERICA

S.I.A. ON THE WEB
• boyslife.org •
Audio, Photos & More!

Robert Kollar, a member of Troop 300, chartered to First Church of the Nazarene, Centralia, Wash., received an Honor Medal With Crossed Palms.

BOY SCOUTS OF AMERICA

FOR SAVING LIFE

- Life Scout **Robert Kollar** arrived one February morning in 1999 at his high school in Centralia, Washington, to find one of his friends in a heated argument with another student. Seeing the dispute was about to turn into a fight, Kollar intervened only to have the second student pull a knife and lunge towards him.

With not even an instant to spare, Robert grabbed the other student's wrist as he stabbed and, pivoting the attacker's arm under his own, he threw the boy over his hip and slammed him to the ground. Then he dove atop him, pinning the attacker down and knocking the knife out of his hand.

Within minutes, teachers from the high school arrived and turned the attacker over to the police. It was only then that Robert looked down at his hand and realized that he had been deeply stabbed. He was taken to the hospital to have the wound treated. Robert returned to class two days later.

In some rescues the victim proves to be the biggest threat:

- Venturer **Thomas Foust**, 17 of Glenview, Illinois, was driving with some friends when they saw a disoriented driver crossing the railroad tracks and suddenly turning right onto them. With wheels still spinning, the car quickly became stuck.

Seeing two trains roaring towards the car from opposite directions, Foust and his buddies jumped out of their car and bolted towards the stuck vehicle and its imperiled driver. There, they encountered Ida Kurtz, 83, confused and not understanding either her predicament or the reason for the young men swarming around her car. They yelled at her to get out. She refused to move.

Finally, with both trains dangerously close, Thomas gave up trying to reason with the woman and dragged her out of the car. They had travelled no more than ten feet when the first, southbound train slammed into Kurtz car at more than 80 miles per hour – spraying glass and automobile parts in every direction and spinning her car around onto the other, northbound track – where it was hit and all-but disintegrated by the second train. Amazing, neither Kurtz, nor Foust, nor any of his friends who had hit the ground just before the impact, were hurt.[51]

Venturer Thomas A. Foust, a member of Venturing Crew 156, chartered to the Glenview Community Church, Glenview, Ill., received an Honor Medal with Crossed Palms for his actions. It is Scouting's highest award for bravery.

S.I.A. ON THE WEB
www.boyslife.org
Audio, Photos & More!

• **Cody Hubl**, 10, a Webelos Scout from Blue Hill, Nebraska, was heading home from school with his brother and fellow students, when the bus they were riding in collided with a truck. Everyone was thrown either into the seat in front or to the floor. Cody briefly was knocked unconscious. When he awakened and looked around he realized that not only were the driver and many of the students injured but both the front and back of the bus were on fire.

Cody ran to find his brother, who had been thrown to the floor but not hurt seriously, and helped him up. Then he went in search of an exit. He noticed that a window above the driver's seat was open. Gathering up his brother and classmates, Cody led them to the window and helped them out one person at a time. He was assisted by people who had stopped to help.

Once out himself, Cody gathered together all of the students and led them to a newly-arrived emergency medical vehicle so they could be treated for their injuries.

• Life Scout **Robert Brown**, 17, was sleeping in a tent with several other Scouts on a campout near North East, Maryland, when an unexpected and massive thunderstorm hit. As trees crashed to the ground around the campsite, Brown, as senior Scout, left his tent to check on the status of his fellow Scouts in surrounding tents.

Realizing that the entire troop was in great danger, Robert roused the other Scouts and led them to a nearby shelter. Once in the shelter, he took a quick headcount and realized that one Scout was missing. In the thick of the storm (and before his fellow Scouts could stop him) Robert ran from the cabin back to the campground with falling branches and trees just missing him. He found the lone Scout in his tent and led him to the shelter.

Over the course of the next few minutes, while Brown and the other Scouts huddled in the cabin, the entire campground was destroyed and several people in the area were killed. But, when the skies cleared, Brown and the Scouts emerged unscathed.

Ranking even above the Heimlich Maneuver, easily the single most important contribution in this century – not to brave Scouts but to the success of their rescues – has been the universal availability of emergency 911 services. It appears, sometimes explicitly but more often embedded, in almost every story in this chapter:

- Scout **Brendan Milliner**, 11, and his brother, Cub Scout **Kelvin Milliner**, 9, of Rochester, Minnesota, were driving home in a van with their parents through a South Dakota blizzard, when Mr. Milliner slumped forward in the midst of a seizure.

Mrs. Milliner grabbed the steering wheel to keep the van on the road, while Brendan dove between the seats and down into the driver's footwell, where he pulled his dad's foot off the gas pedal.

But it wasn't enough – the van smashed into a signpost and spun around, flinging both Mrs. Milliner and Brendan out of the vehicle and onto the snow-covered highway.

Kelvin, who was restrained by a seatbelt, remained in the van, unhurt. He climbed out and saw that both his mother and brother were injured and unconscious. He tried to awaken his father but was unsuccessful. So, the nine-year-old walked out on the highway and tried to flag down a car. Perhaps because the blowing snow made him hard to see, no car stopped for him.

So, Kelvin, feeling desperate and alone, went back to the van. He put snow on his mother's facial cuts to stop the bleeding. When Mrs. Milliner regained consciousness, he instructed her to remain calm.

Then Kelvin went back to the road. Finally, an automobile stopped. Learning of the situation, the driver called 911 and, in short order, an ambulance arrived to take the entire family to the hospital.

Asked later by his mother how he knew not to move her, Kelvin replied that he had learned it in Scouts.

• Scout **Ralph Bryan**, 10, of Happy, Texas (near Amarillo), was driving home with his mother from a rained-out Little League game when they found themselves stuck in high water on a flooded road. With the car unable to move, Ralph and his mom decided to abandon the vehicle and strike out for dry ground.

Instead, the accelerating flood current swept them off their feet and carried them across an open field. Spotting a barbed wire fence ahead, they both grabbed it and clung on despite the fact that the barbs were slicing their fingers to the bone.

Regardless, the two struggled to pull themselves hand over hand along the fence to higher ground. Then Ralph's mother, already weakened from a recent major surgery, became tangled in the wire. While Ralph watched in horror, she lost her grip and was swept away. As the current carried her off, she shouted back at her son, "Don't let go, the water will go down pretty soon. Hang on!" But Ralph refused to listen. Instead, he also let go of the fence and swam in pursuit. When he finally caught up with his mother they still were in eight feet of water. And though she was exhausted and physically larger than her young son, Ralph managed to tow her back nearly 200 yards to the barbed wire fence. After a total of six hours in the water, mother and son finally managed to pull themselves along the fence to higher ground.

At last on solid ground, Ralph and his mother crawled into an abandoned house, where they collapsed in sleep. At dawn, the flood had passed and Ralph hiked out to a nearby road and flagged down a car that happened to be carrying a search party looking for them.[52]

• Largo, Florida: **William B. Davis**, a 17-year-old Eagle Scout, was driving his car when the automobile in front of him stalled on some railroad tracks at an unguarded crossing. As he watched, the young woman, Mrs. Deborah Roberson, desperately tried to get her car restarted, but only managed to stall the vehicle again.

Looking up the track, Davis saw a freight train approaching. Although it was time to act, there was no guarantee he would get either the car started or the woman out in time. So he did the one act left available to him: he used his car to ram the stalled car and shove it forward.

And he was just in time as only moments later the locomotive hit both cars (Roberson's in the trunk and Davis' in the nose). Both were spun around and all-but destroyed. However Roberson and Davis both emerged from their vehicles without major injuries.

Old nightmares
still reappeared
occasionally in
the new century:

- In June 2006, Scout **Colton Penton**, 11, of McNell, Mississippi, his mother and his brother, Dylan, 8, were leaving the home of the boys' grandmother, when her dog suddenly and ferociously attacked young Dylan. Knocking the little boy to the ground, the dog locked his jaws on Dylan's face and refused to let go.

As Dylan screamed, Colton ran up and punched the dog again and again, not stopping until the animal released its bite and ran off.

Next, Colton wrapped his brother in a blanket to keep him warm and fight the inevitable shock. He stopped the bleeding of Dylan's facial wounds by applying pressure with washcloths. Then he sat with his brother while his mother raced them to the emergency room.

In the end, Dylan Penton needed two hours of plastic surgery and 60 stitches. But thanks to his brother's brave intervention, he survived the attack.[53]

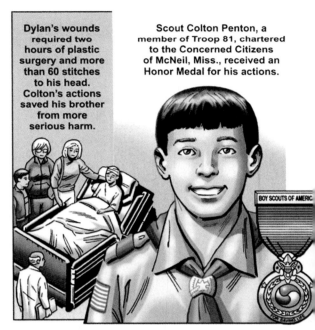

Dylan's wounds required two hours of plastic surgery and more than 60 stitches to his head. Colton's actions saved his brother from more serious harm.

Scout Colton Penton, a member of Troop 81, chartered to the Concerned Citizens of McNeil, Miss., received an Honor Medal for his actions.

- Eagle Scout **Jonathan Mathews**, 17, of Auburn, Georgia, was riding in a car with three friends near Athens when the driver lost control – the car skidded and rolled over three times. It came to rest upside down with its roof crushed in.

Somehow, Jonathan climbed out of the car unhurt, but everyone else was seriously injured – especially the driver, who had suffered a grievous head injury. Meanwhile, the car was leaking gasoline and threatening to engulf them all in flames.

Moving quickly, Jonathan carried the driver away from the car and then used pressure to slow her bleeding. He then returned to the car two more times, each time risking his life, to move the two other victims to safety.

Then, amazingly, Jonathan returned to the car for a fourth and final time to retrieve a gym bag full of clothes. He tore those clothes into strips and used them as bandages. Emergency personnel arrived soon after and were amazed at the risks Jonathan had taken to save his friends.[54]

• A group of friends were kayaking near Lithia Springs, Georgia, when one of the boys fell out of his kayak into a "hydraulic" – a mass of violently churning water in the Class V rapids. Although the boy was a good swimmer and wearing a helmet and life vest, the intensity of the water just was too much. Every time he tried to surface, he was sucked back under. As his energy began to flag, the boy began to lose his fight.

Others in the group found a rescue rope and threw it to him … but it was too short.

That's when Eagle Scout **Oliver Yowell**, 17, appeared in his kayak, fighting his way to the edge of the hydraulic. He timed his approach just right so that when the Scout again surfaced, the nose of Yowell's kayak was just inches away. The boy leaped and managed to hang on.

In that position, Yowell towed the exhausted Scout to an island just downstream. There, he and another Scout pulled the boy from the water and treated him for shock and hypothermia.[55]

• On a night in 2012, Life Scouts and brothers, **James E. Shelton**, 17, and **Patrick Shelton**, 15, were driving with their mother on a highway in their home state of Pennsylvania when, directly in front of them, an accident knocked an SUV off the road, through the guard rails, and down a hillside.

Mrs. Shelton quickly pulled over and dialed 911, while her two boys ran to help the victims.

Joined by a man who also had stopped to help, the brothers followed the screams emerging from the darkness down a steep slope. They found the SUV upside down at the bottom.

The driver of the vehicle was unharmed but his wife was trapped under the SUV. Together, the four braced themselves beside the vehicle and, somehow, managed to lift it high enough to pull the woman out.

That's when the driver of the SUV realized that his daughter was missing as well. The two boys immediately began to search for her, determining that she must have been thrown out of the vehicle as it rolled.

They found her near the top of the hillside, with a cut forehead and a broken hip. They administered first aid and kept her warm to prevent shock.

After the paramedics took the family to recover at the hospital, the Shelton brothers stayed to help the emergency crew clear debris from the road.

As always, there still are heroic Scouts who rise above their own burdens to save others:

• Scout Chad Dulin, 12, of Abilene, Texas, was at a Junior Leadership Training camp in New Mexico. Dulin, Scout Michael Scuttle, 13, and Life Scout **Richard Gregg**, 15, were busy scrubbing pots and pans on a bluff when a gust of wind blew one of the pots over the edge of a nearby cliff.

After warning the younger Dulin to stay put, Gregg and Scuttle took off in pursuit of the pot. As Scuttle went around and down to the base of the cliff as spotter; Gregg descended the cliff. When Gregg was about halfway down, Dulin, peering over the cliff's edge to watch, lost his footing and fell.

Hearing a cry from above and watching him tumble, Gregg scrambled sideways and blocked Dulin's fall. The two rolled together to the base of the cliff. Neither was hurt seriously.

"It happened so fast," Gregg told the *Fort Worth Star-Telegram*, "and I knew I had to catch him. People asked what I was thinking, but I honestly don't remember much of anything. Except I do remember thinking my legs might be broken and I wouldn't be able to play football this year."

Fearlessness seems to have been part of Richard Gregg's character. Not only did he save Chad Dulin's life, make the varsity fall football team as nose guard, *and* run on the track team, but he also suffers from rheumatoid arthritis and severe dyslexia.[56]

RICHARD GREGG'S FAST ACTION EXEMPLIFIED THE SCOUTING TRADITION OF SELFLESS SERVICE. A LIFE SCOUT WITH TROOP 260, CHARTERED TO THE WYLIE UNITED METHODIST CHURCH OF ABILENE, TEXAS, RICHARD RECEIVED THE HONOR MEDAL.

Macho Man

The life of young **Rudy Gonzalez** did not get off to a promising start. By age 13, his existence already was being defined by gangs, drugs, and violence. He had spent time in Houston Texas' juvenile justice system after being arrested for punching a teacher. His education seemed to be nearing its end while Rudy still was in junior high school. In fact, he spent less time studying than breaking into warehouses and stealing from grocery stores.

"I thought I was macho," Rudy later recalled. "I was on a fast track everywhere you don't want to be. I didn't know of any other lifestyle."

It was a chance encounter – and an unexpected one – with a Houston city police officer that changed the trajectory of his life. John Trevino wasn't only a cop, he also was the Scoutmaster of Troop 86. And, in a last ditch attempt to save the troubled boy, Trevino challenged him to prove how tough he really was by going camping with the Boy Scouts.

"He was creative in approach to getting involved in Scoutin Rudy says. "He sold on all the fun and c things about camp and invited me to j him on his next trip. course I accepted."

But then Trevino add one stipulation: "To though, I had to beco a Scout."

Rudy had been look for a way out of a life t had led to the death imprisonment of m of his friends. So, accepted the challe and became a Boy Sco

Just one year la in 1989, he faced ultimate test of what had learned in those months. A neighborh boy fell from the ban a nearby bayou, 20 down into racing muddy water. Rudy did wait to see what wo happen next. Inste he ran along the e of the water u he spotted a tree reaching out over the bank. Climbing up, he made his way out onto a sturdy branch over the water and waited. As the boy passed underneath, Rudy reached down and snatched him – then pulled him up onto the branch and to solid ground.

The boy nearly had drowned. So Rudy and his younger brother linked their hands and wrists to create a "human chair" – a skill they'd learned in Scouting – and carried him to safety.

Scout Rudy Gonzalez as a member of the BSA's *Annual Report to the Nation* contingent in 1991.

"I didn't panic because I knew what to do," Rudy told the media that had rushed to cover the rescue, "I didn't have a choice, anyway. I wasn't going to let the boy drown. As a Scout, I have a duty to help others at all times."

This act of bravery and self-sacrifice by a former troubled youth drew national attention, as well as an invitation to the White House to meet President George H.W. Bush as the first Hispanic member of the select contingent of Scouts to deliver the BSA's *Annual Report to the Nation* to the sitting U.S. president.

Now there was no going back. Rudy resolved to earn Scouting's highest rank, the Eagle medal. For his service project he took on a singular challenge: he managed the efforts of more than 200 prisoners on work detail, as well as a number of volunteers from local community service organizations, to restore an abandoned cemetery for African-American slaves and Civil War soldiers. Rudy Gonzalez earned his Eagle, one of the high points of his life, just before his eighteenth birthday.

His grades turned around as well – enough so to enable his graduation from high school and acceptance into Texas A&M University, where he double-majored in agriculture and international business. Despite the heavy class load, he still found time to help underprivileged kids, founding five Boy Scout troops and four Cub Scout packs in College Station, Texas. "I wanted those kids to see what Scoutmaster Trevino showed me."

"There is more to life than hanging out in the barrio," he said. "There is a whole different world that Boy Scouts can help them see. If it wasn't for the Boy Scouts, I would probably be in the gutter somewhere with the rest of my old crew."

And perhaps, he would not be alive today.

In the years that followed his graduation from Texas A&M in 2000, Gonzalez remained involved with Scouting, first as an intern and then as district executive at the Sam Houston Area Council in Houston. Then he was promoted into the job of district director at the Circle Ten Council in Dallas. Afterward, he moved to the BSA's National office in Irving, Texas, to serve as a business development specialist, membership specialist, and performance coach at Scouting U[niversity]. In May 2015, Rudy Gonzalez was chosen as the Scout executive for the Rio Grande Council in Harlingen, Texas.

A popular public speaker, Rudy uses those occasions to talk about his past to inspire other troubled youth to join him on a different path. He tells them: "There is a way out and Boy Scouts can help you find it." A deeply religious man, he adds, "I feel I am doing what God chose me to do and I am grateful to the Boy Scouts for helping me find my path. Like the Boy Scout slogan says,

¡Scouting – Vale la Pena!" [It's Worth the Effort!]

Millennial Heroes

Some stories showing the new 21st century world of Scouts in action:

• Scouter Gary Buscombe was attending a meeting of **Scout Troop 26** in Tulsa, Oklahoma, in September 2009 when, while answering a question from another adult, he collapsed to the floor in cardiac arrest. The Scouts and adults in attendance immediately went to his aid. One of the fathers, a retired emergency room doctor, instructed another adult to call 911, a third to start chest compression, and a Scout to fetch the troop's Automatic External Defibrillator (AED).

By now Buscombe's face was turning blue and both his heartbeat and breathing had stopped. With the pads attached to his chest, the AED automatically signaled the need for an electric shock and delivered it… then another.

They were successful.

Buscombe later writes: "By the time the ambulance arrived I was already sitting up, asking 'where am I and what happened?'"

At the hospital, and by remarkable coincidence, the cardiologist who was assigned to Buscombe was the same doctor, the father of an Eagle Scout, who had donated the AED to the troop. Thanks to the implantation of an internal defibrillator/pacemaker, Buscombe recovered and embarked on a program of raising money to provide AEDs to other non-profit organizations.

Rocket Boy

In one of the most excruciating rescue stories of Scouting in the 21st century, two Scouts from Dallas, Texas, saved the life of a third Scout from death by model rocket impalement. It is a disturbing preview of what Scout rescues may look like in the age of drones and autonomous vehicles.

On a windy day in October 2007, **Josh Raines**, 14, **Chris Rogers**, 15, and Connor McNeil, 14, were on a Scout trip at Camp Simpson in Oklahoma, several hours north of Dallas. Their group was launching model rockets on a range. All three had shot their rockets and were walking out from the launch site to retrieve them.

Meanwhile, another group of Scouts came up to the launch pad and fired their rockets. By an unlikely chain of events, a gust of wind tipped one of those newly-fired rockets in mid-flight, sending it shooting downwards, directly at Connor.

"I just looked up and it impaled me in the chest," Connor recalled. He screamed in pain. "At first, I just thought it was on top of his shoulder," says Rogers. "It was hot and he was screaming."

But the hard plastic tip of the rocket, still being driven by the now-smoking rocket propellant, had slammed into Connor's chest, breaking two ribs under his right arm and ripping a hole in his lung, stopping just an inch from the boy's heart.

"I felt the rocket moving in my body," Connor later would recall. He thought he was going to die. "I just said, 'Please God, if you want to take me, take me, but I want to stay here for a while.'"

His two fellow Scouts immediately set about saving him. Chris: "I could see that he had a rocket inside of him. I laid him down. And I took off my shirt and put pressure on it. Then I told Josh to keep pressure on it and I went to get help."

An illustration from Boys' Life in 1948.

Josh Raines stayed behind, maintaining pressure on the bleeding wound, treating for shock, and giving his terrified friend words of encouragement. "I kept telling him, 'It's all right; you're going to be fine; you're going to make it through this."

"I remember telling him, 'You'll look back on this and laugh,'" recalled Josh. "I kind of ran out of things to talk to him about."

He continued this until Chris returned, accompanied by two Scoutmasters, one of whom was a doctor.

According to the *Dallas Morning News*: "When [Connor's mother] Linda McNeil got the call about her son's accident, she headed north but didn't initially understand the seriousness. After hearing that a helicopter ambulance had been summoned, she got worried. On the road, she got a call from the hospital's chaplain.

"'He said, 'How long?' I said I was 38 miles out," she said. "He said, 'They want you to be here before they take him into surgery.'"

The BSA's Heroism Medal and uniform knot.

"She didn't recognize her son when she finally saw him. 'He looked like the Elephant Man,' she said. 'His chest was blown up. I laid my head on his shoulder. He turned his head and said 'Mom, it's going to be OK.'"

"Doctors told her the pressure the boys applied immediately after the injury saved Connor's life. She remembered doctors from all over the hospital showing up to view the unusual injury. Some snapped cellphone pictures. They gave her son the projectile in a bag."

Two years later, at the ceremony in which Josh Raines and Chris Rogers received their Heroism Medals, Linda McNeil hugged the boys' parents, saying "They saved his life. Without their Scout training, they wouldn't have known what to do. They are wonderful boys."

As for Connor McNeil, after a long and expensive recovery, he arrived at the ceremony in good health. Said his mom, "You know he's back to normal: He's [just been] grounded for two weeks."

Little Sioux

The disaster that befell the Little Sioux Scout Ranch near the Iowa/Nebraska border on June 11, 2008, ranks along with the Butte Mountain lightning attack and the Tennessee flood both seventy years before, as among the worst tragedies and greatest feats of lifesaving heroism in BSA history.[57]

There were over 100 Scouts, staff members, and adults that day at the 1,800-acre camp. The Scouts, aged 13- to 18-years old, had been invited to participate in a leadership training course at the Ranch, about 40 miles north of Omaha, Nebraska.

"These were some of the top Scouts in the area," Homeland Security spokeswoman, Julie Tack told the *New York Times*.

The Scouts were divided into two troops, "Red" and "Green," each with a different senior patrol leader (SPL) and pursuing a separate leadership training curriculum. According to Green troop SPL, 17-year-old Eagle Scout **Bradley Sundsboe**, "Dinner was at 5 p.m. that day. The weather was overcast but not too bad. All we knew was something big was coming between 2 p.m. and 2 a.m. the next morning."[58]

The Scouts were concerned but not frightened, having practiced emergency preparedness just that day.

After 6 p.m., the Green troop received a call from a local ranger telling them that funnel clouds had appeared over the nearby town of Little Sioux. Recalled Jesse Rothgeb, a 15-year-old Life Scout, "It was really dark. The wind picked up, and it was starting to get worse. So we told Doc [camp doctor Dennis Crabb, M.D.] to hit the sirens." It was almost too late. Until the phone call, the camp had received no official warning – because, it is believed, lightning had hit the emergency transmitter station near town. Now, a desperate Dr. Crabb began to crank the manual siren.

Both troops already had a procedure in place in which, upon hearing the siren, each member of the respective staffs would run off to their campsites to get kids out of their tents and into their assigned shelters. For the Red troop, this was the north shelter, a sizable building with a large brick fireplace and chimney. Red troop member Christian Jones, a 13-year-old Star Scout, recalled:

"I heard the siren, so I yelled to everybody: 'Hey guys, those are tornado sirens. We have to go to the north shelter.' That's when several staff members appeared, running down the road and shouting with urgency, 'Get inside the shelter!'"

Meanwhile, the Green troop, which had taken refuge in the east shelter, realized that its location at the bottom of a large valley made it particularly vulnerable. So the decision was made to evacuate and make a run for the sturdier and more securely located south shelter.

They almost didn't make it.

Bradley Sundsboe: "I got to the east shelter, popped open the door, and yelled, 'We're going down to the south shelter. Run!' I got near the back to make sure we got all the stragglers. Then the moment we got on the road, the wall of wind and rain just hit us, and it was really intense. I had never been in weather like that."

A moment later, Bradley heard on the radio that the tornado had touched down. It later was measured to be of F3 magnitude, with winds of 145 miles per hour, one of 28 tornados believed to have touched down in the state that day. This one went straight through the Scout camp.

Alex Norton, 14, was in the one-room north cabin shelter with his childhood friend, Aaron Eilerts. Eilerts had attended the event the previous year and had come back to teach others, including Alex. Moments after the storm hit, the power went off. The Scoutmaster told the boys to get under the tables. That's when the windows blew out. "It had all happened really fast," Norton recalled.

At the south end of camp, Bradley Sunsdboe knew the situation was desperate: "We were maybe a good 100 feet from the shelter when it got to the point that it was just crazy. I kept looking up... I was blinded by wind and rain, and was half-expecting to see the tornado bearing down on me."

"Then I heard somebody behind me yell,

'Ditch!'

Then I looked behind me and I didn't see anybody there. I just saw trees snapping and falling across the road. The people just weren't there anymore." He decided to push on.

Nearby, Jesse Rothgeb heard the same shout, and made a different choice: "It was kind of a split-second decision. It was just getting so intense. Trees were falling. We didn't know which direction the tornado was going. We figured it was safest to just get down." Into the ditch he went.

Bradley, as SPL, understood his duty: "There was a Scout who was having a bit of trouble going up this hill right by the [south] shelter, so I just grabbed him by the neck and threw him in. I was the last person in. I yelled to everybody, 'Shut up! Get down! Cover your heads!'"

Outside, Jesse was face down in the ditch as the tornado passed: "It was just roaring. It was really loud."

To the north, the disaster was complete. Camp quartermaster, **Alex Losen**, a 20-year-old Eagle Scout, ran for the administration building: "I saw the tornado as it passed... Some of the adults and I got inside the large closet in the center of the building. When part of the roof came off, all of the air in the building got sucked out. I couldn't even breathe. My ears popped so bad I couldn't hear anything."

Christian Jones and his group had made it to the north shelter building: "All of a sudden our Scoutmaster burst into the shelter and said, 'Get under the tables!' So we dove under the tables. The Scoutmaster closed the door, took two steps, and the door was ripped off the hinges."

"I heard the walls cracking and falling, and I heard the fireplace fall in. The sound was coming from everywhere. It was the worst sound I have ever heard in my life. Like the breaking of a thousand bones . . . crunching and cracking...it was terrible."

The estimated eight seconds it took for the tornado to pass through camp felt like hours to the boys along its path. Lying in the ditch, Jesse was astonished by the change: "Then it got really quiet. You could hear it going away. Trees were just littering the ground. We got up and got the last camper into the shelter."

The North Shelter as it stood before the impact.

After the tornado was long past and the skies cleared, Scouts across Little Sioux Ranch slowly emerged from ditches and side buildings, from the south shelter, the wrecked administration building, and the most heart-rending of all – the collapsed north shelter.

Now the rescue began. At first it was just the Scouts and Scouters treating the injured and tearing through the rubble looking for survivors. In time, neighbors of the camp and citizens of Little Sioux made their way through the fallen debris on the access road and joined in.

At the south shelter, the injuries were minimal – just one sprained ankle. Bradley did a roll call to make sure everyone was accounted for, then called up to the north shelter to determine their status. He was told that there were Scouts who were badly wounded and they should bring first aid kits now.

Jesse: "I knew we needed to get up there because I was pretty sure it was bad."

It was a devastating sight. As one young Scout, who arrived with the rescue team told the *Omaha World-Herald*, the camp had been wiped out. The house of the camp attendant had disappeared. "Sights I've seen, I'm never going to forget."

Among those searing images was the bodies of four Scouts killed in the collapse of the chimneys in a north shelter and, possibly, from the impact of a parked pick-up truck that had been blown into it.

Christian Jones:

"After the tornado passed, I stood up right away and I saw it heading away from us. It was really scary. Then I turned around to look at the shelter and all I saw was rubble. My friends were lying there. Some of them I could tell they were OK and some obviously weren't."

"The first person I saw was my friend Ethan. He had a sprained ankle and head trauma. I could tell he was in pain. He was screaming. A big block was on his foot. So we started moving stuff off of him."

Little Sioux hero Jack Pape receiving the 2011 American Spirit Award from Congressional Medal of Honor recipient Leo K. Thorsness representing the Congressional Medal of Honor Foundation.

Star Scout **Zach Jessen**, 14: "When I lifted my head up and looked around, there were no walls or roof or anything. Tables were twisted every different direction. Chairs were scattered everywhere. There were bricks everywhere. I got up. I started helping other people up and moving them to the side so we could get other people out from under the rubble. There were some people crying. We tried to calm everybody down.

"We took our shirts off and used them as bandages. We were tying them around wounds."

Bradley, Jesse, and other Scouts ran to the north end of the camp. Jesse: "We had to run to the administration building to get first-aid kits, and we had to climb over all of these fallen trees just to get there. We grabbed the first-aid kits and started climbing over even more trees. It was horrible. It took forever.

"We got up there to the north shelter and saw the devastation. The building was gone. It just wasn't there anymore. It didn't register at first. Then I realized it just wasn't there."

The Little Sioux Scout Ranch's flag pole - bent as a result of the tornado's force.

Jesse: "I helped one kid – his leg was crushed. Some kids were bleeding pretty bad. One kid couldn't move at all – debris had hit him in his stomach and chest. . ."

When the first ambulances arrived, it still took twenty minutes for volunteers to clear the road to get them through. Then it was a continuous parade of emergency vehicles and helicopters rushing 42 injured boys, including Zach and Christian, to the hospital.

But before he left, Zach had one last chance to look around. "I was still thinking that everybody would be OK, but that didn't happen. I saw that one of the kids in my patrol, Ben, had died. I felt helpless. I was really hoping that everybody would be OK.

"I didn't see Aaron anywhere. I figured he had already gone to get help..."

He wasn't the only Scout looking for Aaron Eilerts. So was Alex Norton, Aaron's best friend. They had been inseparable since preschool. He didn't find out until later that Aaron had been killed in the north shelter collapse, along with Josh Fennen, 13; Sam Thomsen, 13; and Ben Petrzilka, 14.

The National Weather Service's map of the tornado's path and intensity level.

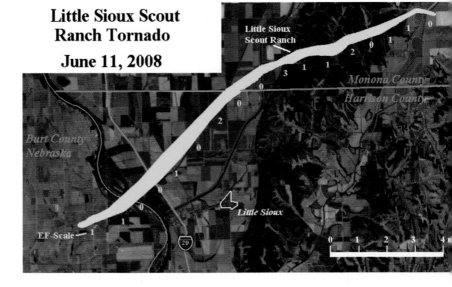

Little Sioux Scout Ranch Tornado

June 11, 2008

Said Steve Foster, a paramedic at the Burgess Health Center in Onawa, Iowa: "Total devastation is what I saw. I'm surprised there weren't more fatalities. I was so amazed by the composure of the Scouts who were able to help us. They were pulling rubble off other Scouts and trying to find their friends. They were offering first responder, first-aid services at the scene. It was great to have that much help."

Dr. Peter Daher, the emergency physician to whom Foster delivered the injured Scouts, said in awe: "They were heroes. These kids were so impressive. They were wet, dirty, and muddy. Nobody complained, nobody whimpered or cried, even the critically injured ones."

Later that day, Nebraska governor Dave Heinemen credited the Little Sioux Ranch survivors for responding "in true Boy Scout fashion." Iowa Governor Chet Culver said, "There were some real heroes at the Scout camp. They set up triage and were taking care of one another and saved many lives before emergency responders arrived. U.S. Secretary of Homeland Security Michael Chertoff was sent by President George W. Bush to visit the camp and express the nation's condolences. Chertoff said he was "particularly touched by the finest young people from this region being caught up in the...terrible tragedy." He added that "the reaction of the Boy Scouts was in the best tradition of what they're being taught."

Interviewed by MS-NBC, Scout survivor Ethan Hession, 13, was asked: "You said, 'If it had to happen it is good it happened at a Boy Scout Camp.' Why would you at the age of 13 say such a thing?"[59]

Hession's reply:

"Because we were prepared. We knew that shock could happen. We knew that we need to place tourniquets on wounds that were bleeding too much. We knew we need to apply pressure and gauze. We had first-aid kits, we had everything."

In the years that followed, Little Sioux Scout Ranch was rebuilt. The Scouts who survived the disaster returned and built a memorial chapel at the site of the north shelter where the four boys were killed. Another survivor, Marcus Ehlinger, for his Eagle Scout service project built a bridge at the Eastern Nebraska 4-H center and dedicated it to his friend Sam Thomsen. Other private memorials have been erected by the families of the victims. And each year, February 24 – now a statewide holiday in Iowa – is officially Aaron Eilerts Day of Service, coordinated by his childhood friend, Alex Norton.

On the fifth anniversary of the tragedy in 2013, a local television news station, interviewed Norton, now a 19-year-old Eagle Scout. He told the reporter:

"Not knowing the extent of the damage, the other campers reacted immediately, putting their emergency training into action. Everyone helped out, moving rocks, administering CPR, and making slings for people who had broken bones.

"It amazes me how well we take in what we learn," Norton said. "You never think you'll have to use it."

He credits the Boy Scouts who were there for saving lives.

"No one complained. We put our worries and our tears aside to help others," he told the reporter. "Our motto is 'Be Prepared,' and after that moment, we were prepared to do what we needed to do."

Looking Back and Ahead

Nearly a century after Dan Beard helped create the Honor Medal – and ninety years after he saved it by redoubling Scouting's commitment to training its Scouts to save lives (while saving their own in the process) the great man's vision faced its greatest test at the Little Sioux Scout Ranch. There, the descendants of Arthur Eldred and Dorris Giles, George Noble and Russell Grimes, in the direst of emergencies, exhibited leadership, resourcefulness, lifesaving, first aid skills, discipline, and most of all, incredible heroism, valor, and guts.

They not only passed this once-in-a-century test with astonishing grace but with unimaginable depth of fortitude. Two months later, the Boy Scouts of America showered the Scouts of Little Sioux Scout Ranch with awards: four "Spirit of the Eagle" posthumous awards for the lost Scouts and 123 Lifesaving awards.

But the biggest honor of all earned by the Scouts of Little Sioux was their validation to the world that Scout training saves lives. It augured well for Scouting and the Boy Scouts of America's Honor Medal program in the 21st century – and the thousands more lives that Scouts are destined to save in the years to come.

The official portrait of the 114 Little Sioux Scouts who met with President George W. Bush in the East Room of the White House on July 31, 2008.

Dan Beard would be proud.

EPILOGUE

*"My first thought was,
'This is going to be the way that I die.'
I then said to myself,
'No, I'm not dying here.'"*
Eagle Scout Matt Moniz
Mount Everest - Himalayas, Nepal.

At 11:56 am on April 25, 2015, the massive, 7.8 magnitude Ghorkha earthquake struck beneath the southern face of the Himalayas and flattened the nation of Nepal. In less than a minute, the quake, felt throughout the region, killed more than 9,000 Nepalese, injured more than 23,000 more, and created more than $5 billion in damage – 25 percent of that poor nation's GNP. Entire regions were destroyed.

On Mount Everest, both the climbers on the peak and those supporting them at the base camp faced their own unique horror. In particular, the sudden shake released a giant avalanche of 400 million metric tons of ice that raced down Everest's face. Nineteen people either suffocated under the wall of snow and ice or were fatally injured when flung against equipment or exposed rock and boulders. It was the single worst day in the history of the world's tallest mountain.

Seventeen-year-old **Matt Moniz** already had known considerable excitement (and fame) when he arrived at Everest Base Camp a few days before. He had set the speed record for reaching the highest points of all 50 states in the U.S. He also was the youngest climber to summit Mt. Makalu in the Himalayas, the world's fifth highest mountain. In 2010, at just 12-years-old, *National Geographic* magazine name Matt as its "Adventurer of the Year."

But it was Mount Everest that first had captured Matt's imagination as a 9-year-old boy. He already had visited the Base Camp three times, including supporting his father's successful attempt; now he was prepared to challenge the mountain himself. And in typical style, Matt also planned to follow a successful ascent by attempting the first ski descent of the Lhotse couloir – a portion of the world's fourth-highest peak nearby.

Just after dawn on the morning of April 25, Matt left the village of Lobuche with his climbing partner, Guillermo "Willie" Benegas (age 41) and Phura Sherpa, their guide. They arrived at the Everest Low Base Camp just before noon and started up the Valley toward their own camp. That's when the earthquake struck with such force that it threw Matt and scores of others, both on the mountain and in Base Camp, off their feet. Then came a roar from above.

Wilie Benegas (left) and Matt Moniz en route to Nepal in April 2015.

"You couldn't really see the avalanche until it was literally coming right through the clouds right on top of you," Moniz told CNN. He later would say, "My first thought was, 'This is going to be the way that I die.' I then said to myself, 'No, I'm not dying here.'"

Matt, Benegas, and their Sherpa guide dove behind a huge rock just before the rolling wave of ice struck. Huddling behind the boulder, they were protected from the impact that killed others with falling projectiles but it didn't spare them from the accompanying blast of arctic air. For nearly 30 seconds, the avalanche filled with "rocks, tents, laptops and debris" tumbled past them and, in Matt's words, "exploded like a bomb." At that moment the three climbers were trapped in a vacuum that sucked the air from their lungs, rendering them almost unconscious.

Then a terrible silence …

They looked around in disbelief. Everything within their sight had been destroyed. They themselves were covered in a heavy coat of powder. Then they saw the victims, dropped their backpacks, and ran to them.

Benegas described the scene as "unexplainable. A few seconds later and our lives would have ended." He knew the only thing to do now was to rescue the survivors. Ordering Matt to stay at the tents, he raced off to start working with doctors, paramedics, and EMTs performing triage on as many victims as possible.

At the triage site, Benegas encountered an unforgettable scene of carnage – "It was a close resemblance to a car bomb in Iraq. Bodies were dismembered. Doctors were frantic trying to remain in control."

Soon after he dove in to help, an animated Benegas was approached by Matt Moniz. Frustrated at not being allowed to assist the wounded and worried that others might die without his help, Matt ignored Willie's orders and hiked down to the camp to help – despite limited visibility and certain aftershocks. Benegas quickly stopped him: "I did not want him to experience this. No 17-year-old kid should experience this scene.

Everest camps

So I told him to go back to our tent and get hot water bottles for the many hypothermic patients."

Confused, Matt nevertheless did as he was told. "I spent the next fifteen minutes running between camps collecting every bottle that I could" and carried them to the triage area. Returning, the carnage was even worse than before and when Matt once again approached Willie, the older man again ordered Matt back his tent. Moniz: "Trying not to be argumentative, I had the same response, 'You got it.'"

But as he made his way back to his tent, Matt Moniz stopped. His conscience told him that he still was needed below. And so, for a second time, he disregarded Willie Benegas' orders.

The first person he encountered upon returning to the triage area was a doctor, who was trying to push a man onto a stretcher. Matt ran over and assisted him. "I asked, 'What do you want me to do with him?'" The doctor replied, "Carry him down to the International Mountain Guide (IMG) camp. With the "true character" and leadership skills that Benegas later would compare to an army general, Moniz gathered up five climbers – three Sherpas, a cook, and a Spanish climber (many of them still in shock) – and organized them to carry the injured man forty minutes over rock and ice to the other camp. After placing the man in a tent in the care of a Dr. Rachel Tullet, the team grabbed another stretcher and headed back up the mountain.

"We repeated the process of loading and carrying the victims for an additional three times, each rotation becoming faster and more coordinated. I felt comfortable and confident leading our team of six people; it was very similar to leading my patrol when I was patrol leader . . . these people didn't have to help, but they did at great risk to themselves."

On the second trip down with a victim, the region was stuck by a major aftershock that set off another avalanche. Not surprisingly, several carriers dropped the laden stretcher and ran for cover. But Matt called to them shouting, "Please, do not just leave him here." Instead, Moniz and his team lay over the injured man to protect him from debris. Happily, the avalanche was smaller and mostly missed them.

After three trips with the stretcher – not to mention having survived a life-threatening event – Matt stumbled back to his tent and collapsed in sleep.

Once he awoke, Matt set out in search of a satellite phone to contact his parents in Colorado. As he recalled, "It was kind of good because in Colorado the avalanche happened at around midnight so ... they didn't hear about it until they woke up."

On the other side of the world, Matt's parents knew nothing of the Everest disaster until the phone rang at 5 a.m.

His father, Mike Moniz, recalled, "It was an odd country code, it wasn't Nepal, and then by the time I woke up enough to realize it was a sat (satellite) phone calling in ... it was gone," Mr. Moniz tried to return the call several times . . . finally someone picked up the phone. "That person was on verge of breaking down and ... at that moment, I was thinking, 'Oh no. It could be incredibly bad news about Matt.'"

Mike Moniz finally realized the voice on the other end was Willie Benegas. "I said 'Is something wrong?' and he said, 'Yes we've been hit by a massive earthquake and an avalanche, and there are people dead around me. I have to go.'"

"He hung up. I could not get back to him. And so at that point, I had no idea what Matt's status was."

It took several minutes before the now-terrified Moniz family finally received a text reading: "Dad, are you there?"

"That was it," Mike said later, still showing his relief. Finally, the two connected by phone: "He was like, 'Dad, I cannot talk to you ... there are people injured everywhere and I have to help.' So it was a pretty emotional moment."

Moniz and Benegas spent another five days at Base Camp, assisting wherever they were needed and helping plan the evacuation. It took another week to reach Kathmandu. By then, news of the devastation across Nepal had reached the survivors on Everest. Moniz, who had developed a deep bond with the Nepalese people over the course of his visits, found himself torn between wanting to get home to his worried parents or staying to help.

Benegas: "As a 17-year-old kid, he had two choices in that moment: He could go home, be with his beautiful girlfriend, hang out with his twin sister, his mother, his father, in the comfort of his home, get a new iPhone, and have the guarantee of a good, warm meal. [Instead] He chose to come back to Nepal ..."

At the same time, the Moniz family did their own best to help. A successful entrepreneur and venture capitalist, Mike Moniz and his wife, Deidra Ann, established a rescue fund for the victims in Nepal. It raised more than $100,000 in emergency monies to hire both helicopters and 1,000 Nepalese porters to carry food to isolated villages across the country before monsoon season made them inaccessible. It was through these funds that Matt returned to Nepal. Just a few days earlier following a presentation to donors in Zurich, Switzerland, his father took him aside and handed him two pieces of paper: "It was a plane ticket back to Colorado and a plane ticket back to Kathmandu," Moniz said. "And my dad was like, 'Matt, you have a choice —(and) I chose Nepal."

For the next two weeks, Matt helped move food supplies to the epicenter of the April 25 earthquake in the Laprak Valley. It was dangerous work. Aftershocks, especially one on May 12 that was a 7.4 magnitude, killed scores more Nepalese and continued to set off avalanches, landslides, and collapsed buildings and homes. Despite this risk, Matt helped build a shelter for a woman who had just lost her husband. To restore sanitation, he dug 25 latrines for a village.

As Matt wrote in a *National Geographic* blog,

"The scene twisted my heart in ways it's hard to comprehend, watching the already traumatized citizens of Kathmandu running through clouds of brown dust, screaming and crying, wondering why this keeps happening to them."

Said his father: "Matt [felt] a tremendous amount of urgency to get some help, and… focus on some of the remote areas that are probably the last to get aid."

Benegas watched all of this with awe: "Throughout this month [Matt] always had a choice. He could have gone home and talked about what he could do; but instead he chose to remain in Nepal and to go outside and do it. The people in Nepal will always be grateful for his courage, charisma, and human kindness."

Aerial image of Mount Everest in Nepal.

Matt Moniz on expedition to the 8,000 feet summits of Cho Oyo and Makalu in the Mahalangur Himalayas in June 2014.

It was Longs Peak Council Executive John L. Coleman Jr. who, upon reading of Matt Moniz's story, approached Matt's parents about nominating him for an Honor Medal with Crossed Palms for his actions on Mount Everest and during the relief effort. It was, after all, an achievement that ranked with the greatest rescues in Honor Medal history, from Arthur Eldred to the Scouts on Devil's Peak Mountain to the boys of Little Sioux. Mr. and Mrs. Moniz admitted that, in all of the activity and excitement, they hadn't even thought of it – but they agreed it would be an appropriate award.

Moniz's nomination for an Honor Medal was signed by Coleman and Council Chairman Stephan K. Hucal. Attached to it was a recommendation/witness letter from Willie Benegas. The packet was mailed to BSA headquarters in Irving, Texas, on July 30, 2015. The application also carried Coleman's suggestion that the medal be awarded at the BSA's Top Hands meeting – a regular gathering at the end of August of the top Scouting professionals from every council in the nation.

The nomination form arrived at Boy Scout national headquarters on Monday, August 3. The first person to see the packet (as happens with every nomination for an Honor Medal, Silver Buffalo or other national BSA award) was Velma Cooks, Senior Secretary with BSA Regional Operations, and the lead administrative support staffer to the National Court of Honor.

Over the course of a year, Velma receives hundreds of these applications. Given their importance, her job is one that requires enormous precision and attention to detail. Moreover, it requires accuracy: even worse than failing to award a worthy recipient would be to successfully deliver the award to someone unworthy – or worse, a fraud. Like her predecessors spanning the previous century, it falls to Cooks as the first "filter" to make sure that these nominees are worthy of Scouting's most prestigious awards and that they will honor the BSA as much as the BSA honors them.

Besides recognizing, organizing, and filing, Velma has a second, equally important, task: *qualifying.* In this task she is assisted by her supervisor, Chuck Ezell, who looks closely through each nomination to make sure that it includes all of the requisite witness statements, factual details (such as dates), and signatures. Any nomination that fails to include all of these items is sent back immediately to the source Council, without judgment, to be completed and returned.

"There's really no rhyme or reason to the number or the timing which these nominations come in," says Ezell, a University of Tennessee graduate who has spent his life in Scouting and currently is the Department Manager of Program Impact and staff advisor to the National Court of Honor. "You would think there'd be more in the autumn, when troops do a lot of camping but our research has shown no particular pattern to lifesaving rescues."

Nor is there a pattern to the number of Honor Medal-worthy rescues, he adds. "In 2014, there were 75 Honor Medals awarded. Of course we looked at more [applications] than that. But other years it might be 30 … or 90. You just never know."

The final task in the qualification process is *categorization*. As it has been since the 1920s, all nominations that arrive at BSA headquarters are divided into two piles: one large and encompassing, the other small and exclusive. The former are those nominations in which not only was a life saved, but also that put the rescuing Scout or Scouter in danger – from moderate to extreme. This pile is on track for the Honor Medal for demonstrating "unusual heroism and skill or resourcefulness in saving or attempting to save life at considerable risk to self." ["Heroism" is defined by the BSA as "conduct exhibiting courage, daring, skill and self-sacrifice." "Skill" is defined as "the ability to use one's knowledge effectively in execution or performance. Special attention is given to skills earned in Scouting."]

Meanwhile, in the most select group in this pile – the dozen or so nominations recognizing rescuers put in extreme danger – are destined, if approved, for Scouting's highest award for lifesaving: the Honor Medal with Crossed Palms. They denote "unusual heroism and extraordinary skill or resourcefulness in saving or attempting to save life at extreme risk to self."

The second pile, that may be one hundred times larger, is a little more difficult to characterize. They are destined, if deemed worthy, to receive either the Medal of Merit or the National Certificate of Merit. The Medal of Merit, by definition, is awarded to the Scout or Scouter who "[h]as performed an act of service of a rare or exceptional character that reflects an uncommon degree of concern for the well-being of others." This description can cover a lot of different activities – a number of Glenn A. and Melinda W. Adams Eagle Scout Service Project Award recipients likely would qualify with their massive projects if they weren't already dedicated to earning their Eagle Scout medal. But, in practice, most Medal of Merit recipients receive their award for saving a life.

As we've seen throughout this book, Medal of Merit recipients, while not risking their own lives, nevertheless often perform rescues exhibiting extraordinary competence and coolness under fire – for example, dealing with a traumatic amputation in which the victim only has seconds to live, or artificial respiration of a drowning victim at a public swimming pool. And, it should be noted, the trauma of failure in one of these attempts can be just as profound.

The nominations deemed not quite sufficient for a Medal of Merit (but still worthy of recognition) are considered for the National Certificate of Merit. Should the nomination fail to earn this award, it can be resubmitted at the local level for a Council Certificate of Merit.

Once this sorting is completed, the two piles continue the process along two very different paths. The large pile (with the fate of each nomination now determined and officially registered by Cooks) is mailed to the appropriate Scout councils around the nation to be awarded to the recipient at Council annual awards dinners, District events, or even troop Courts of Honor. Those who earn the Medal of Merit and the Honor Medal may wear their medal at all Scouting events they attend for the rest of their lives. They also receive a special "square knot" patch, distinct from similar knots earned for other adult Scouting accomplishments that they may wear above the left breast pocket on their uniform as long as they are part of Scouting.

The small pile, now accompanied by brief summaries of the nominations prepared by Ezell and Cooks, moves up through the Scouting channels to the membership of the National Court of Honor. In doing so, they follow the same path as a century's worth of nominations before them.

The National Court of Honor convenes three times per year. Two of those meetings, February and October, take place in conjunction with other national BSA committee meetings. The venue in recent years for all of them meetings is the Dallas-Fort Worth Marriott Hotel. The third meeting of the National Court of Honor takes place at the BSA's National Annual Meeting, which alternates locations each May. Lately, they have been held in Dallas, Nashville, Orlando, San Diego, and Atlanta. In the months between, the National Court of Honor also has regular tele-meetings. In the case of Matt Moniz's nomination, the short time window between nomination and the Top Hands meeting meant that one of these tele-meetings was devoted to voting on his nomination.

Though the venue changes, the content of the meetings remains the same. Indeed, if Dan Beard or Ted Roosevelt were to attend today, they quickly would feel right at home – at least with the selection process. The presence of laptop computers bearing emailed nominations to National Court of Honor members weeks before, certainly would be a surprise.

Probably less expectant would be the fact that the members of the National Court of Honor are less celebrities than individuals with successful professional careers, who have spent most of their lives volunteering with Scouting at the local, regional, and national levels. In fact, National Court of Honor members now are expected to remain involved in Scouting at the troop level to keep them closely attuned to Scouting as it is lived in the real world.

To be certain that this ground level connection is maintained (and no doubt to assure that the decades-long memberships of the National Court of Honor's early days never again occurs), no member is allowed to serve a tenure of more than three years. When the chairman's tenure ends, another member typically is asked to assume that role.

An image of Mount Everest from Base Camp replete with prayer flags flying overhead.

The National Court of Honor's committee meeting traditionally is the first of the day. At 7 a.m., the members gather at one of the hotel's meeting rooms. A buffet breakfast is served, during which time they socialize and catch-up with each other. Afterward, they take their seats at the large board table, where the benediction is delivered and the official session begins.

The membership, consisting of no more than nine distinguished Scouting volunteers, typically is not made public to prevent any sort of outside influence or favoritism.

Staff members, including Ezell and Cooks, also are present, prepared to answer any questions from the members regarding the individual nominations or the nominating process. These questions typically address such matters as how long between the act and the subsequent nomination, the nature of the witnesses, etc.

Normally, however, the discussions are short and the vote follows quickly. "We are always well-briefed before we arrive," says Chairman Kent Clayburn. Clayburn, a third generation Eagle (and the father of a fourth), who has a long family history with Scouting: his college professor grandfather returned from World War I and founded the first Boy Scout troop in Nebraska. Kent, a money manager in Northern California, has spent much of his adult life as a Scouting volunteer at both the local council and National levels.

Besides presiding over the National Court of Honor, he also is a member of BSA's national finance committee: "Sometimes I feel like the Grim Reaper in that job – it's a relief when I get back to the National Court of Honor and get to be a part of such a positive activity."

The conversation may be casual and upbeat, but that doesn't hide the fact that the members of the National Court of Honor take their job very seriously. Says Clayburn, "Crucial to our deliberations about awarding the Honor Medal is that, like the Eagle medal, we maintain the consistency and quality that has developed over the span of the last one hundred years. We see our primary tasks as maintaining that consistency, of never compromising this extraordinary award."

He pauses, trying to encapsulate such a momentous duty in a few words: "We understand the legacy of the Honor Medal. And we understand that we are merely shepherds, merely temporary caretakers of this process. You don't volunteer to be on this committee, you are nominated through a rigorous process. Nominees are expected to not only be involved at the national level, but also to have retained their commitments at the unit and council levels – so as not to be too far detached from Scouting as it is actually lived by the boys themselves."

"Furthermore, this is not a lifetime job. Even a chairman, like myself, must step down after that allotted term and another asked to take our place."

Asked if he feels the weight of his famous predecessors who have led the National Court of Honor, Clayburn forces a brief chuckle and says, "Sometimes. I like to think that Dan Beard is looking over my shoulder and smiling. But the reality is that I'm focused all the time on maintaining the integrity of our organization and the consistent quality of our awards process. That's all I can do."

Still, he admits that sometimes he is awestruck by the quality of the nominations and of the young men and young women they represent, "When I read some of these nominations I just sit there in disbelief at the incredible achievements of these young people. Many of them were already doing remarkable things in their lives – school, sports, philanthropy. They were already living completely enriched and completely filled lives . . . when suddenly an event occurred and they found themselves making life-changing decisions for others and themselves. And because they have the character, the training and the confidence, they not only did the right thing but they performed it successfully. It is simply unbelievable.

"The Honor Medal nominations I see not only give me hope in the next generation of young people, but they also remind me, on almost a daily basis, that Scouting training saves lives; just as it has now for a century."

One of the most popular events during the Top Hands meeting is held on the final evening for top BSA executives and invited guests. Called simply The Campfire, it harkens back to the earliest days of Scouting – and even earlier, to the Native American and Pioneer cultures from which the organization arose.

In format, it is very simple: a communal dinner capped by a presentation on stage around a simulated campfire. The 2015 Top Hands meeting held in Dallas was especially anticipated because of the first appearance of Michael Surbaugh in his new role as BSA's new Chief Scout Executive and for Matt Moniz, Eagle Scout mountain climber and hero of the Mount Everest earthquake.

Weary from a week of meetings that sometime contained explosions of divisiveness of opinion, the professionals were looking for a vision of a new Scouting, and a glimpse of the young people it now would guide and serve.

They got their wish when Matt Moniz began to tell his story. He told the audience about that terrifying and fateful day on Mount Everest...of the avalanche and the survival of his group. Of the disaster and horror at the Base Camp...how, as he sat in the tent desperately wanting to help as it was his Scout training that told him to go. How he had used his experience as a patrol leader to organize men into a stretcher crew...and how, when the aftershocks hit, he kept *his* crew from running away and how they protected the injured climber. Finally, Matt told of his efforts in the aftermath of the tragedy to alleviate the suffering of the Nepalese people, and of his on-going work to improve their lives.

Matt Moniz spoke with tears in his eyes. But there were far more tears in the audience. When he finished, there was silence – followed by a roaring standing ovation.

As the applause ended, current Chief Scout Executive Wayne Brock appeared from the wings and joined the Scouts on stage. He spoke briefly about his pride in Scouting, as exemplified by boys like Matt Moniz. Then, to Matt's surprise, he invited Mr. and Mrs. Moniz to join him onstage.

As the young Eagle and his parents stood before the crowd, Brock read passages from an official document recounting Matt's rescue efforts on Mount Everest. He especially noted the crucial moment when the young man had chosen, in the face of the second avalanche, to shield the injured climber on the stretcher – fully anticipating his own death in the process – rather than abandoning him and running for cover.

Brock then paused and looked up from the document at the boy and his parents, "Now Matt, I know that you had no idea this was going to happen tonight," he said. "You thought we invited you here to speak. But we invited you here because we wanted to honor you.

Matt Moniz (fourth from left) at the Campfire program during the BSA's Top Hands meeting in Dallas, Texas, August 2015.

Honor your courage, honor the example you set for all Scouts around this world. And therefore, as my last act on behalf of the National Council of the Boy Scouts of America and as Chief Scout Executive of the Boy Scouts of America, we want to give you the Lifesaving Honor Award with Crossed Palms."

American Scouting is alive and well.

INDEX

Index

Index

Index

Index

Index

Index

PHOTO

CREDITS

Boston Globe (Massachusetts): 320

George W. Bush Presidential Library and
   Museum/NARA (Texas): 314-5

Rodney D. Carpenter Collection
   (North Carolina): 192

Aaron Derr Collection (Texas): 227

Rudy Gonzalez Collection
   (Texas): 291-2

Dr. Terry Grove Collection (Florida): 16

Robert Hannah & Russell Smart
   Collection (Minnesota & South
   Carolina): v (top, middle), xvi, xxx, 37,
   50-1, 68-9, 78-9, 90, 94, 106, 117, 157,
   208, 297

Knoxville News-Sentinel (Tennessee): 99,
   102-3

Library of Congress (Washington, DC): xxv,
   xxxiii, 6, 26, 30-1, 38, 56, 58-9, 64, 71, 75,
   135, 148

Grant Miehm Collection (Canada): 257

Matt Moniz Collection (Colorado): 318, 324

Minnesota State Archives (Minnesota):
   9 (bottom), 10

National Museum of the USAF
   (Ohio): 198-201

National Archive, Boy Scouts of America
   (Texas): 9 (top), 126, 180, 195, 206,
   214, 218, 221, 229, 234-5, 236, 240-1,
   243-7, 249-50, 252-3, 259-60, 263, 272,
   276-7, 280, 282-4, 288-9, 295, 299,
   307, 309, 330, 333

National Weather Service (Washington,
   DC): 176, 303, 306, 310

Portal to Texas History, *Scouting
   Magazine* Archive (Texas): 173

David C. Scott Collection (Texas):
   xxiii-xxix, 13, 14, 20, 27, 36, 67, 73,
   76-7, 86, 88, 98, 111, 120-2, 124-5, 129,
   136, 138, 140, 142, 145, 153, 155, 159,
   163, 171, 186, 190, 202, 204, 228, 231

Kyle Taylor Collection (England): 323, 328

Troop 90 (Iowa): 312

NOTES

1 Dan Beard, *Boy Heroes of Today* (New York: Brewer, Warren, and Putnam, 1932) p. 5.
2 Why "Court of Honor" for the national body and "Board of Review" for its local and regional counterparts? One possibility is that the former phrase had already been taken by the National Board of Review for Motion Pictures' (also then headquartered in New York City) just a year before, in 1909.
3 http://www.boyscoutcollectibles.com/types-of-boy-scout-collectibles/insignia-items/history-and-value-of-boy-scouts-awards-medals/boy-scout-heroism-medals/ (Accessed May 23, 2015).
4 Boy Heroes of Today, pg. 4.
5 Ibid.
6 Report for the *National Court of Honor*, 1916.
7 Ibid.
8 Ronald Abercrombie, *The Abercrombie's of Baltimore* (Baltimore: Private Publisher, 1940) p. 20.

[9] *Boys' Life*, July 1921, p. 1.

[10] *Boys' Life*, Aug. 1925, p. 36.

[11] Ibid.

[12] Ibid, p. 4.

[13] "Meeting of the Executive Committee of the National Court of Honor of the Boy Scouts of America," Jan. 9, 1924, pp 6-8.

[14] An excellent source is "A History of Senior Scouting Programs of the BSA" — http://www.webring.org/l/rd?ring=geojamboree;id=50;url=http%3A%2F%2Fwww%2Eseniorscoutinghistory%2Eorg%2F (Accessed June 15, 2015).

[15] "How Boy Scout Hero Saved Comrades," *Oakland Tribune*, Jun. 20, 1915, p. 13.

[16] "Lives Saved by Boy Scouts," (Kansas City) *Gazette Globe*, Feb. 17, 1916, p. 1.

[17] "Powell Scout Congratulated by Lindbergh," *Billings*(MT) *Gazette*, Sept. 8, 1927, p. 9.

[18] "Highest Boy Scout Medal Presented Putnam for Heroism in Rescue of Girl," *The* (Syracuse) *Post-Standard*, p. 8, photo pg. 1.

[19] "Kokomo Youth Honored for Saving Father," *Kokomo Tribune*, May 15, 1948, p. 1.

[20] "She Fell Into a Snake-Infested Canal," *Boys' Life*, May 1997, p. 57.

[21] "Harding to Present Boy Scouts with Award of Honor," *Chillicothe* (MO) *Constitution-Tribune*, Jun 20, 1923, p. 5.

[22] *Fort Wayne* (IN) *Daily News*, Sept. 8, 1923, p. 5.

[23] "The Baby Stopped Breathing," *Boys' Life*, Mar. 1985, p. 46.

[24] "The Machine was Mashing His Hand," *Boys' Life*, Feb. 1988, p. 46.

[25] "Glass Sliced his Brother's Wrist!" *Boys' Life*, Feb. 1992, p. 52.

[26] "Three Scouts May Get Medals for Saving Girl's Life from Swift Canal Current," *El Paso* (TX) *Herald*, p. 16.

[27] Maria Cortes Gonzalez, "El Paso Boy Scout to Receive High Honor for Act of Herorism," *El Paso* (TX) *Times*, Sept. 6, 2010.

[28] "National Council Official News," *Boys' Life*, Feb. 1922, p. 22.

[29] Ibid.

[30] "A One-Legged Hero", *The New York Times*, August 27, 1922, pg. 96.

[31] *Indiana Gazette*, May 11, 1928, p. 12.

[32] "Scout Wins Honor Medal and $1600 Scholarship," *Chino Champion*, Mar. 26, 1929, p. 6.

[33] "Victor Boyd, Boy Scout, Recognized as Life Saver," *Honolulu Star-Bulletin*, Nov. 20, 1913, p. 1.

[34] "Rescue on the Danube!" *Boys' Life*, Sept. 1982, p. 41.

[35] "He Lost Consciousness Before He Could Grab the Rope," *Boys' Life*, Jul. 1976, p. 4.

[36] "She Jumped into the Waves," *Boys' Life*, Aug. 1983, p. 46.

[37] Alex Hinojosa, "Texas Gov. Rick Perry in El Paso: Education is a Priority," *El Paso (TX) Times*, Oct. 12, 2012.

[38] http://www.idahostatesman.com/2014/08/20/3332761/vietnam-hero-from-valley-dies.html#storylink=cpy http://www.nytimes.com/2014/09/03/us/bernard-f-fisher-honored-for-bold-vietnam-rescue-dies-at-87.html. (Accessed July 30, 2015).

[39] "The More They Struggled in the Sticky Ooze, the Deeper they Sank," *Boys' Life*, Dec. 1975, p. 52.

[40] "The Smashed Gas Pumps Burst into Flames," *Boys' Life*, Jul. 1975, p. 47.

[41] "The Force of the Current Swept Him into a Deadly Trap," *Boys' Life*, May 1975, p. 38.

[42] "He Fell into the Mower's Cutting Blades," *Boys' Life*, Sep. 1978, p 56.

[43] *Boys' Life*, Oct. 1953, p. 41.

[44] *Boys' Life*, Sept. 1968, p. 53.

[45] "Hit by a Low-Flying Car," *Boys' Life*, Apr. 1979, p. 52.

[46] "Buried by an Avalanche" Scouts in Action, *Boys' Life*, May 1979, pg. 48.

[47] Amy Moss Strong, "Earning their Badges," *Bandon Western World*, May 14, 2015, p. 1.

[48] "Saves Two Lives Within Two Days," Scouts in Action, *Boys' Life*, Oct. 1980, pg. 48.

[49] "Chicago Teen Awarded Honor Medal for Shielding Friend from Gunfire," NBC Chicago.com, Feb. 19, 2014.

[50] "He Saved his Family from a Fire!" Scouts in Action, *Boys' Life*, Nov. 2012, p. 46.

[51] "He Saved Her from the Oncoming Trains," Scouts in Action, *Boys' Life*, Aug. 2008, p. 40.

[52] "Abilene Teen to Receive Scouts' Highest Award," *Abilene Star-Telegram*, Nov. 14, 1982. p. 22.

[53] "He Saved his Brother from a Dog Attack!" *Boys' Life*, Oct. 2006, p. 48.

[54] "He Saved his Friends after a Car Accident!" *Boys' Life*, Mar. 2013, p. 42.

[55] "He Saved a Friend Trapped in a Hydraulic," *Boys' Life*.

[56] "They Saved a Family after the SUV Crashed," Scouts in Action, *Boys' Life*.

[57] All references and quotes in this section not otherwise footnoted are derived from "Tragedy at Little Sioux," *Boys' Life*, Oct. 2008, p. 40.

[58] "Tornado Kills 4 in Iowa Scout Camp," *New York Times*, Jun. 12, 2008.

[59] "Five years after deadly tornado, Eagle Scout reflects on memory of best friend," KETV.com, Jun. 13, 2013.

[60] As reported by the *New York Times*, Jun. 12, 2008.

ABOUT THE

Michael S. Malone is one of the world's best-known technology writers. He has covered Silicon Valley and high-tech for more than 25 years, beginning with the *San Jose Mercury News* as the nation's first daily high-tech reporter, where he was nominated twice for the Pulitzer Prize for investigative reporting. His articles and editorials have appeared in such publications as the *Wall Street Journal, The Economist,* and *Fortune.* And for two years he was a columnist for the *New York Times.* He was editor of *Forbes ASAP,* the world's largest-circulation business-tech magazine, at the height of the dot-com boom.

Malone is the author or co-author of nearly twenty award-winning books, notably the bestselling *The Virtual Corporation, Bill and Dave, The Future Arrived Yesterday, The Intel Trinity, and Four Percent.*

Malone also has hosted three nationally syndicated public television interview series and co-produced the Emmy-nominated primetime PBS miniseries on social entrepreneurs, "The New Heroes." As an entrepreneur, Malone was a founding shareholder of eBay, Siebel Systems (sold to Oracle) and Qik (sold to Skype), and is currently co-founder and director of PatientKey Inc. An Eagle Scout and recipient of both the NESA Outstanding Eagle Scout Award and the Distinguished Eagle Scout Award, Malone was a chapter commander of the Knights of Dunamis and on the staff of the 1973 National Jamboree. He currently is an assistant Scoutmaster of Troop 466 in Sunnyvale, California, president of the Silicon Valley chapter of NESA, and a member of the Santa Clara County Council board of directors.

Malone holds an MBA from Santa Clara University, where he currently is an adjunct professor. He also is an associate fellow of the Said Business School at Oxford University and a Distinguished Friend of Oxford.

AUTHOR

ABOUT WINDRUSH PUBLISHERS

Dallas, Texas

Founded in Dallas, Texas, WindRush Publishers excels at bringing books of exceptional quality and content to the minds of discriminating readers everywhere. With an eye for excellence we always are on the search for new inspirational and motivational topics by expert authors in a variety of subjects.

WindRush is the publisher of the award-winning and bestselling books: ***My Fellow Americans, Lizard Bites & Street Riots,*** along with the Amazon Top 100 ranked ***Four Percent.***

Stay Informed and Inspired at
www.WindRushPub.com